MALTHOUSE

MALTHOUSE

A FOOTBALL LIFE

CHRISTI MALTHOUSE

ALLEN&UNWIN

SYDNEY • MELBOURNE • AUCKLAND • LONDON

For my family

First published in 2012

Allen & Unwin
Sydney, Melbourne, Auckland, London

83 Alexander Street
Crows Nest NSW 2065
Australia
Phone: (61 2) 8425 0100
Email: info@allenandunwin.com
Web: www.allenandunwin.com

Cataloguing-in-Publication details are available
from the National Library of Australia
www.trove.nla.gov.au

ISBN 978 1 74237 814 5

Internal design by Phil Campbell
Set in 11.5/17.25 pt Janson Text LT Std by Bookhouse, Sydney
Printed in Australia by McPherson's Printing Group

10 9 8 7 6 5 4 3 2 1

STOP PRESS

'I'm taking the job.'

Dad had met with Carlton Football Club officials the previous evening and when he woke that spring morning the answer was as clear to him as the blue sky. He called his four children to deliver the news.

I hadn't heard such excitement in his voice for over a year. He had missed coaching. More than I had realised. Even more than he had thought he would.

Here we go again.

CONTENTS

PROLOGUE

'**I**'M NOT COMING BACK, boys.'

Half an hour after the 2011 Grand Final loss to Geelong, Mick Malthouse delivered news of his retirement from the Collingwood Football Club to the club's players, staff and volunteers. He knew this was his only opportunity to have everyone of importance in the one room at the same time, including his family.

Heartbroken, he spoke without tears, but the slightest falter in his voice revealed his pain. He was hurting for the defeat, but more so now for the goodbye.

'I'm not deserting you.' He said it quickly because deep down, he felt like he was. 'I just don't think I can give 100 per cent of myself that you blokes need. This football club was built on the back of hard work. Don't forget your roots, don't forget how it was formed. Be that type of football club going forward.'

He thanked the players for the fond memories built over twelve years at the club. He and his family had cherished every moment spent there. 'I have been enthralled with the journey.'

Then he told them to reflect on what they had already achieved, and wished everyone well for the future.

He never actually mentioned the word 'retirement'—at that moment, his emotions were too raw to give the word voice. He could barely cope with saying goodbye. But he had entered this game knowing it was his last as Collingwood coach before Nathan Buckley would step in, so the farewell was inevitable. Retiring and giving up the game of football just added another element of heartache.

Mick's family listened alongside the players and cried the tears that he couldn't. His daughter Danielle sat on the floor, her head bent forward and her arms wrapped around her legs. She shook with grief as weeks of pent-up anger, frustration and sorrow spilled down her cheeks. Always graceful, Mick's wife, Nanette, held her breath to compose herself for Mick's message. Her swollen red eyes never left his face; her hands remained crossed in her lap. Mick's sons, Cain and Troy, as men do, tried to hide their heartache behind folded arms and gritted teeth, but their hunched shoulders showed their anguish.

Just as I had shed tears on the final siren, I did again in that packed meeting room in the bowels of the MCG. I couldn't swallow for the lump that formed in my throat every time I looked at Dad or my younger sister, Danielle. I could hardly breathe for the pressure I felt in my tightening chest. I wanted to yell that it wasn't fair. I wanted to expel all my feelings of resentment and angst. We didn't want it to finish this way for this coach. Our dad.

It wasn't death. It wasn't tragedy or devastation. But for our family it was loss, and it felt a lot like grief.

That was my last memory of my dad's football career. My first comes from another grand final. I remember watching balloons billowing out from the Melbourne Cricket Ground (MCG) like smoke from a chimney. As though the wind was a parent taking a child by the hand, it tugged and hoisted the balloons up and over the Richmond rooftops and guided them slowly out of sight. I was two months shy of four years old, so the significance of their yellow, black and white colours was lost on me. They represented the two clubs competing in the 1980 Victorian Football League Grand Final: Richmond and Collingwood. Dad was playing in the back pocket for the Tigers that day, and Mum sat in the stands with the other wives and girlfriends, there to support their partners.

We were the footy kids, the players' and coaches' children who attended the Berry Street Crèche on game day. Danielle and I played with the Clokes, the Bourkes and the Bartletts— all famous names in the VFL, but just regular kids to us. Their dads, too, went to the club most days and worked. These kids also watched people line up for their fathers' autographs, feeling a little jealous that strangers were stealing some of their attention. They knew to grab ice from the freezer upon returning home for various injuries suffered during a game. And they'd also concluded from a young age that their dads were special, different in a way from other fathers. We didn't all know it then, but we'd only just begun the roller-coaster existence of a life dominated by Australian Rules football.

Richmond beat Collingwood for the premiership that Saturday in September, and our parents celebrated well into the night. Danielle and I were taken home by our nana. We didn't know what a premiership was, and we certainly didn't realise the huge achievement of winning one until much later in life.

When I think of those balloons now, I can still feel the excitement. There is a distinctive buzz in the air on grand final day in Melbourne, and even at that young age I sensed an anticipation like that of Christmas Eve. People converge on the MCG, some of them having travelled miles, wearing their team colours with pride. Their faces reveal a mixture of emotions—hope, nerves, fear and even joy to have made it this far. People wait years for the opportunity to barrack for their team in a grand final. They can wait decades for a premiership.

In the care of the crèche aides we were taken, hand in hand, to stand outside the Southern Stand and watch the supporters arriving and entering the stadium. Their enthusiasm infected us. We giggled and danced and wondered where these people were going and why it was so important that they got there in a hurry. Then there were no more people to see, but we could hear them, the chorus of their chants carried on the breeze so it seemed like they were standing and singing alongside us.

We saw the balloons next, our squeals of delight spilling into the air above our upturned faces. Too high up to touch but seemingly close enough to try, it felt like magic was happening before us. We watched them disappear in the distance and then we walked in a line back to the crèche.

Those balloons came to be a symbol of optimism for me, for I often thought of that moment throughout Dad's career, comforted by the memory of a little girl's thrill and a father's triumph. The balloons' undulating climb came to represent the rise and fall of our family's football journey. My memory of how they swirled, caught up in a gust of wind, seemed to represent the tough, chaotic times of a season gone wrong. The balloons kept ascending, though, despite the obstacles and perhaps this is most reflective of Dad's career. He made it to the top, overcoming setbacks and hardships, and he carried his family—and his football family—with him.

We feel nothing but pride and love for our dad, but as for football . . . I'm not sure we even like it all that much any more. It's been one long and exhausting experience. We've had rare moments of elation and many moments of strain. We've watched football, spoken football and dreamt football. My sister and brothers and I were born into football and haven't ever known life without it.

This is the story of our dad, the coach.

1 BUSHY

'**M**ICHAEL, GET OUT OF the dirt and come home, now.' Marie had gone looking for her son when he hadn't returned home after school. She found him at a mineshaft.

'I've told you not to play here—it's dangerous,' she said, grabbing his hand and marching him away from the site at the fringe of the city. 'What will it take for you to listen?'

Clay stuck to the ten-year-old's dark hair, his short, square fringe framing a face full of freckles and a toothy grin. He was short for his years, and skinny, with knees too big for his legs.

'I was just playing,' he mumbled, though his mother's mind was already on dinner. She loathed cooking but her family had to eat. Chops and peas it would be, if her eldest child would stop dragging his feet and hurry up.

Michael Raymond Malthouse was often in trouble as a child.

1

His father, Ray, worked full-time with a local plasterer. He'd been born in Ballarat and raised by his grandmother Elizabeth after being abandoned by his own mother at birth. He never knew his father. He earned the nickname 'Hardy' for his bullish approach to a tough life. Ray had been forced to leave school at a young age because an extra pay packet was needed at home, so he lied about his age to get his first job, as a coal stoker at the Victorian railways. It was tough and dirty work, but to be earning a living gave him a sense of pride. Mostly he looked forward to Saturdays, when he could play football, firstly for Railways and then for North Ballarat. He loved playing football and he loved watching football, then he met Marie Canty and felt a different love entirely.

Marie grew up in Gordon, a small town of fewer than 500 people, 25 kilometres east of Ballarat. The middle child of three born to Timothy and Mabel, she witnessed death at an early age when her sister, Cathleen, passed away from meningitis. She looked up to her brother Jack and he looked after her. When she met Ray, though he was four years younger, she knew he was 'the one'. They married in 1952 and had their first child—a son—a year later, then their daughter, Gerardine. Their lives were complete.

Marie stopped working at the local Coles checkout when she had her children and motherhood took over. Michael and Gerardine, who was younger by two years, spent many hours outdoors each day.

They lived in Ballarat Common, an estate built by the Housing Commission of Victoria to address the state's shortage of homes for its growing population. The area would later become known as Wendouree West, but in 1963 it was considered the wrong side of the tracks. Ballarat is one of the original Australian boom towns, built on the nineteenth-century gold rush. Today it is still the fifth-most populated inland city in Australia. The Great Depression stalled Ballarat's growth and it wasn't until the post-war era that it recovered. Though not as prosperous and having lost status to Geelong as the state's second-largest city, Ballarat made a successful transition from gold-mining town to tourist destination in the late 1960s.

Michael attended the local primary school, Our Lady Help of Christians, and from his earliest days as a student, he walked through paddocks of knee-high grass to get there. In winter, his clothing would be wet through from the icy dew by the time he reached the school gates and he would spend the rest of the day trying to dry off and warm up. Ballarat is as famous for its bitterly cold winters, which chill you from the feet up, as it is for gold. The freezing wind blows in with autumn and stays until spring, and a thick grey fog descends over the city in the cooler months.

In winter, it was Mick's job to collect wood for the pot-belly fire in the kitchen of the tiny weatherboard home to keep the family from freezing. Summer or winter, Mick made good use of the large backyard, which was perfect for a game of fetch with his dog. The soil was good for worms so he dug for them among the plants whenever he knew his father was free for a fishing trip to Lake Burrumbeet.

School wasn't Mick's strong point, not from a lack of intelligence, but rather through a shortage of concentration and attention to his studies. He struggled early with reading, noticing that he was slower than the other kids to get through a book. He stumbled over words when he was asked to read aloud, jumbling up the letters and sounds. He was reprimanded for his sloppy spelling, rather than helped, and was often on the receiving end of the leather strap from the school nuns for disturbing his classmates. 'You have the devil in you,' he was often told and he believed it. He enjoyed maths and science and found those lessons a lot easier than his English studies.

His favourite teacher was Sister Austin, a young nun who had grown up on a farm and had the unassuming nature of someone who had spent her life working hard. She also happened to love football and frequently cut her classes short for a kick around in the adjoining paddock. To Michael, this was how school was supposed to be, for his interest in life was in sport. All sports. Any sport. Anything that allowed him to compete and apply his natural athletic ability.

Football was revered above all sports. On his bedroom walls, clippings of his footy idols from *The Herald* clashed with the floral wallpaper. It didn't matter which club they played for—it was their on-field flair that captured his imagination. Collingwood's superstar full-forward Peter McKenna and St Kilda ruckman Carl Ditterich were pin-up regulars. When he was lucky and there was enough money left over from the weekly bills, Michael's father would take him on the hour-long train trip to Melbourne, where they would get off at Spencer Street Station and walk to the MCG or the Lakeside Oval.

It was a special and rare treat for the Malthouse males, cherished by the younger of the two for the time spent alone with his father. Ray would help his son stand on an upturned milk crate so he could watch the game from the grassy banks of the ovals. Michael was inspired by the acts of courage, determination and skill he saw before him and he couldn't wait to get home to practise the moves of his heroes as they slotted goals from difficult angles and rode their opponents' shoulders for a mark. It's what he wanted to do when he grew up, he told his father on the long trips home.

Football took a back seat when Ray was struck down by the debilitating paralysis of Guillain–Barré syndrome and Marie took on the role of full-time carer. The twelve-year-old Michael and ten-year-old Gerardine were regularly shipped off to stay with their maternal grandfather, Timothy Canty, when their mother made fortnightly visits to the Fairfield Infectious Diseases Hospital in Melbourne to be by Ray's side. Michael adored his papa, who took him on long walks through the bush that surrounded his home and taught him to respect nature, so it felt like a sanctuary, away from the worry of his father's health and his mother's ability to cope without her husband. Papa was a kind and gentle soul, always reminding his grandson to slow down and be patient instead of running around without direction and getting nowhere fast.

But tragedy struck for Papa when his wife fell ill. He waited for her to recover from the stroke but she never did.

Michael and Gerardine moved back home permanently, along with their grandfather, after Mabel's death. Papa took over Michael's bedroom, not that the young boy minded because he was shifted into a small caravan in the backyard. The caravan would become Michael's refuge, where he had privacy and too much freedom. (It would later be his children's cubby on their Ballarat visits.)

Ray was close to coming home, having spent almost a year in an iron lung to treat his condition. Barely in his teens, Michael would be the 'man of the house' and help his dad as he battled to overcome semi-paralysis and poor health.

'It's time for Mass, Michael,' Marie called out every Sunday morning. Her faith hadn't faltered through all the difficult times, praying for her husband to return home the man he was when they'd met: the town larrikin who charmed her instantly. She prayed that Michael and Gerardine would stay out of trouble. And she prayed for her mother, that she might rest in peace.

Michael was an altar boy at St Patrick's Cathedral. He didn't understand the Latin hymns and prayers that he was supposed to recite so he mumbled the words and filled in any gaps with language that hadn't been uttered in a Roman Catholic church before. He thought that Sundays really shouldn't be spent kneeling in a chapel wearing a white robe when he could be fishing at Lake Wendouree, or sending a ferret down a rabbit burrow to catch dinner, or riding his battered and muddy bike to the mine sites—or playing football.

Michael lived with his footy in his hands. A prized possession from his father, it was yellow and plastic, unlike the
red leather Sherrins that were too expensive for his parents
to afford, but he loved it like a friend and bounced it as he
walked and aimed it between trees and at the neighbours'
bins—anything he saw as a goal opportunity. He loved to
kick the ball along the narrow corridor of his home, trying
to put enough spin on it to send it through the bathroom
doorway with a crisp bounce, just like Peter McKenna when
he took a difficult chest mark and drilled the ball through
from a tight angle with a drop punt for a goal.

He knew he was a good footballer; everyone at the
Wendouree West junior football club told him so. But he
was a pretty good cricketer, too, enjoying the feel of the heavy
bat in his hands as he swung it to meet a ball bowled at him
with speed. If he connected well, the sound was like a clean
knock. If there was a low thud, he would run for his life to
the opposite stumps, not daring to look at the umpire. He
never took a dismissal well. Cricket was his summer sport;
nothing took away from Aussie Rules in the winter.

As Ray gained strength in his legs, walking with a waddle
now, he encouraged all of Michael's sporting endeavours,
persuading him when he was nearly fourteen to apply his
energies solely to Aussie Rules.

For fitness, Michael ran the seven kilometres to and from
Mount Rowan, a small extinct volcano on the edge of the
city. When there was no one to kick his football back to him,
he kicked it against the side of the garage. Michael's mates

from St Paul's Tech played footy with him but they were too interested in taking joyrides on the back of old utes to get too serious about it.

One day the local cop, Constable Lyon, paid Michael's parents a visit at home. 'I've seen your son around,' he said, 'seen the boys he chooses to hang out with, and I'm worried for him. They're trouble, those kids, and I would hate to see your boy headed the same way.'

Marie and Ray already knew this about Michael—they were concerned too—but he was a teenager and they just hoped he wouldn't get too influenced by the boys who drove cars dangerously fast and were already experimenting with cigarettes and alcohol.

The policeman, who was known to be strict but kind, continued: 'I'd like him to come and play for my team at North Ballarat, where I can watch out for him. Maybe we can use football to distract him from everything else.'

Michael was made to feel instantly welcome at his new club. When he was eight and first started playing football with Wendouree, he and most of his teammates played in school shoes because their families couldn't afford football boots; they walked home in their drenched and dirty uniforms, despite the cold, because there wasn't money to pay for a warm post-match shower. Football was a weekly thrill, a chance to beat an opponent to the ball and kick a goal and get congratulated by all of your mates, but when the game ended normal life resumed. At his new club, it seemed that perhaps his dream of playing VFL football wasn't such a distant hope after all.

He was encouraged to train hard, to practise at home, and to put his heart and soul into the matches he played every Saturday, when his parents and grandfather would sit on the sidelines and cheer him on. He found the battle irresistible and cherished every win. North Ballarat didn't lose a game for two years, but each time he walked from the field victorious, Michael grew a little taller and began counting down the days until he would be part of a team again, working together to be the best. Winning was never taken for granted.

He didn't realise it at the time, but his coach had become his mentor and was guiding Michael to a better life through discipline, responsibility, ambition and a clear direction.

Michael left school when he was sixteen, at the end of 1969, and started work at the Bank of New South Wales in East Ballarat as a cashier. He paid board at home to help with the family finances and the rest of his weekly pay packet was spent on sporting magazines, mostly about boxing. He didn't drink, he didn't smoke and he didn't gamble, so there was always a dollar or two to save. He'd too often seen the effects of alcohol around his hometown and didn't want any part of it, especially if it got in the way of his football dream, as he believed it might. Plus, he just didn't like the taste of it.

In 1970, when he was seventeen, Michael played in the North Ballarat Roosters' under-18 premiership. He was one of the best on the field and basked in the joy he felt at having achieved something so worthwhile. That success made him want more. He was elevated to the seniors the following year.

A few games into the season, there was a rumour going around town that Bruce Eppingstall, Golden Point's centre-half forward, was going to be picked up by St Kilda. He was the star of the local eight-team Ballarat Football League, and Michael didn't doubt that the Saints would be interested in this genuine football talent who happened to reside in their zone. This was the big time.

The two young men played in a Ballarat representative side together, so Michael quizzed his mate: 'Is it true? Have you spoken to St Kilda?'

'Yep. They're coming to watch our carnival in Melbourne, but I reckon I might be a chance,' Bruce said with pride.

Michael thought, I'm going to put on a show for them too.

An almighty show. He was judged best for the lightening carnival held at Moorabbin Oval between three metro teams and one country side. Every player there was from within St Kilda's recruiting zone and they were all equally eager to prove they had what it took to step up to the big league. Bruce broke his hand. Still, the St Kilda recruiters spoke to him, and when they did he slipped in a comment, as asked, about his mate Mickey. The recruiters agreed he could come along to some trial games too.

Michael drove himself to Melbourne in his banged-up Holden, which he'd saved hard for and bought second-hand the moment he got his driver's licence. By the time he arrived, his back was tight and sore from the long journey. He'd been injured in the last match of the season—after which he had been named runner-up in the North Ballarat best-and-fairest to Stewart Gull, who was going to South Melbourne—but he wasn't going to tell anyone in Melbourne about his painful back. No way would he jeopardise his selection now that he'd come this far.

He played in several Saints practice matches that trip, and he struggled. His back pulled every time he bent low to pick up the ball and he felt slow with it, like a large rubber band had been slipped around his waist and was attached to the fence surrounding the ground. After the last game he was by told by an official that St Kilda was declining him and he should go back to Ballarat. He drove home in disgust. He was so disappointed, but his overriding emotion was anger that he had let the opportunity of a lifetime drown with his performance. Michael vowed to redeem himself.

For the remainder of the autumn, he worked on getting his back right, which meant strengthening the muscles and altering his fitness regime. When he wasn't doing that he was working at the bank, watching sci-fi movies at the local cinema, fishing with his dad or his mates, or reading his sports magazines.

In the first game of the 1972 North Ballarat season, he was awarded best-on-ground honours. He got a call from St Kilda that same week. They were giving him a chance to train with the squad for the opportunity to be picked to play with the reserves team—or, better still, the senior side.

Marie was so proud of her son that she asked everyone at Mass to pray for his success. Ray shook his hand and said,

'I knew you had it in you.' His grandfather told him to stay sensible.

Michael packed up the Holden with his belongings immediately and moved to the city, where he joined some Saints rookies—all country and interstate boys like him, who had left home to make a career out of football—at a Moorabbin boarding house run by a middle-aged couple who crammed the bedrooms of their home with extra mattresses and served chops and potatoes for dinner every night. He was transferred to the Beaumaris branch of the bank, so it was just a short drive to work and then back to Moorabbin Oval. He didn't need to be at the oval every day, but he wanted to be surrounded by the sights and smells of a genuine Victorian Football League club.

Michael was thrilled to be living in the city for one reason: the St Kilda Football Club. He had been to Melbourne only a handful of times in his life, each time purely to watch football. His reason for being there now was to play VFL—sightseeing could wait.

2 CITY LIVING

S
T KILDA HAD PLAYED in the 1971 Grand Final and lost
to Hawthorn by seven points after leading by 20 at the
last change. It was an exciting time to be joining the
club, but it also added some pressure. A disappointment like
that doesn't just disappear, so by the start of the 1972 season,
the Saints were looking for redemption, no-one more so that
the coach.

Mick's new leader was Allan Jeans. This was a man who
challenged every boy to grow up, a man who taught discipline
and respect and who wanted hard work and courage in return.
He was the perfect introduction to elite football for the eager
and determined Mick Malthouse.

Such an initiation was almost beyond value for the young
man, who looked at the players who had played in the grand
final—Carl Ditterich, Kevin Neale, Ross Smith, Allan Davis,

Bob Murray—and wondered how on earth it was that he was training alongside them now. He was in awe of them.

Mick was a month off turning nineteen when he debuted for the Saints against Footscray on 15 July 1972. He had been playing in the seconds and was again selected to represent the Saints reserves when Travis Payze pulled out of the senior side injured. Mick was called up on the morning of the game. He sat in the stands of the Western Oval with his father and watched the reserves match, biting his nails and trying to ignore the nervous rumblings in his stomach, and then went down to the St Kilda rooms when the final siren sounded.

'Play well,' his father told him.

In the changeroom, Mick watched the pre-game rituals of the men who had played hundreds of games before, and he copied them. He listened to his coach's instructions and hung on every word. He was reminded by Jeans that to pull on the red, white and black jumper meant that you played with courage and determination, took your chances and backed up your teammates. Mick would do all of that.

He didn't really feel like he was good enough to be wearing the St Kilda jumper, not nearly in the same league as his experienced peers, but he was ready to play football like he had never played it before. He was still skinny and almost six feet tall now, but he was strong and played tall and he was prepared to put every inch of his body on the line for his team.

Mick lasted four minutes before he was knocked out by the Bulldogs' full-forward, Laurie Sandilands. He stayed out on the field, but at half time, when he kept insisting that his boots needed readjusting, the club doctors realised he was concussed and he was sent to hospital for a check-up. He missed the next week's match and couldn't remember anything of his first game.

Mick was undeterred, and he worked harder at training for another opportunity, which came a week later against Richmond. Mick's stamina, pace and pure resolve scored him points with his coach, and his ability to play close-checking defence and win the ball in almost every one-on-one contest forced the selectors to continue picking him. He played all but one of the remaining games of the Saints' season, and then it was finals.

St Kilda had finished fourth and faced Essendon in an elimination final at VFL Park. The lift in intensity on the field and the noise coming from over 50,000 people shocked Mick. It was mind-blowing and exciting and daunting and terrifying. He loved it! The Saints won and advanced to a semi-final against Collingwood. St Kilda beat the Pies by eighteen points.

It was the steepest of learning curves for a rookie footballer, but for once in his life, Mick didn't mind his lessons. He had a brain for football so the answers came easily. He was working as tirelessly off the field as he did on it and his reward was that he remained in the team. Allan Jeans had built a structure around defence, which suited Mick perfectly. He gobbled up any tutorials offered by his coach and took the advice of respected teammates, implementing it all in his own game.

St Kilda lost its preliminary final to the eventual premiers, Carlton, by sixteen points. Mick could only admire the effort of Blues full-forward Alex Jesaulenko's seven goals. That night he told his new girlfriend, Nanette, that it had been the best year of his life. He'd learnt so much and he wanted to learn more. This was the life he had dreamt of living.

Mick had met Nanette a month before that preliminary final, when his teammate Gary Lane had suggested introducing him to the roommate of his girlfriend, Colleen. The two groups of friends decided to meet at the local youth centre they all frequented and as the girls piled out of their car, Mick looked over at Nan and declared, 'Not bad.'

She was appalled at his arrogance and pushed her friend Nicole forward to meet him. 'She's your date, actually,' she quipped and turned away, muttering under her breath, 'and she can have him.'

As the night wore on, Mick became less and less interested in the blonde and giggly Nicole, and kept trying to apologise to the tall and slim Nanette Cromie, whose short auburn hair highlighted her large green eyes.

Nanette was nineteen. She modelled sometimes—he could see why—and was working full-time for a real-estate valuer. She played basketball at the Moorabbin youth club run by Mick's boarding-house 'parents'. She was smart, and he'd assumed highly educated, until she revealed she'd left school at fifteen to enter the workforce and help more with the household. She was one of seven children—Gary's girl, Colleen, was her younger sister. Her father had died when she was eight and they had all been raised by their very strong and very self-sufficient mother, Pat Denning, who had only remarried in 1970.

By the third time the group met, Mick had intrigued Nan enough to encourage her to sit beside him and talk well into the night. She was happy to meet up with him again after his preliminary final loss and listen to his account of an unbelievable year.

After the footy season Mick became a regular at Nanette's basketball matches. She played in a team with two of her sisters and some girlfriends. On one occasion, as he sat in the stand with Nan's brother-in-law Russell, Mick took objection to a referee's call and jumped to his girlfriend's defence, literally—storming onto the court and standing face to face with the official to announce his grievance. He was asked to leave the stadium. After that he watched her games quietly.

When it came to the family introductions, Nanette's mum instantly liked the young gentleman who arrived at the front door of her bayside home. Nanette's siblings, galvanised by the death of their father, and loving and supportive of each other, embraced a shy Mick from the very beginning; Nan's older brother Raymond declared, 'He's a great bloke.' Nanette went to Ballarat with Mick at Christmas to meet his parents. Marie and Ray liked Nan and were happy she came from a good Catholic family.

And so it was that by the start of the 1973 season they were officially an 'item' and Nan attended all of Mick's games, cheering him on with the other players' girlfriends. He made it into the team for Round 2 and stayed in it until Round 19, when he tore a medial ligament in his knee, missing the Saints' two finals. Nanette didn't know it then, but her life was about to be overtaken by football.

On 18 June 1974, a Friday night before a game, Mick arrived unannounced at the unit Nanette still shared with Nicole in Moorabbin.

'I need to talk to you. Alone,' he said. He stuttered and stumbled over his words, until finally he held out a little box containing a gold ring with a small baguette diamond, and proposed.

'Of course,' she said, laughing before the happy tears started. They married six months later, on 6 December. They were just 21.

The bride and groom both wore white. Nanette's sisters Colleen and Leslee and sister-in-law Gerardine wore pale-blue bridesmaids' dresses that matched the suits worn by Michael's best man and St Kilda teammate, Stephen Rae, and groomsman and brother-in-law, Russell Cooper. After a Catholic ceremony at Immaculate Heart of Mary in Hampton, a simple and elegant reception was held at the nearby Bentleigh RSL. Mick's soon-to-be mother-in-law had come to his rescue earlier in the day when he'd forgotten not just his wallet to pay for a haircut, but also for some skin-coloured underwear that wouldn't show through his white bell-bottom pants. Those disasters averted, the rest of the day ran smoothly and Michael and Nanette left happily in the evening for a ten-day honeymoon in Tasmania. When they returned, they moved in to a bright and tidy one-bedroom rented apartment in Caulfield.

Mick played a total of 53 games in the back pocket for the Saints between 1972 and 1976, and while injuries hindered him somewhat, his short time there led to a long career in football. He clicked with his coach in a way that not all players do: Allan Jeans was a man of integrity, a coach who commanded excellence and demanded effort. When Mick was rehabilitating from an injury the two men spent time together in the local police gym, lifting weights for strength, wrestling for coordination, and competing in an invented drill where they would volleyball-dig a medicine ball back and forth. Some time later the coach advised his young student to always lead only as Michael Malthouse, and never try to be anyone else. It remained Mick's mantra in all the years that he coached.

Mick was surprised, then, and gutted when Jeans told him he had slipped to number three, behind Wayne Judson and Billy Mildenhall, as an option for the team's last line of defence and that he was being traded to Richmond. Mick found out soon after that the Saints had been in a financial struggle at the time, and had sold him to the Tigers to help the club's coffers. His coach never offered this explanation, but it was in keeping with Jeans's tough-line approach to spare the details and not too subtly remind the young player to lift his game, nonetheless.

Mick played his final match for St Kilda on 19 June of the 1976 season and played his first game for Richmond on 3 July, for a win in each clash. It would be a fortunate twist in his football fate.

3 SPAGHETTI ON TOAST

IT WASN'T MICK'S CHOICE to leave the Saints, and especially not to go to Richmond—a successful club that he believed from the outside to be arrogant—it was the choice of his St Kilda coach, Allan Jeans, to let him go.

Mick's contract to play at the Richmond Football Club was four pages long. He was offered $185 for every senior match he played, and a bonus of $30 for every one of those games that was won by the club. It was signed on 28 June 1976, two days before the cut-off date to obtain a clearance from the St Kilda Football Club for the move.

Nanette was halfway through her first pregnancy and worried for her husband's career. The $1000 that came with the transfer would help set up the baby's nursery, and the increase in game payments would go towards bills, but a mid-season relocation didn't exactly offer career security and this concerned them both.

Mick called in at Moorabbin Oval on Tuesday, 29 June, to pick up his football boots. The St Kilda reserves coach saw him and asked what he was doing.

'I've been cleared,' Mick said.

His response was met with incomprehension. 'Rubbish!'

'It's true—I'm off to Richmond.'

Mick then went to work at his new job at the Motor Accident Board and afterwards drove to the airport to officially meet his new teammates on a flight to Adelaide to play West Australian team Swan Districts in a competition run parallel with the VFL season. On the plane he sat next to his new coach, Tom Hafey, who told Mick how he wanted him to play at his new club—that was, to play to his strengths. Hafey wanted his new tough and close-checking defender with a poised resolve in one-on-one contests to do what he already did well. It was a confidence-boosting philosophy Mick himself would one day use with his own players.

On 3 July, Mick played his first regular VFL season game for the Tigers, against Collingwood. He felt like he was starting all over again and he was as nervous beforehand as he had been for his first game at St Kilda. But as the match progressed he fell into a familiar rhythm and concentrated on his task. He was glad when the final siren sounded, but already he felt like the move to Richmond was a good one: he'd gathered 21 disposals, including eleven kicks, and the Tigers had won by 95 points.

After that, he played every game of Richmond's season, joining Ian Scrimshaw from Hawthorn, Graeme Robertson from Carlton, Allan 'Dizzy' Lynch from Geelong and Jimmy Jess from Avoca as the new recruits. It was team leaders Francis Bourke, Kevin Bartlett, Royce Hart and Kevin Sheedy who first welcomed Mick to Punt Road: a group of outstanding players who were as friendly off the field as they were fierce on it. Mick and Nanette were invited to the coach's home, where they were further received into the inner circle by Maureen as well as Tom Hafey. No hint of the narcissism Mick and Nanette had previously thought existed at the club; instead, they found a warm culture of mateship and ambition. This was a very talented group of footballers who took nothing for granted and worked hard for success.

The Tigers missed the finals in 1976 and lost their premiership coach at the end of the season, when he defected to Collingwood due to a lack of commitment from the Richmond board. By then, Mick felt as entrenched at his new club as if he had been adopted into a family.

His real family was about to expand, with my arrival in November. In hospital, Nanette received flowers from the club and a huge bouquet from the Richmond girls, now her friends. My parents felt that Punt Road was home.

In 1977 Mick played in 13 of Richmond's 24 games for eight wins and five losses. The Tigers finished fourth and competed in the finals, comfortably beating South Melbourne first in an elimination final and then exiting from the race in the second week with a loss to North Melbourne—in a year made famous by the Collingwood/North Melbourne drawn grand final. North Melbourne won the rematch by 27 points.

In 1978, the Tigers finished seventh. Through consistent form and with a fit body, Mick played all but two games of the season. He was as disappointed as anyone at the club to miss out on the finals by one game. By the end of his third season at Richmond, he had become an integral part of the line-up. He won the club's inaugural most valuable player award, which he accepted humbly, almost embarrassed to receive such an honour ahead of so many gifted teammates. His vivacious personality meant he was well liked at the club and now he was as highly thought of as the stars of the team: Sheedy, who led with flair; Bourke, always the courageous soldier; Bartlett, as skilful as any footballer going around; and Geoff Raines, who could turn a game on its head in a single passage of play.

VFL football then was still fairly amateur. Teams trained on Tuesday and Thursday evenings to fit in with the players' regular job commitments, as their football paychecks required that they earn a full-time salary elsewhere. They played on a Saturday afternoon only, and they attended Sunday-morning recuperation.

Doing weights the day after a game wouldn't be dreamt of in today's football, since scientific advancement of elite sport has determined that ice baths and altitude rooms are a much better form of recovery for athletes, though neither would eating chicken and chips for breakfast and washing it down with a beer. But that's what the players did then.

The recovery sessions ended with a delivery of greasy fast food and a carton of stubbies. Being a teetotaller, Mick passed on the beer, and I delightedly devoured most of his meal, having made the weekly trip in to Richmond to give my pregnant mother a rest.

The Sunday morning get-together was as much a moment of male bonding for Mick as the father–son football trips of his childhood. The team discussed the weekend's results, marvelled at individual highlights in the match, and shared a joke. They jogged laps of the oval almost as an afterthought.

Football in this era was simple, with few demands. Footballers trained, played, and won or lost. They mostly did it for the love of the game. Supporters supported. And the media just reported. Another look at Mick's original Richmond contract reveals that he agreed to 'play the game well and faithfully and to the best of his ability and skill'. He was to keep himself physically fit for football by attending all training sessions organised by the club. That was it. No media commitments, no sponsorship obligations, no diet restrictions, no committees to join, and no promise to maintain—by way of personal representation—the reputation of the league.

In December 1978, I became a big sister to Danielle. It was a very happy Mick who announced to his teammates that he was now the proud father of two girls. Danielle grew up to have all of Dad's natural athletic ability and sporting smarts, but I was the one who eventually followed him into football.

When Mick talks about his days at Richmond, he sometimes speaks of a man called Rudy, who helped him 'dispel his demons'.

Halfway through the 1979 season, Mick dislocated his ankle and strained ligaments in his knee in a training mishap with a teammate. His recovery from the injuries was painful and slow. He lost confidence in his body's ability to mend and wondered what would become of his football future if he didn't regain his strength and pace. The negative thoughts consumed him until he became so tense with worry that when he was picked to play, he performed abysmally. As a result, he underwent a full reconstruction of his lower leg and a partial reconstruction of his knee joint. He was in plaster from hip to toe for six long weeks. It was frustrating in a different way for Nanette, who had a two-year-old, a baby and a husband on crutches unable to even shower himself.

During this time, Mick got his first taste of coaching. Standing on the sidelines of a basketball court with his leg in plaster, he led a group of his Tigers teammates—Mark Lee, Brian Taylor, Michael Roach, Rob Wiley and Greg Strachan—to the Sandringham Men's A-grade premiership. They played every Monday night and were the roughest and most competitive team in the league.

Privately, though, Mick was sinking further into the depressing concern that his football career was over. Finally, he sought help from a West Indian named Rudy Webster. Originally born in Barbados, Rudy was an imposing figure. Tall, dark and with a voice that was deep and resonant,

Rudy was wise, compassionate and experienced in dealing with athletes in distress. He set about altering the way Mick thought of his injuries. Rudy forced him to face the truth that maybe his body wouldn't be the same, and to realise that, by placing so much emphasis on the negative 'what if', he was sabotaging his chance to find out what his body still could do.

Armed with a new resolve to return fitter and stronger, Mick began riding his bike to and from work, still in the city at the Motor Accident Board, every day. The daily outdoor activity helped to rebuild his strength and reaffirm his new positive approach.

Just before Christmas that year, my family was invited to Rudy's home. I found Rudy, with his gentle smile and warm, kind eyes, and his beautiful wife, Lindy, fascinating. They lived in a beautiful old Victorian-style apartment, as I remember it, with a leafy backyard that had plum trees full of fruit, ripe for our picking, and eating. As we entered the formal lounge room, with dark panelling on the walls and bookshelves packed with novels, educational literature and travel souvenirs, we were greeted by a booming welcome.

Lounging on the antique sofas, their legs—longer than I was tall—stretched out in front of them, were several West Indian cricketers. Of course Mum and Dad recognised them straight away. They were world-beaters at the time and in town for a summer Test series against Australia. Rudy had previously worked with the talented athletes and was again counselling his friends for their upcoming Boxing Day Test match.

Danielle and I were mesmerised by the tall, lanky men the colour of chocolate. Dad chatted happily with Michael Holding, Viv Richards, Clive Lloyd and Alvin Kallicharran and, as an enthusiastic cricket fan, could hardly believe that he was in their presence.

The way they spoke amused us kids, and when we laughed at their accents they too let out a chuckle that sounded like a blend of Santa's three-word catchphrase and a laid-back hiccup—'Heh, heh, heh'—their wide shoulders bouncing in rhythm.

When it came time to leave, Joel Garner and Gordon Greenidge were in need of a lift to nearby Toorak, so they squashed into the back seat of our well-used Holden station wagon, baby seat and all. Quite taken with our car guests, I sat squashed between the duo. Their knees were bent up around their ears as they each leant forward to avoid hitting the roof with their heads. It would have been quite a sight for the carloads of people pulling up alongside us at traffic lights.

Mick made a full recovery from his injury and, after a summer spent on the bike and in the weights room, and rarely without a football in his hands, he was motivated for a big return in 1980.

He played in Round 1 and as the season progressed it was evident that the Tigers were going to be a top contender. Michael Roach was fast becoming the epitome of the ultimate VFL full-forward, and with Roach, David Cloke and Kevin

Bartlett up forward, the Richmond team had a balance across the field that was tough to beat.

Danielle and I wouldn't have known how well the Tigers were playing because we didn't see any of those contests. Our only visit to the inside of a football stadium came when Dad took us to the centre of the MCG field on a weekday. The stands were empty and we could hear his echo as he called out 'Cooee' through his hands, coned around his mouth. The Berry Street Crèche, just a short walk from the MCG in the back streets of Richmond, was our introduction to football. We would arrive, already excited for our weekly get-together, two hours before game time. It didn't matter if our dads were teammates or on-field enemies for the day, every child played contentedly with another for the entirety of the match.

Heading into the final month of the season and another finals campaign, Richmond wasn't the cup favourite, having finished the home-and-away season third behind Geelong and Carlton, but it wasn't a team to be underestimated either. The Tigers had an exceptional side, littered with a handful stars but based on a core of hardworking team men. The squad seemed like it could be on the verge of something special.

Richmond easily beat Carlton in the qualifying final, but were more closely matched by Geelong in the semi-final. The Cats led by a point at half time, then, inspired by Kevin Bartlett's sizzling form—he kicked eight for the game— Richmond rediscovered the form that had scored them an eleven-game winning streak during the season and responded with a four-goal win. It earnt the team a week off.

On 27 September, Richmond met Collingwood in the grand final.

Nanette remembers that Mick was quite jittery. They both were. A grand final and a premiership is as much the effort of the families as it is of the individual players.

In the carpark of the MCG grounds, the Richmond wives and girlfriends had gathered for some pre-game festivity with chicken and champagne. The alcohol had been donated by a generous board member, so when game time approached, each woman hid a bottle under her clothing as she entered the ground. They hoped to make good use of the smuggled champagne later in the day, confident their partners would be triumphant.

The Tigers had almost suffered a grand final eve casualty when centre half-back Jimmy Jess stood on a needle at home. It went straight through his bare foot. He called the club doctor at ten o'clock to ask him to snap the tip off, but the doc was able to remove it instead and Jim was clear to play.

By game time, most of Mick's nerves had vanished and been replaced by a determined confidence. His teammates reflected his attitude, fervent and desperate as they ran onto the field. It was clear within five minutes that this grand final was going to be a game to remember for Tigers fans and a day to forget for Pies supporters. Richmond's midfield dominated play, and Geoff Raines was the chief destroyer, with 36 touches. Merv Keane, Robbie Wiley, Bryan Wood and Dale Weightman all played at a level above their Pies' opponents, giving the Richmond forwards every opportunity to excel. Kevin Bartlett was awarded the Norm Smith Medal for his record-equalling seven goals, and David Cloke booted six. It was a little after five o'clock on that Saturday when 113,461 footy-mad people heard the final siren and, Tigers fan or Pies fan, conceded that it had been an extraordinary performance by a brilliant Richmond team. The Tigers more than doubled Collingwood's score, and the 81-point victory stood as the greatest winning margin in a grand final for the next three years.

Mick and Nanette partied well into the night with their teammates and friends, until they could party no more and found themselves sitting on the floor of the Southern Cross ballroom using the wall as support. They weren't inebriated but they were drunk on success and high on life. And now they were tired.

Mick was always a disciplined player, regimented with his fitness, with his training and preparation for games. After the premiership win, he lifted this to a new level, wanting to maintain the edge he felt he might have gained from being a part of a successful season.

The diet of an elite athlete is extremely important for optimal performance. What they consume in the lead-up to an event has a direct effect on their energy output and endurance levels. With the help of scientific research, food preparation for sport has come a long way and nowadays is precisely planned. In 1981, though, it was hit and miss in the small kitchen of a simple weatherboard home in Moorabbin.

Mick had tried eating steak in the morning. It sat heavy in his stomach and too often made an ugly reappearance during a game. He had tried bacon and eggs. The grease left a distracting aftertaste in his mouth. Scrambled eggs left him feeling queasy. Cereal didn't fill him up, and fruit salad also left him hungry. In the end, it was the simplest breakfast that worked: tinned spaghetti on two slices of lightly buttered wholemeal toast.

Every Saturday for the rest of his playing career, Mick ate just that. Nanette did all the cooking, but this was something even Mick could prepare on his own. By this time, Danielle and I were old enough to advance our breakfast repertoire of Weeties and toast and we coveted Dad's game-day morning meal. So began our spaghetti on toast ritual.

Getting ready for a match began with a family breakfast. After a quick, cool shower—because hot water saps your energy—Mick would put on some warm-up music while he packed his footy gear. His teenage years in the 1960s were spent listening to the biggest bands of the time, the Beatles and the Rolling Stones. Years later, it was predictable that those same bands would provide the perfect pre-game vibe. Mick hurried us out the door and the music mix continued in the car on the way to the ground. We heard Elvis, AC/DC—Dad's favourite rev-up music—and, in 1982, the Survivor song 'Eye of the Tiger' became obligatory. It wasn't just Rocky Balboa who was inspired by this track!

One more song was added to our list in 1982. 'Mickey' was a huge hit that year and played widely across the airwaves. Danielle and I pumped our chubby arms in the air, our ponytails bouncing as we wiggled our hips and sang. We were clueless as to the meaning of the lyrics—for us it was a personal tribute to our dad sung by a young American one-hit-wonder named Toni Basil, who had never heard of our football-playing father!

Mick, like many footballers, had his superstitions as a player. He liked to wear a lace-up jumper, and after several years of wearing his socks pushed down, he thought pulling them up might create a change of luck. In one game it seemed to work, so that's how he wore them from then on.

He was also a stickler for routine. Fish and chips for Friday-night dinner before a game; up and out of bed at the sound of the alarm; spaghetti on toast for breakfast; the shower; the music; the packed bag; the family in the car and on our way to the ground by the same time each week. If this happened, and Nanette helped ensure that it did, then he was happy, confident and ready to play.

Mick played almost every match in the 1981 season, missing only one through injury. He had become an unofficial leader of the team, 'the backline coach', as Tony Jewell once described him. He was admired by his teammates for his determination and work ethic, as well as for his ability to harness a group's strengths and talents by providing an extra voice and direction in support of the coach and the captain.

He was also the practical joker of the squad.

Mick and his trusty sidekicks, Jimmy Jess and Merv Keane, regularly found it amusing to hide dead possums—found on their run through the parkland separating the MCG and Punt Road Oval—in their teammates' lockers and cars. This was particularly riotous if the car was a Rolls-Royce and the owner of the car was the club's chairman of selectors.

They also liked to 'borrow' the car keys of certain team-mates from the Richmond property steward, and move their vehicles from the Punt Road carpark to an MCG carpark that was closed and locked up before their evening training sessions were completed. It made for very confused, then very angry, teammates.

It also made for a good laugh, which is required in every rough season: Richmond won just over half of its games in 1981, finishing seventh and missing out on the finals.

Not that Mick dwelt on a loss. He had a rounded life and his children had a way of bringing a smile to almost any situation. At home he wasn't the footballer or the Richmond premiership player or missing with injury or out suspended, he was just Dad. The man who took us walking through apple orchards, getting us tangled on barbed-wire fences. He was the one who picked out movies for us to watch, doubting his choice when in the opening scenes we were already clinging to him with fear.

He was the parent who short-sheeted out beds and wriggled along the floor on his stomach in an attempt to sneak into our bedroom to grip our legs in a ticklish camel bite. Each of us at an early stage found Dad's single strand of chest hair totally fascinating—until he told us that if we pulled it out, he would fall apart. Thus warned, we ceased trying to remove it, imagining his arms and legs falling off and his head rolling along the floor.

Cain and Troy, my brothers, remember eating ants as small boys because of the time they found several of them, dead, in the sugar bowl. Dad pretended to eat the insects, telling the boys he was adding protein to his breakfast cereal. Faces dotted with freckles, the boys looked at their hero with wide eyes, and ate the sugar with the dead ants in it.

Danielle recalls, still with great embarrassment, how Dad delivered her forgotten lunch box directly to her high-school classroom. Realising she had left her lunch behind in her hurry to get to school on time, Dad walked the three blocks to our school and asked the office, 'Where can I find Danielle Malthouse?'

'We can take that for you, Mr Malthouse. We can hand it to your daughter between classes,' the kind receptionist offered.

'No, I'd like to give it to her myself. Thanks, anyway.'

Dad knew the chaos his attendance would cause among a group of footy-aware teenagers. He also knew Danielle would be mortified. It gave him great enjoyment to see the beetroot blush rise up from her neck, to her cheeks, to her entire face, when the teacher announced his arrival. Danielle never forgot her lunch again.

It was always in good humour that he teased his children. Seeing us laugh, and—even better—being the one to make us laugh, was one of life's greatest joys for a man to whom family is everything. Gruelling training sessions, frustrating injuries and disappointing losses were all easier to deal with when his children were laughing.

In 1982, Richmond was once again the formidable outfit that opponents feared. After 22 games of the home-and-away season, the Tigers were on top of the ladder.

Mick was 29 years old and playing close to the best football of his life. It was also his most consistent year, as he lined up in every game of the home-and-away season for the first time in his career.

A dominant performance in the semi-final, albeit for some late Carlton goals in the final term, earned Richmond a trifecta of good fortune—a 40-point win, a week off and a grand final berth. The mood in the Tigers' rooms after was one of cautious glee. The team had been here before so they knew that the really hard work was still to come, but gee, it felt good to get a chance to compete for another premiership.

The changerooms were painted yellow and black, with a large, ferocious-looking tiger baring its teeth on the back wall as if to scare off potential attackers. On the floor in the corner of the room, looking from the Tiger to his teammates, Mick sat alone, wondering if his season was finished. In the first half of the match an innocuous incident in a marking contest had left him with a dislocated right shoulder. It was a severe injury, one that would normally require a reconstruction. As the club medical staff assessed and reassessed his injury, their forlorn looks warned him that any hope of his contesting the biggest match of the season was fading fast.

He had two weeks to get his shoulder right. Not a long time for such an injury, but time enough, he thought. Not usually an optimist—that was Nanette's strongest quality—by the following day, Mick felt strongly that with the right treatment and a strict rehabilitation program of hard work he could put off the surgery and play in the grand final.

He was in constant pain. He would go to the club early each morning for treatment on his shoulder before work and return afterwards, going beyond what was required to maintain his fitness and aid his recovery—physiotherapy, ice packs, heat packs, strapping, massage, ultrasound and precision movement. By the time he returned home, for dinner or sometimes later, his shoulder would throb from the day's therapy. Lying down at night made the ache intensify, so his solution was to prop himself up with pillows and sleep sitting up. It wasn't restful slumber.

It was a very long fortnight, and the family felt his anxiety and distress. Usually the joker, Mick was snappy and agitated. Typically the playmaker, his shoulder was too sore to join in the games he usually played with his daughters. Finally, though, the chance arrived for him to prove his fitness to coach Francis Bourke. It was the Thursday evening before the Saturday grand final. Mick completed the training session with his teammates and felt good about his shoulder. It had held up well in the workout and he was confident it would last an entire game.

His coach wasn't so sure. As his teammates gathered on the sidelines to encourage him, Mick underwent a fitness test. He passed and breathed a sigh of relief, and joy. His strength and mobility were fine.

Premierships are what footballers and coaches work towards. They are rare and difficult to achieve. The chance to win another title had been at the forefront of Mick's mind for two weeks. Having won the flag and carried the cup so recently, the memories were still vibrant and the emotions close to the surface. He knew what it felt like to be a winner. The grind of past years—of unsuccessful seasons, injuries, scrutiny and the general hard slog—are forgotten in the moment the final siren sounds in a grand final, and the winners are crowned premiers.

Some men can play an entire career without this sensation and usually it remains their biggest regret. Mick didn't want regret; he wanted elation—once more. He had dismissed the agony and the doubt and focused only on the hope.

His coach decided to try one last drill, to really 'test the strength of his shoulder'. In a one-on-one contest, Mick was to lead to his left. Thirty metres away, an assistant coach kicked the ball for him to take a chest mark. Before he could complete the simple task, a jolt of excruciating pain coursed through him. He felt his right shoulder tear—muscles, ligaments and bone joint ripped apart.

Coach Francis Bourke had grabbed Mick's suspect arm and twisted in the opposite direction to his momentum. The result was a re-dislocated shoulder, worse than last time, and with it the end of all Mick's hope. It was the coach's prerogative to test that a player could stand up to the rigor of a VFL grand final. His action was the right call in the end, though many would question the way it happened.

Mick was distraught. His Richmond teammates, standing in a group near the entrance of the clubrooms, hung their heads and wondered if the grand final had also just been lost.

At home, Nanette was feeling relieved. She'd been watching the news, which had telecast some of the Tigers' training session live. The reporter had declared Mick fit and passed to play. Thank God for that, she thought.

It was my Uncle Ray who called her from Punt Road moments later. 'You'd better get down here,' he said. 'He's broken down. He's out.'

Mick's mood changed from frustrated and edgy to gloomy and resigned. He still had a role to play for the team, as a motivator and supporter, but it was difficult to lift his spirits enough to find words of encouragement for his teammates. They understood. It was the ultimate slap in the face to play every game of the season and then miss the most important one.

By game day, however, Mick was ready to sit on the reserves bench of the MCG and cheer on his mates. If that was the only part he could play in the season decider, then he would put all of his effort into it. But it was to no avail. After a seesawing first half, Carlton's forwards kicked five unanswered goals in the third term, each one a rock through a glass window for the Tigers defender sitting on the sidelines. The Blues maintained their lead and won by eighteen points.

Mick had surgery in the week after the grand final, spending five days in hospital. It was a big operation and it would take a mammoth effort to fully recover from it. He decided to retire from playing immediately.

What he hadn't given enough thought to, though, was the longing in his heart that would grip him every Tuesday and Thursday night as he caught the train from his city office past Punt Road Oval. His teammates were on the track—training, competing and laughing—and it made him realise, each time, how much he missed the group and would miss the contest.

When Francis Bourke asked him to return to the team and play one more season, it didn't take much convincing for Mick to say yes.

By this stage of our lives we were used to Dad's injuries and the prompt attention they usually required. We'd seen him vomiting blood from a broken rib and a punctured lung. We'd visited him in hospital after reconstructive ankle and knee surgery. Mum's worried looks were so common that they appeared normal to us. Usually, his pain didn't bother us. But I remember the day Dad had his jaw broken and lost his front teeth. Danielle and I were beside ourselves, not for the injury and the pain it caused our father, but for what the injury meant—we would miss the Richmond 'aftermatch', as we called it.

The injury happened in the second quarter of a match against Carlton after a spiteful collision. Mum quickly made her way from her seat in the grandstand to the changerooms below, and waited just outside the door in the bitter cold. From there she could hear the game continuing as a loud section of the crowd shouted their disapproval of an umpiring decision but she couldn't tell which team they barracked for. The Tigers' club doctor came to the door and told her that Dad would need to have the two teeth that were still lodged in his mouthguard surgically reimplanted and then wired.

As the doctors made hasty arrangements with a dentist, Mum collected Danielle and me from the crèche. We were then supposed to pick up Dad, groggy and hurting, from the dentist's rooms and take him home to rest.

But at five and three years of age, we had been attending the Tigers' post-game function—family gatherings at the Riverside Inn in Richmond—after almost every Richmond home game since we were born. We'd come to love the aftermatch. What wasn't there to like about extended playtime with the other footy kids, who were like step-brothers and -sisters to us, or sneaking a glass of fizzy drink from Dad's teammates when it wasn't allowed at home? Being spoilt occasionally is every child's right, and in this environment, the team's offspring were utterly indulged.

Here we would ask innocently for a glass of 'wy-an' and be given a small cup of orange juice, believing it to be the same alcoholic drink our mothers sipped from wine glasses.

The Richmond rover and Dad's best mate, Robbie Wiley, was the king of the kids. Jimmy Jess and Stephen Mount were the troublemakers, always causing mischief, while Kevin Bartlett and Barry Rowlings were the soothers, calming us all back down again after we'd been stirred up.

Hence, the question had to be asked as Mum reversed out of the MCG carpark: 'Why can't we just drop Dad off at home and go back to the aftermatch?' Danielle's query was met with a stern response, although at the time I thought it was reasonable. Two missing teeth didn't seem all *that* bad to two small girls who didn't want to miss the highlight of their winter weekends.

As adults, we now laugh at our brazen suggestion to leave an injured father to fend for himself, but in 1981 it led to a backseat double tantrum that lasted until Dad cautiously sat down in the front passenger seat, his front teeth held to his jaw with wire and dried blood still staining his lips. He was in a daze and his mouth was numb from the anesthetic. His pale face made his bleary eyes look frightful. He couldn't talk and he couldn't focus on his daughters. The drive home must have been hell for both Dad and Mum.

'What happened, Dad?'

Groan.

'Why can't you talk?'

Shrug.

'Why does your mouth look like that?'

Grunt.

'Be quiet, girls—Dad is sick, he needs to rest.'

Eventually we let him.

It was one of the very few times during Dad's playing career that we didn't make it to the aftermatch—until 1983, when we became infrequent visitors, at best.

For all the pain he'd suffered throughout his career, Mick's shoulder injury was different. His football comeback was proving far more difficult than he'd allowed himself to contemplate. Spending time in the reserves, he struggled to find form and when he did, his body would once again fail him, as he succumbed to soft-tissue injuries.

At the end of May, he managed to string two senior games together. Nanette was heavily pregnant, but still she sat in the stands, cheering him on. The first match was against his former team, St Kilda, at Moorabbin Oval in Round 9. Mick got seventeen kicks, including one behind. The Saints won by fifteen points. The second match was at the MCG against the Sydney—until 1981, the South Melbourne—Swans. Level at three-quarter time at 8.8 apiece, Richmond kicked a further eight goals in the final term to win by twelve points. Mick had ten disposals and gave away two free kicks.

They were the last games of VFL football Mick ever played.

When Mick retired this time, he was content with his decision. He accepted the fact that, at almost 30 years old, he had achieved the most he would get from his body. After flogging it for so long, the brutal pre-seasons, the injuries and the surgeries had taken their toll. He had played 174 VFL games.

Richmond finished tenth that year and played its last game of the season on the final Saturday of August, losing to Fitzroy by 34 points. Mick went to watch and afterwards farewelled his teammates properly. He spent the night talking to his teammates; some he knew he would never see again, while others, like Robbie Wiley, would remain close friends. They asked him what he would do next and he said he wasn't sure; he'd probably continue his studies to become an accountant. He kept his coaching ambitions to himself, because he wasn't sure yet if it was a realistic aim. He needed to give it some more thought.

On Tuesday, 30 August 1983, Mick celebrated the arrival of his third child. Cain was a chubby, placid and content baby boy, with a full head of soft brown hair and a round pink face. The family had moved recently to Vermont South and a bigger home with a large backyard for a cubby house and a swing set. Mick was still working hard at the Motor Accident Board and studying at night school, so he didn't have much time to wonder about his football future.

The family took a holiday in the Victorian coastal town of Coronet Bay just after New Year's Day 1984, something we hadn't been able to do before as pre-season training usually got in the way of summer breaks. It was a blissful time. There were no mobile phones then, no laptop computers. There wasn't even a phone at the house.

One particularly warm morning, towards the end of the second week, the family was once again enjoying the sun and the sand, just one kilometre from their temporary home. On this day, Mick had brought a small portable transistor radio to the beach, so he could listen to the Test match being played at the SCG between Australia and Pakistan. During the lunch break, the radio broadcasters held a cricket quiz. Mick listened as they revealed the winner to be a woman from the west of Melbourne.

'While we're speaking of the western suburbs,' continued the commentator, 'there's been some big football news today with the resignation of Footscray coach Ian "Bluey" Hampshire.'

Mick sat bolt upright and held the radio closer to his ear. As the announcer wrapped up his comments, Nanette moved closer to her husband, sensing that something was up. 'What are you thinking?' she asked.

'I think we should go home. I have a feeling they might want to talk to me,' Mick said.

They packed up and drove home that very afternoon.

In October 1983, Mick had applied for a coaching position in the South Australian Football League but had been beaten to the Central Districts role by St Kilda great Kevin 'Cowboy' Neale. It had wounded his fragile hope that coaching could be his next profession. But then he was approached by Wangaratta, from the Victorian Country Football League, to be its coach. He was flattered and eager, but a move to the bush with three young children presented more of a challenge than he and Nanette were ready for. It did renew his hope, however, that he was on the right career path. Now, as he drove home, he recalled a conversation from partway through the previous year with Shane O'Sullivan, Footscray's general manager. He'd wondered where Mick thought his football career was headed. Mick had been taken by surprise by the question at the time but was pleased when the Bulldogs' boss revealed that they saw him as a potential coach. Nothing eventuated from the discussion but now the memory of it increased Mick's urgency to get home.

That evening Mick met with Shane again, along with Footscray vice president Nick Collum and football manager Steven Nash, who all visited him at home. Nanette sat on the sofa in the small and tidy family room, exhausted from the long drive and the night-time ritual of getting three children to bed.

In the room next door, Mick was offered the Bulldogs coaching job.

4 A BULLDOG CALLED SCRAGGER

MICK HAD KNOWN FOR quite a few years that he wanted to remain in football beyond his playing days and instinctively felt that he had the right make-up to coach. It had dawned on him at a young age, when injuries were a regular occurrence instead of an occasional inconvenience, that he needed to look beyond playing if he wanted to stay in the game, for his playing days would be limited.

He had long been collecting information from his own coaches by watching them, talking to them and learning from them, and now he wrote lengthy notes—which he still has: crumpled pieces of lined paper now gathering dust in a box at the back of a wardrobe—to make sense of the newly attained knowledge. Mick agreed with many of the principles passed on by his coaches, but also disagreed with some. When he began to question and challenge their thoughts and processes more and more often, particularly as he matured as a player and started forming his own ideas on how to improve a team's performance, he confirmed for himself that coaching was a genuine option for his future.

He'd been lucky to have been taught by a diverse group of football men, beginning with the legendary Allan Jeans. His style was highly defensive, which suited Mick's own game in the backline. Jeans made his teams train smart and play smart.

In complete contrast, Tom Hafey's focus was attack. As a leader, he placed a lot of emphasis on forming strong relationships with his players and made them work hard on the training track. In Mick's view, Barry Richardson was well before his time but had perhaps lacked a suitable chance to display and develop his unique coaching strategies.

The Tigers' premiership coach Tony Jewell was another who liked to push his troops to their physical limit, preparing their bodies well for the rigours of elite football; he encouraged ruthless football. Francis Bourke's approach reflected his own personality and playing style—intelligent, composed, courageous and determined. Not every player can be a Francis Bourke, though, and trying to make each man play that way may have been his weakness.

From these five men, Mick gained an invaluable comprehension of the game. He learnt from the masters—Jeans and Hafey—and watched the others. As coaches, they all contrasted greatly, but one element bound them: they were winners. Through this, they passed on a positive attitude to a determined coach in the making. As a leader himself, Mick was a mixture of all five, developing his own style as the years progressed and his confidence grew.

In his final year at Richmond, Mick's mind posed the question: What if? He felt he knew football well enough by now. He also felt prepared by his years of listening, watching, discussing and self-educating. And he felt he knew people, and the intricate and delicate art of dealing with the sensitivities of a group of individuals. So he finally voiced his ambition to coach. He didn't dare to aim for the VFL yet, considering country Victoria, or even the South Australian Football League, as more viable options for his introduction to coaching.

The offer from Footscray in 1984 wasn't totally unexpected, but the timing was awkward. It was mid-January, over three months since the end of the previous football season, and his competitors had been preparing for the new season during that time. Mick says now that he felt thrust into the job and overwhelmed by how much catching up had to be done. But at the time he took it all in his stride.

On his first day on the job, 16 January—the date comes easily to mind even now—he was extremely nervous. As he turned into the short driveway at the back of the Western Oval, he looked through the passenger window at the large Bulldog statue positioned above the office doors, dwarfing the entrance, and gave in to the butterflies that had settled in the pit of his stomach that morning.

It was windy—it was always windy at the Western Oval. The smells from a nearby abattoir and the Dunlop rubber factory around the corner combined to form a stench that burnt the back of his throat and stung his eyes. Walking across the dusty, loose-gravel carpark, Mick glanced over the entire exterior of the club, noticing the peeling paint and ageing framework of the grandstand, which was named after Bulldog great Ted Whitten. This was his new home and the team wasn't the only thing in need of rebuilding.

A self-confessed stickler for regimentation, Mick had already spent hours planning his approach to the squad, their training sessions for the week and the schedule to come, plus the structure of a new game plan. Discipline was high on his agenda, as was an ethos of 'rehearsal, rehearsal, rehearsal'.

Of all the tips and advice he'd been given, the comment that stood out most was to always be himself. And that's how he intended to begin his tenure at the Bulldogs. He was confident in his own abilities and thought he knew what the team needed to do to be successful. Though younger than many of his players at just 30 years of age, he wasn't intimidated by the age gap. But he was cautious at the start, and tried to imagine what the likes of Doug Hawkins, Brian Royal and Simon Beasley, seasoned footballers with impressive reputations, were thinking. All the players, from rookies to veterans, would be keen to impress, he knew, for they would want to get a game. But how would his recent on-field opponents react to him as their new coach?

Jim Edmond, Footscray's captain at the time, was a feisty half-forward who lacked height but played tall, making him a perfect match-up for Mick as Richmond's hardy back pocket when the two sides had clashed. Mick had come off second-best in one contest with the Bulldog forward: Edmond's elbow had connected with his head, just behind his ear, leaving him bruised and barely able to remember the remainder of the game.

They were now face to face again, and this time, as coach, Mick had the upper hand. Jimmy grinned, his knowing smile instantly relaxing his new leader. They shook hands and laughed and the ice was broken. 'He was terrific for us,' Mick says of the Scotsman with the short fuse.

A loyal band of Footscray supporters was an entirely different problem for the new coach. Outgoing coach Royce Hart's failings—just eight wins in two-and-a-half seasons—had left its legacy and the fans were nervous of a repeat with another novice at the helm. Mick needed to make them believe in him and prove he was worthy of their support. That would only come with on-field improvement and, ultimately, success.

That first Monday went quickly—in fact, the week passed in a rapid flash of introductions, outlines, preparations, orders and training drills. There was no time for a leisurely transition. It was a sprint, uphill. The team seemed to enjoy Mick's thoroughly planned and diverse training sessions. He stamped his authority and outlined what he wanted the club to achieve that year and how they would do it. He introduced a new strategy—a power game off the backline with a defensive structure and hard running. It was very different to their previous style—it had to be—but to Mick's relief his players' embraced the new concept and even took ownership of it, to an extent. It was a good start and it increased his confidence that he knew the game, that he could lead a group with discipline and good communication and that he could coach.

From the very beginning of his time at the Western Oval, Mick said that 'the Bulldog boys would rather a fight than a feed'. He meant it affectionately. They were a bunch of good blokes, and as diverse as their cultural and football backgrounds were, he would have no trouble getting them to play, as a group, for the red, white and blue jumper. It was what they instinctively did at Footscray.

Mick's first true test as a disciplinarian came quite early on. On a return flight from a practice match in Perth, he had imposed a no-drinking rule on the team. He wanted to start a new culture at the club, one of order, restraint and commitment, and he felt a difference could be made by banning alcohol during the season.

Star player Doug Hawkins felt differently and, without trying to hide it, drank several glasses of beer on the way home. Mick waited until the following day to reprimand him, taking the evening to consider his options. If his rules were ever going to have effect and his authority remain intact, he had to penalise Hawkins. More than anything in this world, Mick knew that Doug Hawkins just wanted to play football. He lived for the game: missing one, even a practice match, would be punishment for him, so that's what Mick imposed the following weekend. Hawkins was apologetic and regretful and the lesson was learnt.

When speaking about Dougy, a smile always crosses Mick's face. He named Doug Hawkins as one of the greatest players he ever coached for the way he 'massaged' the ball, and his ability to use both sides of his body equally. A knee injury in 1986 that required a reconstruction and a year on the sidelines hugely affected Hawkins' natural game and, Mick believes, is possibly the only reason this great football talent never won a Brownlow Medal. As different as their personalities were, Mick always admired and respected Hawkins and remembered fondly his infectious laugh.

At home we were making our own adjustments to a new, more public life. If we thought that being children of a VFL player put us in a distinctive league, then being the children of a football coach was like going from baseball's minors to the majors. The boys won't ever remember the relative anonymity of our surname in footy-mad Melbourne because suddenly it was 'famous' and our dad's every move was chronicled in the media and judged by the public. Kids we went to school with had parents who read newspapers and formed opinions that were spoken aloud around the breakfast table. Those views were repeated to us in the classroom, whether as praise or criticism. More commonly it was the latter.

At the announcement of Dad's new position, our family was front-page news. A photographer and a journalist from *The Sun* came to our home one morning. Mum had tidied our hair, washed our faces and dressed us in cute, matching summer outfits. We are all smiling in the photo: Dad, Mum, Cain as a baby, Danielle and me. Genuine smiles.

As the five of us sat huddled unnaturally close together on one small couch, we were excited about the prospect of a bright future. Football—for us kids, anyway—had always been fun. We didn't know the pitfalls that the family of an elite coach could face. That, we would find out soon enough, but in a single frozen moment of time on the front page of a big Melbourne newspaper, we were happy and looking forward to a life of football. That life meant that Dad was at home less and less. Coaching was yet to be considered a full-time job, so each weekday he would leave home before we had even woken and head to his day job as an administration officer at the Motor Accident Board. After work he would drive 45 minutes to the western suburbs, for training sessions, football meetings, team selection and other general work around the club. By the time he arrived home, his three children were tucked up in bed, fast asleep, and his wife was exhausted.

Perhaps out of guilt or as compensation for his increasing absence, Dad would often come home bearing bags full of lollies. He would wait for the weekends to spoil us with chocolate-covered honeycomb (my favourite) and soft multi-coloured lollies dipped in sugar (Danielle's favourite). Excited as we were to finally see him for the first time in the week, our enthusiastic greeting was exaggerated when we knew goodies were on offer, as we guessed in which hand behind his back he was concealing the bags of treats. Being a sweet tooth himself, he didn't make us wait to rip into the clear cellophane bags—as long as we shared the sweets with him!

*

The start of the 1984 football season brought with it hopes and dreams and a whole list of new elements and conditions to adjust to.

Mick's first game as Footscray coach was against the club he had only just stopped playing for, Richmond. He was nervous, especially when he allowed himself to think that he was about to coach against the club he'd bled for as a player. Remembering a conversation he'd once had with football great Leigh Matthews, Mick reflects: 'When you've literally bled for a club, it remains a part of you and it is where your heart will always belong. Coaching will give you memories and acquaintances, but a true emotional attachment comes only from a team for which you've pushed yourself to the physical limit alongside your teammates.' The connection is made stronger by a shared premiership. In this sense, Mick's heart lay with Richmond; as Matthews told Dad, his heart still lies with Hawthorn. Now was the time to put those thoughts aside, though, because as Footscray's coach, Mick needed to turn his nervous energy into a positive force to focus his mind for an entire match.

On paper, the side he'd picked was a good one: Simon Beasley up forward, Doug Hawkins on the wing, Andrew Purser in the ruck and Neil Cordy down back. In preparing for a game, Mick spent as much time on the opposition as on his own team, placing equal importance on knowing an opponent's strengths and weaknesses. He briefed his players on their direct opponents for the day, informing each one of his man's dominant foot, aerial strengths, what he was like in a one-on-one contest, and his pace of mind and of foot. Some of Mick's players joked that he even told them what colour underwear their rival wore! Considering that this contest was against his former teammates, Mick felt confident that he knew them well.

When he took his seat for the very first time in the unique Western Oval coach's box, Mick was so close to the ground that he could lean out of the side of it to call to his players to tighten up, pull back or to attack through a certain area. He emphasised these instructions with signals he'd created for the players, who could see him through the box's window. Surrounded by a small team of part-time selectors—there were no assistant coaches then—it felt strange to be coaching against his mates, but he felt electric now, alive. Mick had always loved the competition, the thrill of the contest, and today he would experience it on an entirely different level.

The final siren came sooner than he'd expected—the game was over, it seemed, in a second. He'd rotated player positions, responded to opposition moves and addressed the team as if he'd been doing it for years. There hadn't been room to enjoy the match—it was all business.

Footscray won that first game easily. Mick was thrilled.

After the match, Nanette gave him a congratulatory kiss and said she was going to the opposition rooms to find

Richmond's club doctor. Dr Benjamin Weiss had become our family GP in the years we had known him at the Tigers, and a switch of clubs hadn't changed that. Nanette had been feeling unwell for a few weeks, but put it down to the stress of Mick's career change and the tireless duties of being a mother of three, including a seven-month-old baby.

'I think I need to come in and see you,' she told Ben, explaining how she'd been feeling.

'You could be pregnant.'

Mum scoffed at the doctor's suggestion, but made an appointment to see him that week. The test came back positive. Four children. A football team. A whole season ahead. A husband who was never home. Nanette cried at the unexpected news and when she told Mick, he was taken aback too.

By the next day, Nanette and Mick had put their concerns behind them and rejoiced in the thought of a new addition to their family. A pregnancy would just be another part of Mick's first season as coach.

We very quickly aligned with the rhythm of a new season.

The morning routine wasn't much different to when Dad had been playing, and we still went to the crèche on game day. This wasn't a purpose-built childcare centre like Berry Street, though; the Footscray crèche was a 100-year-old weatherboard house that sprouted like a tree in the Western Oval's carpark. It was small, rundown and smelly, and it was our sanctuary in those early weeks of the season. Halfway through the year, Mum began walking us back over to the ground at three-quarter time and up a steep flight of stairs to an area of the grandstand reserved for the partners of the players.

The very first time we witnessed a quarter of live football, we were in awe. From where we sat, undercover but front and centre, we could actually hear the players on the rare occasion that the crowd went quiet. The deep thud of the football as it ricocheted off a boot. The heart-stopping clash of two hard bodies in a contest for the ball, the air in their lungs escaping with a forceful sigh as they collided. The whistle of the umpire and the resulting cheer or jeer of the crowd. That sound was magnificent. It was so loud that at times it felt like 50,000 people had crawled into your ears to yell at the same exact moment. Even as the roar dulled, the shouts of individual supporters travelled clearly across the ground: 'Open your eyes, ump!' 'Is that all you're good for, Beasley?' 'Bloody do something!' As if the players weren't trying their hearts out.

Someone—I can't remember who—gave Danielle and me a line to shout at Footscray's opposition: 'You're dead meat!' We yelled it with gusto, giving emphasis to the word 'dead' as if we were genuinely encouraging murder. We weren't, of course, we were merely caught up in an exuberant moment, glad to be supporting our father, and blissfully aware that we were both now part of a select group of people. The Footscray girls. The players' wives and girlfriends looked like beautifully groomed supermodels, with fancy careers and amazing lives to match. Really, they were a lovely bunch of girls who had gathered to support their partners. By treating us as equals they made us feel very special, every weekend.

We quickly came to love those 30 minutes of football each week. During one home game, when we had wandered down to ground level to wait for Mum as she lined up to buy us a drink, we were met by an elderly lady with a stumpy, over-weight bulldog on a lead. He had a Footscray scarf wrapped around his neck that caught his drool before it dripped to the ground. He was introduced to us as Scragger, the Bulldogs' mascot, and we were encouraged to pat him. He was so placid, or perhaps lazy, that he barely registered our interest, but there was something very loveable about him. His owners had a chair, just for him, on which he would slump to watch the game, and he was at every home match until he died and was replaced by another Scragger.

The Footscray aftermatch had the same party vibe as we'd experienced after games at Richmond, but now that we were older, and the coach's children, we noticed more than we had before. We spotted celebrities in the crowd: newsreaders, actors and musicians, themselves excited about meeting their favourite footballers. We saw supporters getting drunk and being politely asked to leave without a fuss. We saw men in suits and ties whispering their assessments of the match and Dad's performance in the coach's box.

We saw how people pounced on Dad as he entered the room, before he even had a chance to say hello to us. How they questioned the result, his tactics, his choice of players for the game. We saw children line up for photos and autographs, pushing in front of us to get to our dad.

We started to despise it a little, especially after one particular occasion when Dad joked with us at the wrong time.

A group of children, some of them boys, had noticed Danielle and me sitting on a rarely used staircase watching *Young Talent Time* on a nearby television and they started teasing us about our program choice. We loved the variety show so we defended it. The exchange didn't last long, but when they got bored and left us alone we headed back to the aftermatch for our parents' protection. When we finally reached Dad, he was surrounded by kids clambering for his signature, among them the outspoken pint-sized offenders we'd just encountered.

We tried pushing our way through the crowd. 'Dad, Dad,' we called out, hoping to be heard above the invasive hum of a room full of people. 'Dad, those kids were being mean to us.'

'He's not your dad, he's Mick Malthouse,' one of the boys hissed.

'He is our dad,' I replied as Danielle nodded her head, her face forming a frown. 'Daaad!'

The boys continued to tease us. 'Ha, ha, they think he's their dad.'

We were finally at the front of the queue. Grabbing at Dad's hand, we tried to explain about the hurtful boys.

'Yes, little girl, what do you want, my autograph?' Dad asked in a high-pitched voice. The boys roared laughing.

Danielle and I started crying. 'Dad, tell them you're our dad,' we pleaded, our bravado all gone.

In the car on the way home, Dad apologised for his poor joke. We didn't stay mad at him for long, but we did make him promise to acknowledge us as his daughters at every possible opportunity. We didn't always want to share him with everyone else.

As we crossed the West Gate Bridge, separating the western suburbs from the city of Melbourne, we looked through our windows at the flickering lights of homes in the distance. There didn't appear to be a seam between where the lights finished and the stars in the sky began. 'It's fairyland, girls,' Mum whispered, as she did every time we crossed the bridge on a Saturday night after a home game.

Long before *The Footy Show* was dreamt up by Eddie McGuire, Channel Seven's *World of Sport* was a Sunday-morning institution for every footy fan in Victoria. Anchored by famous radio commentator Ron Casey, it featured a group of former football greats, including Bobby Davis and Jack Dyer, with Lou Richards hamming it up for the weekly handball competition. The program showcased the previous day's VFL matches and had the coaches dissect and discuss the results.

The first time Dad was introduced on the panel as 'Bulldogs coach Mickey Malthouse', my sister and I stood in the shadows of the studio cameras, watching with excitement. It was a novelty for Dad to appear on the show, having enjoyed the program for years, particularly the exaggerated banter between Dyer and Richards.

As a thankyou to the coaches for coming on the show each week, they were presented with a goodie box. When we got home, the big brown package virtually burst apart without help, it was packed so full of treats: Four'N Twenty pies, party-size sausage rolls, six-packs of Coke, bags of chips, chocolates and lollies—it contained every food item that wasn't usually found in our house.

Every Sunday—especially after the time we made our own appearance on the *World of Sport* panel, showing off our newly pierced ears—we ate our way through the treats in that big brown box. It wasn't until Mum and Dad realised that Danielle was becoming addicted to the Coca-Cola that they started giving the weekly prize away to family and friends. By that stage we'd been fortunate enough to redeem offers from elsewhere also: the very committed and extremely generous Denny Schwarz, the owner of Footscray's major sponsor, Eastcoast Jeans, dressed us all for the winter. The salary of a rookie, part-time football coach didn't amount to much in those days and it certainly didn't stretch very far for a family of five with another one on the way. So some new wardrobe items were greatly appreciated, not to mention admired.

With the perks came the drawbacks, and one of them was that every student at our small primary school knew who our dad was and what his job entailed. For most, that didn't mean too much, but for a significant few, it was a dagger with which they could stab us at any moment. Footscray's losses were shot at us like bullets: 'Your dad couldn't win a raffle if he bought all the tickets!' It hurt. Perhaps if we'd previously gloated about Dad's job and revelled in the Bulldogs' wins, we could have expected retaliation. But we didn't speak of Dad or the Bulldogs—how many seven-year-old girls do spend their lunch breaks discussing their father's career? So the teasing came without warning and felt like a very personal attack. It happened right through our school years, at some times worse than others, and during all of that time, I never got used to it. It had a way of sticking to you like paint, leaving a sore red mark when you tried to scrub it off.

It extended into other areas of our lives too. Danielle can recall a basketball match played against a particularly outspoken opponent. (Danielle was a very good basketballer, eventually joining Perth's WNBL team, the Breakers, at the age of sixteen.) On this occasion, as Dad sat in the stand making a rare appearance, Danielle's team was beaten. Danielle herself was on the receiving end of a nasty outburst from her adversary. At the end of the game, that same girl went to Dad and asked for an autograph, a request with which he complied. Danielle was livid.

'How could you sign an autograph for a girl who was so mean to me, and who just beat us?' she questioned, the only words she spoke to Dad for the remainder of the evening. I don't think Dad had a reply for that.

During our first year at Footscray, Dad started the ritual of having players, a few at a time, over to our house for dinner.

It was a way of getting to know them away from the football club, while introducing them to his family.

Mum cooked the delicious meals, and Danielle and I waitressed. It was exciting to meet the players Dad had spoken about so often and whom we saw regularly on the field.

So we came to know the players for more than their goal-kicking ability or their tackle count. We knew that they were sons and brothers, and young uncertain men, eager to make a career—a life—out of football. Dad's players, all of them, wouldn't have been aware that we copped abuse on their behalf from schoolmates for their weekly performances, or that we defended them—and that missed goal, that report, that dropped mark—like we were defending siblings.

By the end of Mick's first year in charge of the Bulldogs, the club had broken even: eleven wins, eleven losses—a fair start. The coach had plenty to build on.

He went to the annual VFL Coaches' Conference at the end of that season. He walked in to the meeting room and found a scene that could later have reflected an Australian Football Hall of Fame gathering. Already seated around the table were Allan Jeans, Tom Hafey, Ron Barassi, David Parkin, John Kennedy and Kevin Sheedy. Mick was immediately struck by the thought that he didn't belong there, that he was an imposter. He worried that he hadn't earned his stripes yet.

'What are you doing, laddy?' Jeans asked him, creating a gap between himself and Parkin for Mick to take a seat.

Mick sat and listened to the group of wise footy men discussing the season just past and proposing alterations for the future. He'd never felt as intimidated and unsure of himself as at that moment. He barely said a word.

By the meeting's end, he felt slightly more accepted, but not any more sure of himself. He wondered if they viewed him in the same way that he himself—in the years to come—looked at the new coaches joining the table each year: meeting David Parkin's knowing gaze with a slight nod of the head, each man privately wondering if these new boys would cut it.

The first training session of early pre-season had only just begun when Mick was called off the track to take a phone call. Nanette and Cain had been in a serious car accident. An out-of-control truck had swerved into their car as Nanette sat at a red light. She had no room to move before the truck smashed into the driver's side of her car.

The steering wheel collapsed onto her lap as her head hit the dashboard. Seven months pregnant, she was rushed to hospital as she went into labour. Cain, just a year old and suffering from shock, was with a nurse and screaming for his parents. Mick arrived in record time to take him, and find out what was happening with his wife.

Doctors managed to hold off the labour, but explained that Nanette was still at risk of delivering the baby early—she was concussed, a nasty gash above her forehead had required heavy stitching, and her body was badly bruised. Her seatbelt had saved her and the unborn baby's life. Cain's car seat—which Nanette had, without explanation, moved to the centre of the backseat that morning—had protected him from major harm.

As Mum recovered in hospital, Dad took over running the house. He didn't have a clue what he was doing! He couldn't cook so the family either had takeaway each night or burnt toast. He pulled his daughters' hair and made them scream as he tried to tie their ponytails for school. He did the washing, then left the clothes to pile up unfolded and unironed in the laundry. Beds were left unmade and Cain was shipped off to his nana's through the day. It was a relief for all the family when Nanette came home a week later.

On 4 December 1984, at full term, Troy was born—all ten pounds of him. The year had finished on a high note.

The following year was perhaps the season that fixed Mick's destiny in football.

Firstly, he left the Motor Accident Board to concentrate more of his time on Footscray. Club director Peter Sidwell—who became Mick's best mate and manager—offered Mick a job at a newly launched magazine called *Your Sport* selling advertising space. This job allowed him the luxury of working fewer and more flexible hours and meant he was now—virtually—a full-time coach. These days, a coach works not only full-time for his team, but is on call for every hour not spent at the club. With the travelling involved in a national competition, recovery sessions to attend, opposition and reserve grade matches to view, and media commitments, AFL coaching in the 2010s isn't just about training and the game—it's a seven-day-a-week job.

In 1985, Footscray recorded its most successful home-and-away season in 30 years, with sixteen wins. They finished second on the ladder and with that, got a double chance in the finals. Mick puts their performance down to having a good balance of players on each line: a solid backline, a high possession midfield and a productive forward line. The supporters were excited, highlighting the similarities between Mick's squad and that of the 1954 Footscray Premiership team. Their collective hope was energising, their expectations suffocating. Mick carried the anticipation on his shoulders like a bag of bricks.

A mini street parade was held for the team through the streets of Footscray on the eve of the finals. Mick knew it was good for the town, but he felt it wouldn't be good for the football side. And it wasn't. They were flogged by Hawthorn in the first final.

Mick refocused the team for their clash the following weekend against North Melbourne. Simon Beasley kicked his 100th goal for the season and was mobbed by the crowd on the field, and Doug Hawkins played the greatest game Mick had ever seen an individual play. With a best-on-ground voting system of three, two and one votes given out to three players, Mick would have awarded all six votes to his wingman that day. Footscray won and advanced to a preliminary final against Hawthorn.

Inwardly, the Bulldog boys believed they could beat premiership favourite, Essendon, if they could get past the Hawks. They'd won at Windy Hill during the season and Mick had heard that the Bombers were worried about the possibility of facing Footscray in the grand final.

But the star-filled Hawthorn team didn't give the Bulldogs that chance, winning again, this time by ten points. Mick hadn't felt disappointment like this before, not as the coach of a team whose season had come to a premature end.

Footscray's first-year star Brad Hardie won the Brownlow Medal that year. The look of genuine joy and pride on Mick's face when the cameras panned to capture his reaction revealed the intensity of emotion to which he had committed himself as the leader of a group of young men who were learning football and learning life.

Soon after, Nanette learnt the hard way that when your husband is the coach, football takes over your life. Following the 1985 Grand Final, won by Essendon, the Footscray boys, along with Mick, left for their end-of-year footy trip to Los Angeles. On the first leg of the flight, a small group of players began a food fight among themselves. The airline wasn't impressed and dumped the team from the plane in Hawaii.

There was uproar at home. Thinking that her husband was still on a long flight to LA, Nanette began receiving calls from the media at six in the morning: 'Can you tell us what went on on the plane?' The question came without introduction. 'Who was involved in the incident? Have you spoken to Mick? Does he condone what his players did?'

The calls and the questions kept coming. Nanette hadn't spoken to Mick so she had no idea what they were talking about, and now she was worried. With four children in need of breakfast, she tried calling several people from the club for help in dealing with the media, but they were either with the team or away on holiday, which is why she had become the media's point of contact.

Journalists may have been chasing the real story, but the kids at my school already thought they knew the truth. 'Your dad's going to jail,' one boy stated, as if the police had just confirmed it to him.

By the time we returned home from school we were inconsolable. Nanette—still in her pyjamas after spending the day answering phone calls and trying to clean up a mess she hadn't made—tried to decipher our words as they spilt out between sobs.

'Is Dad going to jail?' we asked. She knew then that the situation was out of control and she wanted her husband home immediately.

The players at the centre of the 'scandal' that the media had painted the incident to be were punished accordingly. An apology actually came from Qantas months later, stating that their staff had overreacted to the situation. By then the media wasn't interested in the story—it was yesterday's news, so to speak. Dad was regretful that anything untoward had occurred at all, and especially disappointed that the effect of some player mischief had been escalated in Melbourne, putting undue stress on his wife and family. My parents were both relieved when he returned home and things got back to normal.

An eventful year gave way to a string of disappointments. After climbing to the top end of the ladder and competing in three finals, winning just half of their games and finishing eighth the following year felt like a major let-down for both coach and club. They weren't completely deflated, taking heart from the tight nature of the season, in which the fifth-, sixth- and seventh-placed Essendon, Collingwood and North Melbourne all finished on equal points; the Bulldogs were just a game behind them, well ahead of the ninth-placed Geelong. They all knew, though, that there was a lot of improving to be done.

Mick made the headlines once again when, during a match late in the 1986 season, he dragged Brad Hardie for not picking up his man. In a show of contempt, Hardie took off his jumper and swung it around several times above his head as he stood on the sidelines in front of the Footscray members.

The event divided the supporters. Some congratulated Mick for his courage in removing a star player from the ground for not doing his job. Others opposed his judgement and applauded Hardie's petulant show of frustration.

Danielle and I copped another school taunting session: some older boys inserted sticks in the spokes of our bicycles in an attempt to trip us up and injure us. We arrived home shaking, angry and miserable. Once again, Mum's protective instincts emerged and she bristled at the unfairness of her children having to deal with public controversy created by someone else.

At the end of that year Brad Hardie was sold to the newly formed Brisbane Bears for enough money to save the Bulldogs from financial collapse. Every year that Mick was coach of Footscray, he had to 'sell' big-name players at season's end to help top up the coffers. It was frustrating, limiting and far from ideal as far as team performance went, but it was essential in order to keep the club afloat.

By the mid 1980s, the media devoted to football had increased. More and more journalists were VFL-accredited and the footy-mad Victorian public was impatient for news of their favourite teams and players.

We became used to seeing television cameras and reporters at our home. Dad's face on the news and in the papers was now commonplace. The boys had both gone through a stage of looking behind the television set to find their dad whenever they saw him appear on the screen. By this time, though, they'd realised, like their sisters before them, that the man answering questions on TV wasn't really their dad—he was the coach of Footscray.

In 1987, Footscray lost the first three matches of the season by a total of 42 goals, but in the fourth round took on the reigning premiers, Hawthorn, and won. Having sold good players to other clubs at the end of the previous season to raise funds, new players were brought into the Bulldogs' side from the reserves and the Under-19s just to make up the numbers.

Of all the successful seasons he's coached, Mick describes 1987 as one of his greatest triumphs due to the effort and commitment of the young and inexperienced players who pushed through that season, showing courage and grit, only to miss the finals by just half a win.

They were further stretched in 1988 and struggled with consistency, winning and losing eleven games. Still, they had a chance to finish in the top five and it all came down to the last match of the year against the most recent team to enter the competition, the West Coast Eagles. In front of their home crowd, the Bulldogs stayed close to their opponents for three quarters. But as the Eagles kicked away with three goals, in a low-scoring contest, Footscray failed to register a goal in the final term and were eventually beaten by 24 points, 3.11 (29) to 7.11 (53). The Dogs' season ended instantly.

Far from breaking his spirit, those two tough years strengthened Mick's resolve. The introduction of the Brisbane Bears and West Coast Eagles to the VFL had made it exciting for a young coach—new opponents to analyse, more travelling, and games on a Sunday as well as a Saturday—it was fast becoming a professional competition. On the downside, resources were stretched, particularly for the financially drained clubs like Footscray that were increasingly losing players to their richer rivals.

For Mick, these times were horrific. Players would come to him asking if he knew of the club's future, if he knew where they would be playing the following year. He didn't have answers for them because he himself didn't know how bad the club's situation was. But he did pass on some advice: 'Play the best football you can to make sure you're playing football somewhere next year.'

It was a time he would never want repeated. Trying to focus the minds of insecure and uncertain players was complicated, demanding and difficult—perhaps the hardest thing he would ever do in coaching.

By 1989, Footscray's fragile financial existence extended to our family's finances. On more than one occasion, Mum was left in panic at the local shopping centre when her attempt to withdraw money from the bank was declined. Dad's paychecks had started to bounce and our family savings were drying up.

Our parents kept their worries and stresses concealed as best they could, but there was a significant shift in the home dynamics and, as curious and perceptive children, we knew something was wrong. What led to Mum and Dad's total devastation wasn't money troubles, though, it was cancer.

In the weeks leading up to Christmas in 1987, our family was stunned when Mum's brother, Ray, was diagnosed with cancer of the oesophagus. Ray was a man full of life. Tall, rounded at the edges, with a moustache to rival that of Merv Hughes, he was the person who cracked everyone up with his impersonations and well-delivered punchlines. Just two years older than Mum, he was quite possibly the family favourite. His three children were of a similar age to us and Lucas, Ben and Kate were our frequent playmates. Mum and Aunty

Coralie were close friends, and Dad was as tight as a brother with Ray. Watching him battle the illness—losing his hair from the treatment and turning yellow when it spread to his liver—was perhaps the most difficult thing Mum and Dad had lived through.

Uncle Ray had begun working at Footscray years earlier as the game-day bench assistant. His jovial personality shone in the football club environment and 'Muddy' was accepted as one of Footscray's own. A park ranger for the Melbourne and Metropolitan Board of Works, he actually became a mentor of sorts to several young Bulldog players by helping them get jobs there. In 1988, the player group held a sportsman's night at the Western Oval to raise funds for Uncle Ray's chemotherapy. He was eternally grateful, as were Mum and Dad.

But by the start of the 1989 football season, Uncle Ray had exhausted every avenue of treatment. He was weak, tired and very ill.

I knew why my cousin Joely was picking me up from school on 26 April even before she told me. It was quiet at home, though the house was full of family. Everyone had returned to our place after offering their love at Uncle Ray's bedside as he passed. The air was thick with grief and felt suffocating from the moment we walked through the front door.

The team wore black armbands for the match against Melbourne that weekend.

It was one thing after another in a distressing year. A severe asthma attack had almost taken Troy's life, leaving Mum and Dad on high alert to his condition. Mum had to undergo a hysterectomy and the rest of us suffered an acute bout of gastro during her stay in hospital.

It wouldn't be the last time Dad would coach with a soul that was numb, but for the first time he began to doubt himself and his role in life. Football didn't seem important any more. But he pulled himself together—he had to. A football team relied on him. And our family needed him also.

While he put every effort into his job for the remainder of the season as usual, Dad was still grieving for Uncle Ray and the year had become overwhelming. He needed to get away and rethink life. He didn't know what he would do next, but he knew he couldn't remain in the Footscray position any longer. He wasn't sure if he even wanted to coach any more. There was a mutual understanding in the end between coach and club.

That season Footscray finished thirteenth. They were broke and a merger with Fitzroy had become a real possibility. Thankfully, Footscray was saved from folding by the generosity of a large supporter group. But our life was about to be turned upside down again.

'We have something to speak to you about,' Mum told us one October afternoon, asking Danielle and me to sit down for a talk with her and Dad. We'd had so much bad news that year that I couldn't help but wonder if more was about to be delivered.

'How would you feel about moving to Perth?' Dad asked.

5 A TWO-YEAR EXPERIMENT

Iᴛ ᴡᴀs Mɪᴄᴋ's ᴍᴀᴛᴇ Robbie Wiley who alerted him that West Coast was looking for a new coach and helped convince him to apply for the position. In October 1989, Mick was unemployed, with four children to look after, and worrying about the future. Several candidates had been interviewed for the role and in the end it came down to Wayne Schimmelbusch, Robert Walls and Mick. There didn't appear to be any rush by the Eagles to make an appointment, which worried Mick further.

So he was surprised but relieved when the Eagles chose him. It turned out that Alan Schwab, chief executive officer of the VFL at the time, had recommended him. It seems Mick Malthouse was part of his plan to turn the VFL into a truly national competition. West Coast would need to succeed on the field for that to become a reality and, in Schwab's eyes, Mick was the man for the job.

The West Coast Eagles had entered the competition in 1987 and in their first three seasons, Mick had noticed the team's huge potential. With the right approach, new structures and a better fitness program, the possibilities were exciting.

The year just ending had been traumatic and the black cloud left by Ray's death was hovering too close overhead to give anyone in the family breathing space. Quite often Dad referred to a small note of advice, handwritten on a yellow post-it and framed, left to him by his brother-in-law: 'Never, ever get to a stage in your life where you think I wish I had of, or worse still, why didn't I?' So when the opportunity to relocate first presented itself, Dad was open to the idea in a way he may not have been previously. 'I think I can win a premiership with this team,' he told us.

When the West Coast position was confirmed, Mum and Dad were excited, even happy. It would be the fresh start they felt we all needed, away from Melbourne and the lingering heartache. Now they just had to get us on board.

'You'll love it there,' Mum told us, painting a picture of Perth as being always warm, close to the beach, and just a four-hour flight for our Melbourne friends to come and visit.

'Your dad has signed a two-year contract, so we'll go for that long and if it doesn't work out, we'll come home.' Dad always signed his contracts with the kids' schooling in mind. Two years would get me to Year 10, Danielle to the start of high school and the boys through the early years of primary school, so if we needed to move back to Melbourne, it wouldn't be too disruptive.

My thirteenth birthday party became a tearful farewell to my friends. The three things I knew about the Eagles were:

1. They were newish.
2. They had finished eleventh on the ladder for the season just gone.
3. They had a player named Karl Langdon who had peroxide white hair and seemed to show off whenever he got the ball . . . and who argued a lot with the umpires.

'Why do you want to coach them?' I asked, perplexed, when Dad told us of his new job.

Not that his answer in any way consoled us. I cried the whole way to Perth on our Boxing Day flight. Moving to the other side of the country to start at a new school without friends felt like the end of the world. Danielle was just as upset, but remained dry-eyed on the plane, having cried all her tears in the weeks leading up to our departure. Cain and Troy were too young to understand and thought that a house near the beach sounded brilliant.

Two months isn't a long time to plan a new life for a family of six, but our parents were lucky to find a house to rent that was big enough for us, and close to schools and the football club. When we arrived in Perth, the things that stood out to me, as a teenage girl, were different to the things that consumed my parents. They were concerned with how to transport us all and whether our furniture would arrive intact and on time. They worried about how the dry heat would affect Troy's asthma and about our schooling, which hadn't yet been fully arranged. And they kept a close eye on how all of us kids were coping with the move.

I remember we ate Hungry Jacks—a take-away food chain that didn't yet exist in Melbourne—for lunch. Hungry Jacks was the Eagles' major sponsor and we'd been given vouchers for free food. I remember that a flame-grilled Whopper was delicious!

I remember, too, that we stayed in a hotel for our first two nights in Western Australia. Danielle and I had our own room adjoining our parents' and we could watch TV from bed if we liked. Our rooms had a view of the Swan River, and Kings Park in the distance, two Perth landmarks we would come to recognise well. By the time we moved into our new house by the sea, it felt like we had been on a mini holiday, which was perhaps the best way to be introduced to our new life.

Our new house lacked an air conditioner but it was a four-minute walk along a grassy track to the beach. The seaside in Perth is so different to Melbourne's bay. Huge, powerful waves welcomed us by grabbing hold of our legs, sucking us back into the undercurrent and dumping us on the sea floor with a mouthful of white sand and a head full of saltwater. Not exactly a happy hello.

The Victorian Football League was to be officially renamed as the Australian Football League in 1990, so Mick felt that he was becoming a part of history. If the Eagles could make the most of their home-ground advantage and learn to win in Melbourne, they could be unstoppable.

Mick's first task was to introduce himself to the players, staff and board members. Then he had to change the mindset of them all.

Western Australians in general place a lot of emphasis on sport, perhaps because of the warm climate, which encourages an outdoor, active lifestyle. Perth's sporting teams—the Wildcats (basketball), the Warriors (cricket), the Heat (baseball) and, in particular, the teams of the local football competition, the West Australian Football League (WAFL), which was hugely respected and greatly supported—were held in high regard.

This was where the problem was for Mick. His new players thought their first allegiance was to their WAFL clubs. Indeed, the West Coast Corporation as a whole lacked an understanding of the AFL and its long history, and this stood in the way of a true commitment to the national league. Mick's players listened to ABC Radio broadcasts of WAFL games on their flights home from interstate clashes instead of sharing his interest in the details of matches played between the Eagles' own AFL rivals. So he began requesting newspaper clippings from Melbourne on everything AFL, and covered the walls of the Subiaco Oval changerooms with the articles. Each week he highlighted anything to do with their opponents and insisted that his players read the press. Half of their weekly team meetings were dedicated to their upcoming challengers. He was very deliberately flooding his players with information on the AFL and in turn diminishing the time they spent thinking about the WAFL season.

'I want you to know your foe,' Mick told his team, introducing homework to their weekly schedules. He gave them tapes to view, and notes on their opposition to work through. He was surprised it hadn't been done before. It worked instantly to give each man a boost ahead of meeting his rival face to face in a game.

To further explain this WAFL dedication, it is interesting to note that the Eagles rarely appeared on the back page of *The West Australian* newspaper in those early years, with the local football teams or the successful Wildcats dominating the sport news instead. These days AFL news is the biggest sporting news on most days.

Thus, Mick was taking on more than just his player group when he began breaking down the barriers. Many Perth people despised the AFL concept, believing its success to be at the expense of the WAFL.

On the field, Mick had complete autonomy and implemented all his methodologies, which had been shaped from his six years at the Bulldogs and reworked for his new team. He felt confident and comfortable in his initial training sessions, especially when he saw his players respond positively to his drills and strategies. He introduced a very structured game style to the West Coast Eagles.

The team was highly skilled in its use of the football and the new coach wanted his players to capitalise on this strength of their game. He raised with them the issue of mental toughness. He knew they possessed it, but believed that their opponents underestimated their courage. He highlighted John Worsfold, Guy McKenna, Troy Ugle and Dean Kemp as examples of men who kept their heads over the ball, and pointed out Dwayne Lamb, Karl Langdon, Chris Mainwaring and Murray Rance as the players who could be counted on to never back off. These were the positives that just needed honing. What he wanted to do now was create a more defensive game plan to take advantage of West Coast's tough and talented backline and its quick and hardworking midfield. He had a strong belief that instant improvement could be made from the implementation of a solid armour.

Big changes occurred by giving fitness coordinator Brian Dawson free rein over a new regime that included a different approach to weight training. The players' dramatic size and strength gain was immediate and even led to accusations of steroid use—which were laughed off—such was the transformation. The Eagles' new look was imposing and the players lapped it up. The likes of Worsfold, McKenna and Michael Brennan took on the training with enthusiasm and the effect was powerful.

The promise that Mick had seen in the Eagles was becoming the reality. The next issue to be addressed was their home ground—Subiaco Oval—and how best to use it. A big stadium, built specifically for football, set in sunny and warm Perth, with perfect drainage, was both a positive and a negative for the team that played there often. Mick believed that sometimes your apparent strength can be your biggest weakness. The size of the ground had dictated West Coast's game style: the team scattered when they had the ball, and waited for a perfectly delivered pass on the run. When the team played in Victoria at grounds that varied in size, that were heavy from the rain and regularly flooded, that had cricket pitches in the centre and lacked protection from the howling winter wind, this game plan fell apart. Melbourne teams ran towards the man with the ball when he was under duress and searching for options, and it worked for them. Mick needed the Eagles to do the same.

Tweaking a game plan means a minor adjustment for the playing group. Changing it completely, as Mick was doing, is revolutionary and requires the rewiring of the footballers' brains. To his relief, his players embraced the new strategies wholeheartedly.

Mick knew the team was gaining confidence in the new structure when they played Essendon at Waverley Park in a Foster's Cup pre-season match. The Eagles lost by three points but it was a significant improvement on the 24-goal defeat they had suffered to the Bombers at the end of the previous season, in which West Coast had scored just one goal for the game. That humiliating demolition had left its mark on the team. This narrow pre-season loss helped erase that mark and prove to the new coach and to the team that they were on the right track.

And this led to the final issue—travel.

West Coast was on the road every second week of the season, at least. They would fly to Melbourne and try to find a ground to train on, but they'd find that walls were going up everywhere. The Victorian clubs were either denying permission for the Eagles to train at their home grounds or leaving obstacles on the ovals for them to train around. 'We were given no favours,' Mick recalled. In retaliation to their treatment in Melbourne, West Coast began its own diversionary tactics on opposing teams travelling to Perth. After finding out when each team had requested to train at Subiaco Oval—through the very accommodating West Australian Football Commission—Mick would set his training session for that exact time, forcing his rivals to make last-minute changes to their plans. It wasn't illegal—it was just fighting fire with fire.

When Mick took over at West Coast, no West Australian team had ever won at the Melbourne Cricket Ground: not the Eagles, not the state side, not even the junior state side. It was more than a bogey—losing there was simply expected.

Mick decided to change the team's travel schedule. He put great importance on the final training session of the week, so they trained on the day before the game and then flew to Melbourne.

'It became get in, get out,' he recalls. He reduced the stay in Melbourne by returning straight after a match. And he imposed a no-drinking rule on the team, believing that the mix of alcohol and flying would work against the players' recovery. Simply put, he brought professionalism to the club.

It was with his mind on huge possibilities that Mick was able to leave us at home, miserable, every time he got on a plane to Melbourne. Even now, Mum's heart constricts with the memory of an eleven-year-old Danielle sitting on the stairs crying her eyes out, after pleading with Dad to 'please take me with you', every time he left.

We were still adjusting to life in Perth, and it was slow going. Being introduced as the daughter of the new Eagles' coach didn't help to endear me to my classmates. And it seemed that the kids who did talk to me were only doing so because they wanted free tickets to the footy—it was alarming how many 'friends' came out of the woodwork at finals time over the years. Danielle, as the only new girl entering grade six, felt isolated and shy. Her anxiety led to stomach pains that occasionally sent her home from school. It took six months for the stomach and heart aches to ease and for friendships to be formed.

It was sport—basketball, in particular—that helped us find our feet in WA. Both Mum and Dad had played basketball from their late teens, and while Dad no longer had the time, Mum continued to play twice weekly, just as she'd done since before we were born. It was natural that all four kids followed suit.

It was easier to make friends with children who shared a common interest in basketball. The Perth Wildcats were enjoying a successful run in the National Basketball League (NBL), which had resulted in a popularity surge for the sport. Mum found a team to join through a girlfriend from Footscray, Dianne Rance. Dianne's husband, Murray Rance, played for the Bulldogs in 1986 and 1987, moved back to the west in 1988 and was still playing at West Coast in Dad's first year there. Pretty soon Danielle and I were playing district basketball, and travelling—with Mum as our taxi—some long distances for our games.

Dad came to as many games as he could to cheer us on, though our weekend schedule didn't allow for him to attend as often as he, or we, would have liked. When Mum coached our team—Danielle and I played together in the Under-20 division when I was sixteen and she was fourteen—to a memorable win over the reigning champs, we joked that she had taken over the mantle of 'top coach' in our household.

The Eagles were having a good season. The new, more defensive game plan and the alterations to the team's travel schedule were producing the results the club wanted. West Coast recorded several pivotal victories, including a 63-point win over the Bulldogs at a windy Western Oval; a 31-point defeat of Carlton at its home ground, Princes Park in Round 17; and success by seven points against Geelong at Kardinia Park in Round 22. The club had finally won a game at the Mecca of football, the MCG, in Round 6 against Richmond. It was all worth celebrating, and further evidence that the team's talent was finally being maximised—Mick was succeeding in getting the best out of his players.

They were winning at home too. In fact, they won every game, bar one, from the eleven matches played in the home-and-away season in Perth, both at Subiaco Oval and the West

Australian Cricket Association ground, where night games were held.

Mick created an 'us versus them' mantra for his players to recite. When he first took up the coaching position in the west, he raised several issues with AFL CEO Alan Schwab, particularly pertaining to an unevenness he had noticed between Victorian teams and the WA club. For a start, West Coast had 39 players on its list, compared to the 42 players rounding out other squads. They had no local zone, unlike the suburban zones of other teams. They were already at a disadvantage due to their distance from Victoria and the travel required in a season, so Mick wanted changes made to create a more level playing field. It ended in an argument, but Schwab eventually gave ground and allowed for the last three picks of the 1989 draft to be taken by West Coast, increasing its list to 42. One of the men drafted was Dean Kemp.

There were other small anomalies that would take years to straighten out. In the meantime, instead of letting his players dwell on the imbalance of the system, Mick used it to motivate them. By sticking together and treating everyone else as the enemy, including the opposition fans, the Eagles' team played united and fierce football. Their home crowds encouraged and lifted them. Victorian supporters maddened and spurred them. It worked to produce a noticeable improvement in the team dynamics.

Off the field, things weren't working quite as well. Halfway through 1990, Nanette and Mick had begun to question the merit of the move west. They were financially strained. Mick's contract with the Eagles wasn't a plentiful one—certainly not enough to cover the rent of a City Beach home while sending four children to a Catholic college, plus paying for all of life's necessities. They had almost cleaned out their savings and the thought of amassing debt worried Mick greatly. Back in Victoria, Nanette's mother's health was deteriorating and she felt guilty at having left her care to her sisters in Melbourne. The two-year experiment looked shaky.

But as the Eagles continued to win matches, and win over the West Australian public, the reason for the move became the reason to stay. Just maybe, Mick and his new team could win a premiership.

The family moved to a suburb closer to the football club; the mortgage for an old, half-renovated weatherboard was cheaper than the rent for a double-storey contemporary home with sea views. Every cent saved helped to ease the financial pressure.

By season's end, West Coast was placed higher on the ladder than it had ever been, claiming third spot with sixteen wins. Confidence had been gained from a defensive structure that was difficult to penetrate and masterful in turning the ball over to the defender's advantage. The players were stronger, fitter and more determined than ever. They had gelled as a unit and had belief in their new coach.

The Eagles were in the finals and playing like a team possessed. They had been on the road two weeks in a row by the time they faced Collingwood in a qualifying final at Waverley Park. The Pies had finished one place above West

Coast on the ladder and the ledger was squared from the clubs' two encounters during the season. But no-one could have predicted the outcome of this final.

Collingwood led by two points at three-quarter time and the last term saw each team score three goals. With less than two minutes remaining in the match, the Pies, up by a point, worked the ball forward to the top of the 50-metre arc, where John 'Woosha' Worsfold intercepted and kicked long downfield. An infringement by the Eagles' runner Robbie Wiley resulted in a boundary throw-in on West Coast's half-forward flank. Laurie Keene tapped the ball to Karl Langdon, who put it straight to his boot. It travelled high across the goals, and was marked in the forward pocket by Peter Sumich.

'I don't think the Eagles can lose from here—it's a question of whether they can win,' said Dennis Cometti in the Channel Seven commentary box.

Every West Coast supporter was asking the same question. On a difficult angle, on the wrong side of the goals for a left-footer, the Eagles' full-forward ran in and kicked the ball with ten seconds left on the clock. He missed to the left for a point. The siren sounded immediately—scores were level.

In an interview after the game, a furious Mick said: 'The simple facts are we drew the bloody game, and we came over here to win.'

West Coast was to return to Melbourne the next weekend for a rematch, the team's fourth road trip in a row. Signs of fatigue were beginning to show. After dwelling too much on the draw during the week, the team consequently lost its focus and, by the time the game began, they were a bundle of nerves. The Pies thrashed them by 59 points.

Yet again the Eagles made their way to Melbourne the following weekend for a semi-final clash with the Demons. Mick was desperate for a win, knowing that the club's first finals victory would provide what their breakthrough win at the MCG had done—confidence and belief. It was in the second quarter of the match that he saw his desperation mirrored by his players. The Eagles kicked six goals to Melbourne's seven points and retained the lead for the remainder of the match. In the end it was a 30-point victory that was worth gold.

For the sixth straight week, West Coast was back in Victoria, this time to play league leaders Essendon at Waverley Park. Mentally and physically exhausted, Mick urged his team to fight off the excuse of overtiredness, but he was met with a flat response and feared that beating the Bombers was an almost impossible challenge. He was right. By half time the deficit was 36 points, too high a hill to climb for a side that was fighting its own demons. They went down by 63 points to the eventual grand finalists, but what remained after the loss was a powerful motivation to go further. The club's first ever September win a week before had formed an important expectation for the following year.

Collingwood won the 1990 Premiership.

*

The inconsistency and hardship of travel bonded Mick's West Coast team. He felt a measurable shift in the attitude of his players by the start of the 1991 season, recognising the mental strength gained through adversity. They were now capable of beating anyone, anywhere, he thought.

His observations were confirmed by the scoreboard when West Coast won its first twelve games of the season. It was three matches in particular in the middle of that successful trot that really stood out to the Eagles' coach as further evidence of his team's growing confidence in their leader, the game plan, and the combined abilities of a group of determined athletes.

For Rounds 6, 7 and 8, the Eagles were booked to play on the road. It would be a test, Mick knew, of the squad's resolve and fitness. At Waverley Park they faced Geelong. It was level at the first change, then—kicking with the breeze—West Coast piled on seven goals for a handy half-time lead. The Cats clawed their way back into the contest to halve the deficit by the last quarter. Craig Turley and Chris Mainwaring swung into action, steering the ball forward to Peter Sumich, who finished the match with eight goals. It paved the way for a classy 45-point win.

Next they met Hawthorn at Princes Park. Again it was close early, before the visiting team managed to quieten the stunned home crowd with a stifling performance. West Coast won by 82 points.

The body language of the players the next week suggested they were jaded, but their focus remained sharp. They headed to Windy Hill to take on Essendon. A good start was important in this clash and they got it with a five-goal opening term. The Bombers failed to kick a major. Holding sway in the centre, Simon Madden hoisted his teammates up off the pitch and got them back in contention. Just a goal separated the sides at three-quarter time. Fatigue was creeping into the Eagles' game but their coach implored them to stick to the plan and rest when the match was over. Swapping goals in a tense last term, Mick's men looked out on their feet. But from somewhere deep inside they drew energy from a belief that had been building like a tidal wave since the previous season. They no longer played trying not to lose, they now played to win. With enough ambition to quell the burnout, West Coast landed the final blow. A breathtaking seven-point victory had just raised the bar of what the club could do.

The Eagles' twelfth straight win was a big one, 118 points over Footscray at the WACA. The team had hit full stride: now a game in the west induced fear in West Coast's opposition, who faced the hurdles of travel, of a vocal and passionate Perth crowd, of playing at grounds they weren't used to and of a team whose strength and talent and toughness had been harnessed in a way that produced a lethal brick wall. It wasn't an impenetrable barricade—the Eagles faltered three times in the remaining ten games of the season—but it was no longer a flimsy wire fence.

Coaching is all-absorbing. For Mick it was a 24-hour-a-day, seven-day-a-week job, literally. If a thought came to him while he was on the loo, he would jot down notes on the toilet roll. When he woke from a dream about a game he would write that down too, on the notebook he kept next to the bed. While he insisted on his assistant coaches taking a day off during the week to spend time with their families, he himself would analyse videos of the opposition from home. At night, as the family lounged in front of the television, Mick would sit with a small magnetic board on his lap, adjusting match-ups and team structures. There was a thin red strip with a name written in black ink for every player in the competition. (We had fun changing the names of players or moving the team around when Dad wasn't looking, doubtless helping to create some inspired match-ups!) While driving, he was working out how to penetrate the opposition's backline. When eating lunch, he was thinking about who best to use to tag a rival midfielder.

During a game he had tunnel-vision and a one-track mind. Sometimes when he walked across the field before a match observing his team's warm-up, he would search for us in the crowd and wave when he saw us. But after the umpire's first bounce, he could run straight past us from the coach's box to the ground at the breaks and not even notice that we were within arms' reach. During a match against St Kilda after the Eagles' first loss of the 1991 season, Mick decided to sit on the bench in the second half to be closer to the action. After an error-ridden passage of play, Mick picked up the phone and shouted a message for Robbie Wiley to relay to the player at fault. He felt a tap on his shoulder. 'Ah, Mick, I'm right here,' said Robbie, standing directly beside him. The players on the bench giggled and the Eagles' runner muffled a laugh. Mick glared at him. 'Just get out there,' he yelled. For Mick, coaching really was all or nothing.

The only times Mick didn't think about football were in moments in the company of his family—around the dinner table conversing about the day's events, watching his children's sporting endeavours, or helping them with homework. His favourite books are stories about war, but even those got put aside until after the footy season, when his mind would finally allow him to complete a page without veering off to thoughts of a game or a player. Crossword puzzles—and later Sudoku—were, and remain, an off-season enjoyment for a man who likes to keep his brain sharp.

Mick was appointed the WA State of Origin coach midway through 1991. The WA team played at the WACA and quite convincingly beat Victoria. It was a huge win, mainly due to the extra confidence gained by the Eagles players who contested the match. However, it was after this win that Mick's positive outlook of his team's season took a dive. His men thought they had already climbed the mountain and West Coast lost some of its momentum.

Defeated in the last game of the season by Fitzroy, the club still finished top of the ladder, having found a formula to defeat previously unbeatable combinations. Tony Lockett and Stuart Loewe; Jason Dunstall and Dermott Brereton; Gary Ablett and Barry Stoneham rarely had an easy shot at goal anymore against an imposing Eagles defence consisting of Dwayne Lamb, Glen Jakovich, John Worsfold, Guy McKenna, Ashley McIntosh and Chris Waterman. In the middle, the ball was held up by Craig Turley, Don Pyke and Dean Kemp, with Peter Matera and Chris Mainwaring running on the wings. It was a formidable outfit, but Mick felt uneasy about the approaching finals.

In a qualifying final at Subiaco Oval between West Coast and Hawthorn, neither side gave an inch in the opening quarter and the home team led by five points heading into the second. Seasoned finals performer Jason Dunstall was proving difficult to contain as John Platten tore through the centre to repeatedly deliver the ball to him. Hawthorn hit the lead and maintained it, just, until the last quarter, when several goals in succession went unanswered and the gap became impossible for the Eagles to reduce. The Hawks won by 23 points and taught West Coast a valuable lesson in humility.

Time for a reality check. Winning comes from hard work, no matter how much talent you possess. Responding to a lecture from their coach, a recharged Eagles team travelled to Melbourne for a semi-final clash with the Demons. After a slow start, the Eagles found the form that had recently gone missing. A second-half blitz with multiple goalkickers led to an assured 38-point victory.

Mick's unease was lifting, or perhaps it was just our fervency at home that was rubbing off on him as we played 'One Day in September' on repeat on the CD player.

It was a wet and freezing Melbourne day the following weekend when the Eagles took on Geelong at Waverley Park. The mud in the carpark alone slowed arriving supporters to a dawdle. Every goal in this match would be worth double, so a four-goal-to-one opening term was a handy start for West Coast. Scoring slowed as the rain pelted harder, but you should never underestimate a talented team. Missing Gary Ablett and Billy Brownless from their forward line, the Cats fought hard to resurrect their season—but the Eagles fought harder. With a grand final berth in sight, every act became one of desperation. West Coast withstood Geelong's comeback and held on for a fifteen-point win. It was a defining victory for the courage and determination shown. It was also possibly the coldest game Mick was ever involved in. The players didn't even strip before entering the showers after the match, standing under the taps until the hot water ran out.

Within the space of two seasons, the Eagles had been catapulted from the bottom half of the AFL ladder to the top. It was a leap more than a climb, propelled by discipline and structure, and a more purposeful use of talent and skill. With a fresh desire to succeed and a belief that it was possible, West Coast had booked its place in the 1991 Grand Final. Perth erupted into Eagles mania.

6 PAIN AND GAIN

THERE IS ONLY ONE night of the year that comes close to the excitement and thrill of Christmas Eve in our family, and that is grand final eve. The anticipation on the Friday night before the biggest game of the football season is almost the same as that before the arrival of a stocking full of gifts from a big jolly man dressed in red. But instead of Santa, it's two coaches and their teams who hold the hopes and dreams of supporters in their grasp; unlike Santa, they won't make everyone happy.

The 1991 Grand Final was played at Waverley Park for the first and last time in the current era, because the MCG was under heavy reconstruction. Mick had been nervous, not just because of the enormity of the occasion, but because he knew how tough it was going to be to win. The Eagles had made their way to this final encounter the hard way, and they were exhausted from so much travelling. Hawthorn had had plenty of finals experience over the years and were a very good team.

We didn't go to Melbourne. Logistically and financially it was too difficult to fly four children across the country for one game, so we stayed—separately—with friends. I was fourteen, Danielle twelve, Cain seven and Troy six.

I woke grand final morning missing my siblings. Only they could understand the nerves and impatience I was feeling for our dad. We had each wished him good luck over the phone the night before, and now we waited for the game to begin. I went with my friend Belinda and her family to another school friend's house in the lofty suburb of Dalkeith. People had gathered to sip champagne, snack on prawns and socialise. The footy was on the TV in the background.

I sat in an adjoining room on the floor, legs crossed and eyes glued to the set. I didn't move for over two and a half hours. Children played games around me. My friends disappeared to a bedroom to read magazines and discuss boys. Parents laughed at Angry Anderson's 'Bound For Glory' rendition and talked about their kids, every once in a while glancing towards the television before turning back to the group, unfazed by the build-up of tension.

The game began and back in Perth I took a deep breath in, and exhaled slowly and deliberately like I was inflating a balloon. I knew my sister and brothers were doing the same in nearby homes, trying to calm the nerves that churned our stomachs. The start was physical but the Eagles flexed their muscles as aggressively as their opponents did. By quarter time we had a nine-point lead.

Hawthorn's stars—Dermot Brereton, Jason Dunstall and Gary Ayres—were well matched by West Coast's soldiers—Brett Heady, Chris Lewis and Peter Sumich—but by half time the Hawks had taken back the lead.

There's an AFL expression that 'the third quarter is the premiership quarter'. In this case, the third term was a dead tie as both sides scored five goals and three behinds in a determined clash of strength and skill. With half an hour of football remaining to determine the 1991 premiers, my heart raced as it tried to keep up with the thoughts that darted through my mind. Can we do this? Who looks more tired, us or them? What is Dad saying to the team right now? The umpire bounced the ball to start the last quarter and again I exhaled a loud sigh. 'COME ON, EAGLES!' I shouted, not caring that someone laughed at my outburst.

Then it happened. Hawthorn took off. And West Coast got left behind. Every goal the Hawks kicked was like a punch to my ribs. It made me feel sick. I felt like crying. But I took the hits and sat and watched what was now a horror movie, silently praying for a miracle.

The Eagles kicked one goal in the last quarter. Hawthorn kicked eight—it was their ninth premiership win. It was the first grand final loss for a team coached by Dad.

I went for a walk with my friends soon after the final siren and they repeated their parents' words: 'Oh well, bad luck, they'll do it next year.' It wasn't comforting. When I finally spoke to Mum on the phone a few hours later, she wasn't very comforting either. Her words were slow with sorrow. She said Dad couldn't take the call because he had just broken down on the phone to Danielle. My sister was inconsolable after hearing the crack in her father's voice, and the boys weren't talking at all.

I shed my own tears then, for all of us. For Dad, hiding his head in his hands back in his hotel room. For Mum, embracing a young and visibly upset Glen Jakovich outside the Waverley change rooms. For Danielle, feeling as alone as me, trying to fall asleep in her friend's bedroom. For Cain and Troy, old enough to feel the unhappy emotion but too young to know how to deal with it.

Losing a grand final is like losing a friend named Hope. Sure, there'll possibly be chances to make new friends in the future, mates called Joy, Triumph and perhaps Relief. But you will always feel an element of regret that you couldn't hold on to that one friendship. That you let Hope go without so much as a hug goodbye. A grand final loss is gut-wrenching.

Of course, I can't speak for the players who put their total physical and mental selves into training, preparing for, and playing the games. I don't know how their hurt feels. But I believe I can speak on behalf of the families of those players and coaches, who invest as much heart and spirit into the team's efforts as the men themselves do. We hurt seeing them hurt.

At a grand final dinner held for West Coast at Melbourne's Southern Cross Hotel that night, Dad made a speech that some considered harsh. He told his players they should never want to feel this way again, that given the opportunity over they should want to avoid finishing second, at all costs. He told everyone gathered in the ballroom to harness the hurt and use it to drive their purpose in future seasons. It wasn't insensitive, and it certainly wasn't unsympathetic. It was how he felt.

By Monday morning, my siblings and I braced ourselves for what we might encounter at school. I'd often found myself the unwitting defender of Peter Sumich. As the Eagles' full-forward—now an assistant coach at the Fremantle Dockers—he broke all sorts of records in those early years, including becoming the first left-footer to kick more than 100 goals in a season. He also holds an AFL record for kicking the most points in a season: 89 behinds came with those 111 goals booted in 1991—not including those that went out of bounds—and for every point he kicked I copped an earful. The only other person to defend him as vigorously as I did was my girlfriend Samantha, who had been in love with 'Suma' since his South Fremantle days. We were always a fired-up duo on a Monday after a game if he missed more goals than he kicked.

But that particular Monday—despite Peter Sumich actually kicking five straight goals in the losing grand final—the kids kept quiet. I actually think they didn't know what to say. 'I'm sorry for your loss, my condolences' seemed a little over the top for a game of football. 'Who cares?' Heartless. 'Next year' didn't cut it, because another grand final isn't ever guaranteed. So they said nothing. Which was fine by me.

The loss galvanised the squad, and as Mick had predicted in his post-game speech, his players' appetite for a premiership had become more than a hunger—they were now starving for one. They started their own traditions, enhancing the sense of team and the new feeling that West Coast was finally a genuine AFL club.

Thursday night became steak night. A T-bone for every man, cooked medium rare on the barbecue after training. My brothers started going to the club for this weekly ritual, and just as Danielle and I had felt while sitting among the players' partners at Footscray, Cain and Troy felt like they belonged. It became common practice on those nights for the players to give the boys boxing gloves and encourage them to duel in a playful bout. Chris Mainwaring found it particularly amusing to hide Cain and Troy in the lockers of his teammates, who were taken by great surprise when they tried to collect their boots and a lanky, boisterous kid jumped out at them. The boys often had to wait a while for the locker doors to be reopened so I'm sure his trick was also a way to keep them quiet for a short period!

Chris was one of Mick's players for whom the whole family felt real affection. His death in 2007 stunned and deeply saddened Mick and Nanette. He may have had troubles away from football that later became difficult to deal with, but in all the time that Mick knew him, 'Mainy' was nothing but genuine and friendly. And happy. It doesn't take much for me to conjure up his smile—a grin that was as infectious as chickenpox. Mick remembers Chris Mainwaring as one of his hardest workers at training, leaving nothing of himself on the track. His natural talent and footy smarts were evident for all to see as he turned every possession into a gift for his team. It was his work ethic that made him a footballer of elite quality and his exuberant personality made him a friend to everyone.

Two years had come and gone and we were still in Perth. Dad's contract had been extended and with it came a pay rise—to my parents' relief. As a family we were established in the community through school and basketball. Clearly our 'experiment' had been successful. We were staying put.

Every West Coast player from those years—John Worsfold, Guy McKenna, Peter Matera, Dean Kemp, Ashley McIntosh, Tony Evans, Don Pyke, Brett Heady, Dwayne Lamb, Peter Sumich, Chris Mainwaring, Glen Jakovich—very quickly became a household name in Perth. Sporting achievements are glorified in WA, and as football is the number-one sport, Eagles players are considered, like Hollywood movie stars, as role models, whether they deserve it or not.

But the Eagles didn't exactly get off to a flying start in the 1992 season, winning and losing games by the smallest of margins and even drawing with Brisbane in Round 5. By stringing four wins together three times throughout the season, they remained a top-four threat. Then two big losses—in Rounds 18 and 23, when they scored fewer than

30 points against their opposition—left some football critics questioning how far West Coast could actually go.

They finished fourth at the end of the season proper: Geelong was on top, Footscray second and Collingwood third, in what was then the top six. Mick, dismissing statistics for a 'gut feel', felt at ease with the season and confident about the approaching finals. West Coast had defeated the reigning premiers, Hawthorn, by two goals at the midpoint of the season, shaking off any lingering memories from the grand final loss, so facing them in an elimination final held less fear. In Round 19, the Eagles had downed Geelong at Kardinia Park by nineteen points, so should they advance and contest with the Cats, they would be armed with confidence.

Mick had built a solid team around him in the coach's box and at the selection table, and they all shared a close bond: Robbie Wiley, Ian Miller, Tim Gepp, George Young, Trevor Sprigg and Trevor Nisbett as football manager.

On Melbourne trips the match committee would rise before the player group and jog to a nearby tennis club to compete in a quite competitive doubles match, and Mick laughs to this day at the memory of 'Spriggy' puffing on a cigarette between games. He says the tennis relaxed them before a match, and they continued their friendly tournament right through the finals series.

The 1991 Grand Final loss had matured the team. They were hardened to finals and understood what was required of them. Its late entry into the league meant West Coast was years behind the other teams in experience. Melbourne crowds are large and vocal, particularly so during finals, when more is at stake. The intensity of these matches lifts to a level of brain-zapping electricity. In the previous two years, the Eagles had been fast-tracked in these football lessons.

A first-up win in September 1992 was vital. Playing at home, West Coast was in need of the extra support at quarter time after stumbling through the first term. 'E-guls, E-guls, E-guls,' the crowd cheered, and clapped in time. We joined in from where we sat, having drunk our hot chocolates and eaten the egg and bacon rolls that Mum always packed for home games. Away from us, she gritted her teeth and clenched her hands in her lap, surrounded by club directors and sponsors.

By three-quarter time, the margin had been reduced to three points in Hawthorn's favour.

When Mick was asked what he said to his teams in the huddles during close games he would always shrug and answer, 'I can't really remember.' He was in an adrenaline haze in those moments, when the game is in the balance and his players need a lift. He would speak from experience and intuition, guiding the team through the challenge like a pilot landing an airplane. Whatever he said this time, his men were inspired, grappling for a two-goal lead and holding it until the final siren. It was a huge confidence-booster for everyone involved.

AFL footballers can be a superstitious lot, and while Dad didn't have too many of his own superstitions as a coach, his wife and children made up for it. For the first final, Mum had decorated the house with blue and yellow irises, so she bought them again for West Coast's semi-final against Geelong at the MCG. We watched the game on television at home. I wore the 'lucky' jumper that I'd worn all season (even when the weather didn't call for long sleeves), we ate nachos with extra cheese, as we had done for most of the Eagles' away games that year, and we all reclaimed the same 'tested' positions on the couch. How could West Coast lose?

They didn't. In fact, in a game that was described at the time as having all the hallmarks of a grand final, the Eagles led from start to finish, improving the scoreline each quarter to win by 38 points. The victory earned the team a week off, time to recover and to prepare. In a fortnight, West Coast would compete in its second grand final in two years.

I can so clearly remember my train ride into the MCG on the Saturday morning of the grand final. West Coast faced Geelong, who had beaten Footscray in the preliminary final. I was with my uncle and two cousins and we had dressed in as much blue and yellow as we could—not exactly a fashion statement—so we stood out in a carriage full of dark blue and white. Following a throng of people walking from the train station to the stadium, we passed buskers who sang the Geelong club theme song and were asked five times if we wanted to buy the *Football Record*. Repeatedly we were told to 'go home' by several Cats supporters who claimed that the Eagles stood no chance. Mum had reserved a seat for me next to her in the stand, though once I sat down there was little pre-game chatter between us as we both fought our nerves.

Dad's own concerns intensified when he saw the fired-up Cats team in the race before the game. When midfielder Don Pyke was knocked out by Gary Ablett in the early minutes of the opening term, Dad's suspicion that his opposition would be over the top with aggression was confirmed. As soon as Pyke was upright and coherent, he was returned to field 'to prove to Geelong that we wouldn't be intimidated'.

The Cats took an early lead—and didn't we know about it where we sat, adjacent to the Geelong members. Having worked out that our group was related to the West Coast players and coach, the Geelong supporters turned to us after all five of the Cats' first-term goals, and not so politely appealed to us to return to Perth before the game was out. We barracked louder.

By half time Geelong had a lead of twelve points and still the crowd beside us continued to challenge our resolve. They clearly didn't notice what Dad saw as he made his way from the field: the Geelong players were looking tired. With this observation he spurred his players on, knowing they 'had plenty left in them'.

The Eagles out-ran, out-scored and out-played the Cats in the second half, led by Tony Evans' courage and attack on the ball, Brett Heady's tagging efforts on Paul Couch, and Peter Matera's outstanding ball work. At the final siren, Chris Mainwaring jumped for joy despite having a broken ankle, such was the rapture of the players at having won a premiership. He didn't even flinch, as though the jubilation had completely numbed his pain.

Near us, it was like the mute button had been pressed on a TV remote: the once rowdy group of Cats supporters had gone quiet. Some of them had already gone home. We didn't mock them—we didn't need to, we were too busy cheering on our team. With joyful tears spilling down our cheeks, Mum and I turned to each other and hugged.

Danielle, who had been training for the opening match of the Under-16 National Basketball Championships, was struck by the empty streets of Perth as her team drove back to their hotel to watch the medal presentation.

The boys had stayed with family friends, and showed their support by pumping their small fists in the air and shouting at the television as our dad appeared on the screen, being congratulated by the men he shared the coach's box with. They shook his hand, smacked his back and roughly rubbed his head in a masculine display of affection.

Mick felt nothing but relief to have won, but his full-face smile and enthusiastic embrace of his players on the ground revealed the true joy that he would graciously accept later. Seeing him hold the Premiership Cup with John Worsfold and raise it high above his head in the middle of the MCG gave me goosebumps. The memory of it still does.

This time, the grand final dinner was one of pure delight. We posed with the cup as the players danced to Daddy Cool's 'Eagle Rock', which played on repeat all night. It was an evening to savour.

What we would encounter the following day at Perth airport, as our plane came in to land, was a welcome of surreal proportions. Two fire trucks formed an archway of water for the plane to travel through. We were bundled off the aircraft and into a bus to keep the ecstatic crowd at a safe distance. Cars lined the lengthy exit of the airport and were parked on the side of every road leading to Subiaco Oval, where the team was to be presented to their supporters. It was madness.

The Premiership Cup had never left Victoria before, and on this day it was greeted in great West Australian style.

Cain and Troy met us at the ground and walked with Dad onto the stage. They remember the crowd, which almost covered the entire oval, as wild. Each player was greeted by a deafening cheer as he was introduced. The applause for Dad could have been heard five suburbs away, and even over the roar of the waves at Trigg Beach. It was a wonderful acknowledgement.

We arrived home in the afternoon to find that our neighbours had decorated the front of our house in blue and yellow balloons and streamers. A nice touch. A sign, also, that our family had been accepted into the neighbourhood.

Danielle had her first-ever state basketball match that night, and after a quick stop at home, Mum and Dad were the first parents to arrive at the basketball stadium. Dad was eager to show Danielle the gold premiership medal he had been awarded the day before. She was already on court warming up with her team, so after waving hello he walked to the baseline and motioned for Danielle to meet him.

'Hello, darling,' he said as they quickly hugged. She congratulated him again and went to return to her team.

'Look!' Dad produced his newly acquired prize, holding it up for her to see.

'Dad, I'm warming up for a game! I don't have time to look at your medal right now,' said Danielle, direct as always.

Dad laughed with Mum as he sat down beside her to watch his thirteen-year-old daughter represent Western Australia in a sport she loved. He had been put back in his place.

Everything is brighter after a grand final win. Birthdays, Christmas and New Year celebrations are all somehow sweeter. Even trade week and the National Draft—times when Mick was always stressed each year—couldn't dampen the spring in his step. Then came the start of another season. The premiership medallion was hidden in the bottom drawer of the bedroom dresser and along with it the feeling of success was put away. It was time to prepare from scratch for another long and fickle year. It kind of brought the mood down.

Mick believed that—after such a high—his players' hunger for triumph might diminish with the summer heat. It was his job as the coach to keep a lid on the excitement and expectations of his team at times, and at other times to motivate and urge his players to aim higher. It's a hard task to pick them up and keep them grounded at the same time.

West Coast had become the hunted, as each team tried with increasing vigour to upset the reigning champs, and 1993 was a true roller-coaster season. Mick seemed to be always tired and stressed. Nanette absorbed the negativity and tried to keep a happy balance at home, but for their children at school there was no escaping the season—their father was either a hero or a traitor, depending on the week.

The Eagles staggered into the 1993 finals with twelve wins and eight losses and then convincingly beat North Melbourne in the elimination final. The Kangaroos had finished third on the ladder and had beaten West Coast by a goal in their only other encounter during the season. By now, the Glen Jakovich and Wayne Carey duels had become a contest of strength and cunning that many football fans looked forward to witnessing. At Waverley Park on this occasion it was Jakovich who trumped his rival, keeping the North Melbourne superstar goalless, and helping the Eagles to a 51-point win.

In the MCG semi-final the following Sunday, Essendon proved to be a tougher opponent, stamping its authority from the outset. West Coast failed to recover, going down to the eventual premiers by 32 points.

Season over.

Life went on despite football, and as a family, we rode the changes together.

We moved house to a new suburb at the edge of our school. A relatively new redbrick home, it came complete with air-conditioning, a pool and landscaped gardens. It would be a happy home for us.

*

The Eagles' 1994 season started with a close loss to the reigning premiers, Essendon, though far from being a red flag alert, the three-point defeat—a big improvement on the result of the last encounter between the two teams—was a positive sign.

As winter approached, West Coast's dominance emerged, with half of its eventual sixteen wins resulting in a margin of more than seven goals. The team didn't suffer back-to-back losses for the entire season, and for the second time in Mick's reign, the Eagles finished on top of the ladder. It was a season to be proud of and gave reason for spring excitement.

In the last game of the home-and-away season, however, the mood changed. Just before half time in the match at Subiaco Oval, an all-in brawl erupted between the West Coast and Footscray players at the boundary line on the wing. As the players wrestled and swung fists at one another, someone in the crowd yelled, 'He's choking him!'

Bulldogs defender Danny Southern had Peter Sumich in a stranglehold and the Eagles forward had gone limp. Glen Jakovich tried desperately to pull Southern off his mate, realising the seriousness of the situation. By the time the umpires regained control, Peter Sumich lay slumped face-down on the grass. The crowd was quiet and scared. People wondered if he was dead but didn't dare ask, fearful of the enormity of what was occurring in front of them. Medical staff carried the Eagles' leading goal-kicker down the race and into the rooms.

Mick later revealed that Peter Sumich had blacked out due to the strangulation and was very close to suffering permanent damage through a lack of oxygen to the brain. Upon his retirement in 2000, Southern admitted that he feared at the time that he had killed the Eagles' full-forward.

It was an ugly day for football that led to a worrying week for West Coast as it waited for the AFL tribunal to hand out its punishment to a host of players reported for the melee. All eight of the reported footballers from both sides were heavily fined. Southern was ordered to pay ten thousand dollars. No-one was suspended.

Mum had just waved us all off to school when the shrill of the phone broke the silence of a house empty of children. She answered, listened to the caller at the other end, then dropped the phone in fright. It was a man claiming to be Danny Southern: 'Tell Mick if he doesn't shut up about me, I'll fucken' shut him up.' And he hung up.

Mum called Dad in tears. He assured her it was a prank, though they were both unnerved that the caller had somehow acquired our silent phone number. Dad told the Eagles' CEO, who alerted the Western Australia Police. They weren't prepared to take any chances that it wasn't just a hoax and ordered protection for our family by way of a patrol car keeping close tabs on the house, and on us.

I'm not sure that the sight of a police car by the front nature strip was really all that comforting to my parents, as it acted as a reminder of the threat and the price of fame. Would somebody really harm a member of our family because of a football match? It was a scary thought. After a week with no further phone calls or any sign of trouble, the police packed up and left our street.

It wasn't exactly a great lead-up to a final and Dad and the West Coast team went into the qualifying final still trying to get their focus back on football.

In a twilight match at the WACA, the Eagles built on a two-goal margin at quarter time to lead by 24 points at three-quarter time. But the Pies, having beaten the Eagles by 37 points during the season, issued a final-term challenge.

Kicking six straight goals, Collingwood had all the momentum. Magpies fans sensed an upset and though they were outnumbered at the Perth stadium, their support could be heard across the ground. It was the inspiration the visitors needed for one last push for victory. I screamed with my siblings until our throats were sore, trying to outdo the visiting black-and-white army. It was all we could do. We didn't even know how much time was left.

It felt like hours before the sound of the siren finally drowned out the Pies' cheer squad and ended the match, just in time. West Coast had won by two points.

Almost losing scared the Eagles into purpose and it was the Demons who suffered the effects. For four quarters of the preliminary final at the WACA, West Coast played with determination and poise, beating Melbourne by 65 points. It seemed like the team had reached its full potential.

The Eagles were in the grand final, and another premiership beckoned.

*

I was in the middle of Year 12 mock exams but there was no way I was going to miss it. Danielle would go too, but the boys, much to their annoyance, would stay in Perth again. I completed my Human Biology examination on the Friday afternoon and travelled to Melbourne that night, taking with me my study notes for an English exam on the Monday.

I don't think I was nervous on grand final morning—at least, not as nervous as I had been for the grand final in 1992. Danielle probably felt more anxious for her first live grand final with Dad coaching. There were more Eagles supporters for this third tilt, a sea of royal blue and yellow making the players feel right at home. They'd begun a chant at Subiaco Oval that season, similar to the cheering heard at Premier League soccer matches: 'Eeee–guuuulls,' they sang together, each syllable stretched to its limit as they pronounced the name with purpose. Over and over like a mantra they chanted it, getting louder and louder as the game progressed until you couldn't hear anything else.

The Cats led at quarter time by a point. Then West Coast, with its backing track of support, took over. Once again, Dean Kemp, Guy McKenna, Michael Brennan, Glen Jakovich, Don Pyke and Tony Evans dominated their opponents. While some inaccurate kicking belied the team's true supremacy on the scoreboard, there was no doubting how in control of the match they were. Mick actually remembers enjoying the game, a rarity for him, stealing a moment to sit back and take in all the elements of this immense achievement. He felt relaxed for most of the match—which is surprising, given he can count on one hand how many times he's felt like that during the 28 years he coached AFL!

The Eagles won by 80 points for their second premiership in three years. When Mick held the cup aloft in the centre of the ground, his transformation of the West Coast Eagles was complete.

When children reach milestones or do something to impress, it is the parent who feels proudest. In this case, it was Mick's kids, his wife, his parents and his in-laws, all at the game, who wanted to shout to the 93,000 people in attendance: 'He's ours! That man who just coached the Eagles to their second premiership, that gifted and talented and wise and humble man, belongs to us. We are so happy for him and we are so goddamned proud of him!'

The response in Perth was even crazier than it had been two years previously. The Eagles and Mick were given the keys to the city by the lord mayor, after a parade through the streets of Perth. They were all kings of Western Australia.

7 THE WESTERN FRONT

A POLL IN *The West Australian* newspaper once asked its readers to list who they thought were the most famous people in the state. Mick Malthouse came in at number one, above actors, politicians, musicians, other athletes and footballers, and business tycoons, of which there are many in very wealthy Perth. It basically confirmed what the family already knew: Dad was the most famous person in the city. That probably sounds better than the reality of living with a father who is recognised everywhere he goes.

The more someone stands out in the public eye, the more people will feel an affinity with them. Society is fed glimpses of a personality, but when those pieces are put together to form a whole, it doesn't necessarily match the real person. In WA, people thought they knew my dad, but in reality, they didn't know him at all. Rarely did other people get to see the father who made us laugh at the kitchen table, or the man who played practical jokes on his players. They didn't know he cooled his young sons down at bedtime on a hot night by washing them with a cold facecloth, or that he sat with his daughters while they did their homework, helping with mathematical equations and looking up science answers he didn't know in the encyclopedia.

Every time Dad's contract came up for renewal, it made back-page news. His salary—never once reported accurately, and always overestimated—was discussed often. People voiced their opinions on the way he coached. They assumed from the snippets of interviews they saw on TV that he always spoke in short, abrupt sentences. They talked about our family as if we were close acquaintances. And now and then, someone would just make something up to cause trouble—for their own amusement, or just because they could.

We had very little privacy as a family, but we learnt to live with it by becoming private. Mick Malthouse, the Eagles' coach, wasn't the same person as Michael, our father, and we were happy for them to be two different people. We were different in public too; much more guarded than we were in our home. In this way, we protected who we really were. We needed to do that more and more often after the 1994 Premiership win.

Western Australia's support of the Eagles was about to be tested, with a second Perth club joining the AFL competition in 1995. There had been so much talk and argument about the introduction of this new club. Could Perth support two AFL teams? Where would it be located? What would it be called? Who would coach them? Should the Claremont Football Club just be elevated from the WAFL to the AFL? This last suggestion came from some very vocal Claremont associates, including the club's coach, Gerard Neesham.

But there must have been a few sceptics, because the Claremont idea never took off. The new club was built from the same basis as the other fifteen AFL clubs—recruits and draftees from across the country formed the team list, and support from the league set the standards and guidelines of participation.

And so it happened that the sixteenth AFL club became known as the Fremantle Dockers, named to pay tribute to the long history of football in the port city. Their inaugural coach was Gerard Neesham, their captain was Hawthorn premiership player Ben Allan and their first match was against Richmond at the MCG on 1 April 1995. They lost.

It was Round 7 when West Coast and Fremantle met in the first ever 'Western Derby'—pronounced as it's written, and named after the customary clashes between East and South Fremantle. My brothers told Dad, 'You can't lose to Fremantle—we won't be able to go back to school.' Danielle and I agreed.

The upcoming contest seemed to divide the state as the 'south of the river' populace jumped on board the Dockers' bandwagon, and the 'north of the river' inhabitants stayed firm with the Eagles. Fremantle fans called West Coast supporters 'snobby', and they retaliated by labelling the Freo crowd 'feral'.

It was all very amusing until the Eagles thumped the Dockers by almost 90 points, and the name-calling became serious.

In many ways, the introduction of a second AFL team in Perth took the pressure off the Eagles. For a start, there were now two clubs, two coaches and two squads for the media to focus on. Fremantle's fan base was a lot smaller than that of the Eagles, but it allowed for comparison of performance and eased, somewhat, the unrealistic expectation of West Coast supporters that their club would play in a grand final every year.

What Mick hadn't really considered until the first Derby was the significance to his players of a neighbouring team. He was astounded at the ferocity shown by the players during that first clash. They were marking their territory, he realised, making a statement that Perth was their backyard and they were the number-one team in it. John Worsfold led the act and the team followed.

The Round 22 Derby didn't get any better for Fremantle, with West Coast rounding off the home-and-away season with an eight-goal victory over its cross-town rivals. Mick believes that suffering a big loss in the first Derby had affected the psychology of the Dockers squad and would for many years to come.

Fremantle completed its season with eight wins, finishing thirteenth on the ladder. The Eagles were once again in the finals, having sealed fifth spot with fourteen wins.

West Coast's form had been affected by injuries. The club had had a fairly good run with the availability of key players until now, which had helped greatly. In 1995, though, Peter Sumich, Karl Langdon and Ashley McIntosh were among the big-name players to miss several games through injury. Chris Mainwaring suffered two dislocated shoulders during the season and managed only nine games. And Tony Evans—who Mick used as the barometer for the team since he was 'as hard as a cat's head'—missed eight games in the second half of the season. The Eagles had become ragged around the edges.

Football coaches won't ever use injuries as an excuse for a below-par season, but behind closed doors they will lament the loss of key players. Or at least, my dad always did. We were almost more afraid of seeing him after a game in which a player was injured than if the team had suffered a loss. And we could always tell if an incident had occurred at training by the way he walked through the front door of our home—stealthily, like a ghost, as if he thought that by not disturbing us, we couldn't disturb him and his negative thoughts. It was Mum who so often became the voice of reason. She was the yin to his yang, staying positive and reminding him of the benefits of debuting a rookie or elevating a reserves player to fill the role of the injured man.

In saying that, injuries do affect the balance of the team, the dynamics of the player group and the structures, and sometimes even the mood of the whole club. When several players are missing together, the team can become like a patchwork quilt.

One versatile utility player who made his debut during the season was Fraser Gehrig—whom Mick describes as a superb athlete and as strong as an ox. He would go on to become an important part of the forward line at West Coast, before dominating as a full-forward for the St Kilda Football Club, winning back-to-back Coleman Medals in 2004 and 2005.

The Eagles played Essendon at Waverley Park in a qualifying final. In a sign of the team's fatigue, they scored just 2.2 in the second half, to lose by nineteen points.

At the MCG the following weekend, North Melbourne took advantage of West Coast's slump in form and sent the visitors home with a 58-point loss. Mick hates losing—it's one of the things that makes him a good coach—so it's fair to say he was down in the dumps when he returned home from that game.

Needing a break, Mum and Dad took advantage of an offer from a friend who owned a beautiful beach house in Peaceful Bay, near Denmark in southern WA. They took Cain and Troy with them, who, at twelve and eleven, were still young enough to miss a few days of school without concern.

They'd been gone just a day when the home phone started ringing. It was a journalist wanting to speak to Dad. Because of the seclusion of the coastal town there was no mobile phone service so Dad was unreachable. The reporter wanted to confirm whether or not Dad was going to Richmond. Ah, excuse me?

Danielle and I hadn't heard anything of the sort from our parents but when the calls kept coming we wondered what was going on. Finally, Mum called home from a payphone she'd located in town.

'Mum, the media keeps calling to see if Dad is going to Richmond,' Danielle said before Mum had finished saying hello and asking how we were coping on our own.

'What? What are you talking about?' Mum asked while motioning for Dad to join her in the phone box. Danielle explained the calls we'd received and Mum and Dad laughed it off, saying, 'It must be the latest rumour. Don't worry, if they keep calling, tell them to ring someone at the club.'

By the time they returned home, tanned and relaxed from their week at the beach, the rumour of a Malthouse defection to Punt Road had became news and I was being quizzed by my Channel Seven and *Sunday Times* work colleagues, and Danielle by friends, as to the truth of it.

One early morning, as Mum and Dad lay in bed listening to the radio, a caller declared on the station's 'rumour file' that she could confirm that Mick Malthouse was going to Richmond because his two boys were enrolled at Richmond Grammar. She knew that for a fact, apparently.

'Is that true?' worried Troy, who had stepped into their bedroom to say good morning.

'Of course it isn't.'

Firstly, Dad was contracted to the Eagles—he hadn't even spoken to Richmond, and he didn't know where this ridiculous notion had come from. Secondly, that school didn't even exist—and never had.

It didn't stop people's curiosity, though. Mum couldn't even go to the supermarket without being stopped by other shoppers who asked her if we were leaving. Down the track,

Robert Walls' appointment as the Tigers' coach finally put an end to the story.

*

In 1996, Ben Cousins made his debut for the Eagles, the Fitzroy Football Club played its final season in its own right, and an AFL regulation caused finals mayhem.

But first things first. The Eagles started the season with another win over Fremantle. In Round 2, they hosted Brisbane at the WACA. Late in the first term, Mick saw something that made him shiver. From the back pocket, John Worsfold ran from the field. Unless a mistake had been made on the bench, the Eagles' captain wasn't supposed to be coming off, which meant one thing: he needed to come off.

As tough as always, Worsfold disguised his pain by running instead of limping off the ground. Mick made a beeline for the club doctor at quarter time to ask about his skipper. 'It's bad,' he was told. Bad enough to keep Worsfold sidelined for a year, as it turned out. A tear to his anterior cruciate ligament (ACL) meant he had to undergo a knee reconstruction.

The eventual loss to Brisbane was the first of four defeats in a row for West Coast. The fourth defeat was against Carlton, but the television replays showed it shouldn't have been a loss at all.

Certain games will stick in your mind: for the result, the performance of the team or a particular player, or because of a single incident that affected the outcome of the match. This was a single-incident game. In the third quarter, the ball was in Carlton's forward 50 when Tony Evans soccered it through for a point. Evans' opponent, Blues midfielder Greg Williams, celebrated from within the pack at the top of the goalsquare as if he had kicked the ball himself. The umpires awarded Williams the goal. Eagles players vigorously protested the decision and a slow-motion replay on Channel Seven revealed that, in fact, Williams' boot hadn't even touched the ball. It was a rushed behind and should have been called so. That goal made all the difference, too, because West Coast lost the match by a point, and the loss would come back to haunt them in September.

Perhaps, though, it was also the catalyst for the winning streak that followed—eleven in a row. The seventh win, against St Kilda in Round 12, came at a cost, however.

After a week of rain, the Subiaco Oval surface was slippery. One particular area of the ground—near the forward pocket at the western end—had earned a bad reputation in recent times and been nicknamed 'wounded knee'. It was about to claim its next, and perhaps most significant, victim.

In the final term of the match against St Kilda, the Eagles' medical staff rushed to the aid of a player who lay crumpled on the ground. One hand was in the air to signify that he needed assistance, and the other hand on his right knee. The number on the back of his jumper wasn't clear to the crowd, but still Mick knew who it was.

In career-best form, after a three-peat of club best-and-fairest wins, Glen Jakovich came off the field in distress. Mick's heart sank for a player with whom he shared a close bond, and then his mind went into overdrive: What has he done? How long will he be out for? Will he be the same when he comes back? Who will I replace him with?

Glen Jakovich underwent a knee reconstruction on the Monday to repair a ruptured ACL. He had been a star performer in West Coast's backline and replacing him would be like switching to soy milk for your morning coffee. It would take a lot of team adjustment to accommodate the absence of a regular performer. Mick was in a sombre mood all week.

Mick had a soft spot for Glen: he spoke of him often and in a way that a parent speaks of a son. He was more than a coach to Glen, he was a mentor, and in the absence of his own father, who had passed away years earlier, Glen himself called Mick a father-figure. They actually teamed up, long after their West Coast days, in the coach's box in 2008 and 2010, when Mick invited Glen to be one of his assistants for the Australian team against Ireland in the International Rules series.

Now, it would be remiss of me here not to admit to something quite embarrassing to do with Glen Jakovich. So here goes. Through my early years of high school I had a crush on him. A major crush. The type of crush where even your hair changes colour at the sight of him. And talk about tongue-tied! I would either launch into tangled gibberish or greet him with monosyllabic sounds if ever we crossed paths long enough to attempt a conversation. Thankfully, Glen, at just eighteen years of age and with a mouthful of braces, was just as shy as I was, so our verbal exchanges were always brief.

I'm not speaking (or writing) out of line here, either, because, to my great humiliation and mortification, Robbie Wiley, a once trusted family friend, teased Glen about my adolescent affections. 'Beetroot red' doesn't even describe my blushing when next I saw him after Robbie's betrayal. Knowing that the coach's fifteen-year-old daughter had a crush on him must have been hell for the poor guy, but luckily Dad found it amusing, and hopefully that lessened any anxiety Glen had over the situation. I got past my crush pretty quickly after it was no longer a secret and even now I am abashed as I write about it. Danielle wanted to marry Tony McGuinness when we were at Footscray, but as she was only seven then, it doesn't really count.

By late July in 1996, and after eleven wins, West Coast succumbed to the Brisbane Bears at the Gabba in Round 17. At season's end, they'd finished fourth on the ladder with fifteen wins, an equal record to Brisbane in third, and just one win behind Sydney and North Melbourne in the top two positions. If only that one-point loss to Carlton had ended differently . . .

The Eagles met the Blues in the qualifying final at Subiaco Oval and got a jump start on their rivals, kicking six goals to one in the opening term. Carlton staged a fightback in the third quarter, keeping West Coast to a solitary goal. But a dominant Eagles backline, led by Guy McKenna, quelled the run-on, and they strode into the semi-final with a 55-point win.

In the top-eight system, as it was played then, first played eighth, second played seventh, and so on, in the first round of finals. The top four teams all won, which meant the bottom two losing teams—Geelong and Hawthorn—were eliminated. As the lowest-ranked winner of the first week, West Coast was to play the lowest-ranked loser, Essendon, at home in the next final.

But this scheduling didn't take into account the contract the AFL had with the Melbourne Cricket Ground, which stated: 'at least one game will be played at the MCG in every week of the finals.' This MCC requirement hadn't been updated since the AFL competition had become a national league. No amount of lobbying, pleading or legal challenges would alter the decree, so the final was to be played at the MCG and the Eagles would have to travel again.

The rule has since been modernised and now the highest-ranked competing team will always receive a home final. With the emergence of non-Victorian clubs, the MCG has been left empty on several occasions during September in the past decade. The grand final will always remain there, however.

There was a chorus of disapproval in Perth at the decision, and perhaps it was too loud, for it distracted the players' attention and added to the pressure they were already carrying. As a coach, Mick says one thing you must always try to avoid is outside influences and bias. At this point, though, it was

Mick's dad Ray, 1951, Ballarat

Mick's mum Marie, 1951, Ballarat

Mick as a baby, 1954,
Ballarat

Fishing near Ballarat with mum and dad, 1963

Ready for a North Ballarat football match, 1968

St Kilda, 1973

Mick in action for St Kilda v Carlton, 1973

Nanette modelling for the Wool Awards, Melbourne, 1971

Nanette and Mick, Christmas, 1972

Nanette and Mick's wedding,
Immaculate Heart of Mary,
Hampton, 1974

Mick in action for Richmond v Hawthorn, MCG

Richmond premiership, 1980

With Tiger legends Kevin Bartlett and Francis Bourke, 1980

Christi, Mick
and Danielle,
Moorabbin, 1979

With Kevin Sheedy and Merv Keane, Dreamworld, Queensland, 1985

Christi, Troy, Danielle and Cain, Glen Waverley, 1985

The coach with his boys, Footscray, 1986

The family, from left: Troy, Mick, Danielle, Nanette, Cain and Christi, Nunawading Basketball Stadium, 1989

Footscray coach's box with Ted Whitten Jnr

A victorious West Coast team leaves the field, including Mick and Scott Watters

1992 West Coast Eagles Premiership, Mick with Russell Cooper and Stephen Rae at the MCG

1992 West Coast Eagles Premiership, Mick and captain John Worsfold accept the cup

A contemplative moment, Victoria Park gymnasium, 1990

2010 Collingwood Premiership, Mick and the team hold up the cup at the MCG *Photo courtesy of Joe Armao, Fairfax*

Mick leads his boys off the field after the 2011 Grand Final against Geelong at the MCG. *Photo courtesy of AFL Media.*

Mick and Christi on her wedding day, Port Melbourne, 2007

Nanette and Mick at the Brownlow Medal

Christmas 2003, from left: Cain, Nanette, Christi, Mick as Santa, Danielle and Troy, Hampton

Marie and Ray's 50th wedding anniversary, Mick with his parents and sister
Gerardine, Ballarat 2002

Mick with three of
his grandchildren,
from left: Zac,
Lillia and Holly
© *Newspix / Tim
Carrafa*

difficult to do that. 'Unfair' was never a word he used to describe the mess; 'disgraceful' was the adjective that best summed up the situation. A team that works hard enough to finish fourth and win its first final deserves the reward of a home final in its next match.

At the club, Mick played down the furore, but in the end it became an excuse to lose. They were belted by the Bombers from the first bounce, and the match finished 22.12 (144) to 8.19 (67).

Essendon coach Kevin Sheedy had appealed to all football supporters to come to the game and 'support the Victorians', which heightened the frenzy in Perth. I can vouch for the fact that it worked on the Malthouse children. We were outraged that Sheedy was using the 'Victorian' card when he didn't deserve to be hosting the final in the first place.

His plea drew a massive anti-West Coast Eagles crowd and led to a kaleidoscope of twirling black and red at the MCG at the final siren. This mirrored Sheedy's 1993 antics after a close game late in the season against West Coast, when Essendon ruckman Paul Salmon kicked a goal in the last 30 seconds to break the deadlock and seal the win. Sheedy stormed out of the coach's box, took off his jacket and swung it vigorously above his head. He was celebrating the win, but by demonstrating his joy beside the Eagles' box, he was also sending a message to Dad: 'I won, Mickey!' He always called him Mickey, never Mick or Michael.

Kevin is a man for whom I have plenty of admiration—for his success at the Bombers, and also for his work in promoting the game of football. I have actually known Kevin Sheedy since I was a little girl running around at Punt Road. I know his children and I read with interest recently an article containing an interview with Geraldine Sheedy, Kevin's wife, describing the hurt the family felt at his departure from Windy Hill. I can sympathise with that. But on those two 'jacket-waving' occasions, my family wasn't very impressed with Kevin Sheedy.

Dad and Kevin have known each other since they were teammates at Richmond, before they coached against one another for 24 years. It's fair to say they know each other pretty well. They're not mates, but they share a mutual respect; as fierce competitors, each knows how to rile the other. We often joke that Dad is the 'nutty professor' for his sometimes vague behaviour at home and his bizarre quotes in press conferences. He says only a crazy man would be a coach. I think both Dad and Kevin Sheedy epitomise the ultimate mad coach.

There are many Eagles supporters who today still rue 'the season that got away'. West Coast had defeated the eventual premiers, North Melbourne, by 67 points during the year and the club's dominance during its mid-season winning streak made it clear that it was once again a genuine premiership threat. Still, there are many factors in every season that lead to the final result and the eventual winner. Sometimes it goes your way and sometimes it doesn't. The Eagles didn't play in the grand final that year and Mick wears the 1996 season like a scar.

A highlight from the year was Ben Cousins' debut in the midfield in Round 4 against Geelong. In that game he kicked two of his 34 goals for the season. He didn't miss a match for the rest of the year and won the AFL's Rising Star award. Perth had a new hero.

Mick had watched Ben play for Wesley College as a teenager. 'He was this little chubby bloke who was extraordinarily gifted and skilful, but he looked like he didn't want to work hard,' he says. 'He looked a little lazy.'

Ben Cousins had the choice to go to the Geelong Football Club, as part of the AFL's father–son rule or to the Eagles or the Dockers. All three clubs wanted him. West Coast invited him to do some weights training at the club. Alongside players like Dean Kemp and Guy McKenna, who had strong work ethics and demanded a lot of themselves, Ben learnt what it took to be an elite footballer.

'Within three or four months, Ben's attitude to training had changed completely,' Mick says. 'He was a different player. He now had the work ethic to match his talent.' Mick adds that Ben was a revelation to the Eagles once he decided to debut with them. 'I could see that he was going to be a great player.' It was with pride, and no great surprise, that Mick saw Ben win the Brownlow Medal in 2005.

I remember a family conversation at the breakfast table once, the morning after a game early in Ben's career. West Coast had played the Bulldogs and Ben had been heavily tagged, and beaten by Brownlow medallist Tony Liberatore.

Dad described to us scratches the length of a ruler that covered Ben's torso after the game.

'You should see him,' Dad said to us then. 'He has big red welts, and the scratches are deep.'

'What did Ben say?' we asked Dad.

'Nothing.' And that was Dad's point. Ben never complained—not about an opponent, not about his asthma, not about the conditions—he just got on with the game. Ben had been so frustrated at his inability to break the tag in that game that he vowed to get fitter and stronger than his opposition. 'He took his game to a new level then,' says Mick.

Mick and Ben remained in contact over the years, if ever Ben needed football advice or if they were just in the mood for a catch-up and it was with great regret and disappointment that Mick witnessed, from afar, Ben's struggle with drugs.

After Ben's one-year ban from football—for 'bringing the game into disrepute'—Mick courted the idea of drafting him to Collingwood late in 2008, but on the advice of medical experts, the Pies decided against the move. Mick was pleased, though, that Ben did return to the AFL, with Richmond, and even attended his final game in 2010 to wish him luck for the match and for his life after football.

Mick has lasting memories of 'footballer' Ben at the end of the last training session of every week: 'Ben needed that one-on-one time, some touch work, and it became a habit—to the point that we couldn't not do it each week. It was almost like a superstition.' So much so that, at Collingwood, Mick did the same ball work with Scott Pendlebury and Luke Ball at training, and with Dale Thomas before a game. If 'Daisy' missed a match, Mick said, he wouldn't feel right until he found another player to complete the drill with.

After the 1996 season, the Fitzroy Football Club merged with the Brisbane Bears to become the Brisbane Lions. The once great club played its final game against Fremantle at Subiaco Oval. The Brisbane-based Lions went on to become the most dominant team of the early 2000s, playing four successive grand finals for three premierships in 2001, 2002 and 2003.

Our family got on with life. Cain completed his first year of high school in 1996 and Troy was farewelling primary school. Danielle had also finished her studies and was concentrating on forging a career in basketball. She was a member of the Perth Breakers squad, with high-profile teammates like Michele Timms, Robyn Maher and Tully Bevilaqua. Having a father involved in elite sport probably helped her with the logistics of a professional career—the training, the meetings, the travel, the diet, the mental preparation—but it may have also increased the expectations she placed on herself.

One June evening, during an innocuous training drill, Danielle landed awkwardly and dislocated her kneecap, straining the medial ligament. Her physio feared that she'd also torn her ACL. An MRI scan the following day revealed the worst—she would have to undergo a knee reconstruction. She was inconsolable.

A few days later Danielle amazed us all with her courage and strength as she underwent the excruciating surgery and painful recovery in hospital. Dad, knowing first-hand the importance of a sporting dream, wanted Danielle to have the best of care, so he arranged for her to do her rehabilitation at the club with the Eagles medical staff. It was at the same time that Glen Jakovich had undergone his reconstruction, so Danielle made a bet with him that she would recover faster and be back playing sooner than he would.

Danielle went to the Eagles' treatment rooms three times a week for vigorous physiotherapy, ultrasound, ice therapy and strengthening exercises. She recalls how Guy McKenna— always the joker—would make her laugh: pretending he didn't know she was behind the curtain of the next bed, he would criticise his coach with a booming voice.

I think it helped her recovery to be alongside people who understood her desperate need to get back on the court while undergoing such a long and intense process.

My own rehabilitation experience was much more intimidating. After surgery for compartment syndrome in 1993, I needed to build up the strength in the muscles of my lower legs with some deep-water running, so Dad took me to the Eagles' rehab centre to use the pool there. After I changed into my bathers, Dad hurried me to get into the water. When I opened the bathroom door, however, a sickening sight confronted me—the whole West Coast team was in the pool. It was a Sunday morning after a game and they were swimming laps as part of their recovery.

I felt like the kid wearing a school uniform on casual-dress day. As I dropped my towel and entered the water as fast as I possibly could, the players looked to me briefly before turning away. But I knew that they knew I was horrified to be sharing a pool with them.

I never forgave Dad for that humiliating event, and I never returned to that pool.

I recovered and so did my sister, and true to her word she beat Glen Jakovich back to the playing arena by six months. Danielle's knee gave her lasting troubles, though, and eventually caused her to give the game away.

I joined the world of television journalism in 1996. I had been writing for Perth's *Sunday Times* newspaper for over a year, covering NBL and WAFL games, and I had completed a brief stint at a country newspaper, *The Bunbury Mail*, after deferring my university studies. My surname helped, I'm sure, in getting me an interview for a job as a research assistant for the popular *Today Tonight* program. I got the job and had to work hard to keep it in the cut-throat television industry.

Halfway through the 1996 season, my producer considered me 'ready' to try reporting. My first assignment wasn't too much of a stretch for me! It was to interview a group of young, talented, hard-working and idolised Eagles players. I stood next to the camera, held the microphone and, with a slight wobble in my voice, asked my dad's young players about their debut season. Their answers were thoughtful, amusing and intelligent, and we got a pretty good story out of it. I didn't begin reporting regularly for a while after that, but when I did, I continued in the field of sports journalism.

The boys had started joining Dad on the Eagles' pre-season camps. If the team camped, they would share a tent with Dad. If they slept in dormitories, Cain and Troy would be designated their own bunkbed. They joined in cricket matches, hiked through bushland and swam in cool river water. They loved it, and through these experiences became much more a part of the football club than Danielle and I had ever been at West Coast or Footscray.

They were both playing school football now too: Cain in the ruck, and Troy in the forward line. Troy didn't mind Dad going along to watch his games, knowing that his father was there to support, not judge. Dad would stand in the background, refrain from being vocal—that's not his style—and applaud his son's efforts. Cain—who was more self-conscious—resented Dad's attendance at his matches. I think it made Cain feel like he was on display, when he just wanted to play footy for fun.

So Dad resorted to finding alternative ways to watch Cain's games. Our school was at the base of a tall overhang, where some large homes had recently been built to take in a beautiful view of the Perth city. One particular Wednesday afternoon, Dad walked from our home to the top of the hill that overlooked our school and perched himself on a low sandstone wall. He'd brought a pair of binoculars and, at the sound of a hand-held air horn, he adjusted the lenses and focused on the second half of Cain's footy match. He'd been there for a short while when he a heard a snigger behind him. He turned and saw two women walking past, shooting a look of disgust at him as they did.

'I'm just watching my son play football,' Dad said with a smile to the women, who were now well past him.

As he turned back to the school oval, he looked for the first time directly below where he was seated on the brick wall. At the very base of the cliff-face were the school netball courts, and two games were in progress. Dad wanted to run after the two women to explain that he hadn't even been aware they were there. He hoped that the women hadn't recognised him. We laughed so hard when he told us later at home that we were literally in tears.

Cain told him: 'It serves you right for not telling me you were watching my game!' But he did allow Dad to attend a few more of his matches after that.

Port Adelaide Power joined the competition in 1997, along with the new-look Brisbane Lions, and Footscray had a name change to the Western Bulldogs.

The Eagles hosted the Sydney Swans at the partly redeveloped Subiaco Oval in Round 1. This development was really just the introduction of lights for night games, and the laying of a new surface—which, to Mick's horror, was thoroughly tested by a few of his players, who used it as a driving range one afternoon. Their coach caught them teeing off from the goal square, where they managed to leave divots in the freshly laid turf.

There was excitement in the air for the start of a new season helped by a big first-up 41-point win over the Swans.

West Coast were back on the road for Round 2, travelling to Geelong. In a low-scoring match, the Eagles' opening three goals went unanswered for a lead of thirteen points at the first break. As Mick addressed his players in the huddle, in the Eagles' rooms, Chris Mainwaring, the team's star wingman, was being told that his season was over. The curse of the knee had struck again. An awkward landing had left him injured.

West Coast struggled to stay on top of its opponents, and in the final term the Cats turned a one-point deficit into a six-point win.

The Eagles were a morose group of men on the flight home that night, and Chris Mainwaring was a dejected figure at the front of the aircraft, his left leg elevated and his knee wrapped in ice. He underwent a reconstruction that week and remained sidelined for almost two seasons. His knee was never the same again.

In what can only be considered bad luck, the Eagles lost yet another key performer to a serious knee injury when defender Mitchell White went down during a big win over Melbourne at the MCG in Round 5.

There was no explanation for the absurd number of knee injuries occurring to West Coast players in those years, but Mick had his own theory. He believed the constant strain of flying took a toll on the body and it was this fatigue that perhaps weakened the muscles and joints. He would know—he spent a decade flying across the country and back again for a quarter of each year.

Consider the process: the setting of the alarm for an early wake-up call to arrive at the airport on time; the hour-long wait at the airport after checking in; the dehydrating air-conditioning on the flight; the bus rides to hotels and football grounds; the hotel rooms themselves, with artificial air and uncomfortable beds; the two-hour time difference; a game of hard-hitting football; and the long flight back, into the headwind, late at night, with only a few hours' sleep at home before returning to the club to begin another week. It's a draining schedule for anyone.

Mick believes that the career of an AFL footballer from an interstate team may be cut short by up to two seasons due to the strain of travel. He names Brett Heady, Karl Langdon, Don Pyke and Tony Evans as examples.

Whatever the case, it was with great relief for Mick and all West Coast supporters that John Worsfold returned from his extended layoff in Round 3 of the 1997 season, while Glen Jakovich took to the field again in Round 6. But it was a season of mixed results. The highlight was a 79-point demolition of the Brisbane Lions in Round 7, and the low point a belting of similar proportions by Adelaide at Football Park in Round 14. In the end, a cluster of wins to finish off the year kept the Eagles' season on track, and they finished fifth.

With memories still fresh from the Round 14 disaster, West Coast headed back to Adelaide for their qualifying final.

After starting well, the home side wore the Eagles down and won comfortably. Facing a week of criticism and analysis at home, the Eagles squad regathered and refocused for a big semi-final encounter at the MCG. North Melbourne had finished seventh and only just beaten Geelong in the previous final, but West Coast was wary. In their only encounter during the season, North Melbourne had won by 45 points.

Wayne Carey was well held by Glen Jakovich again and the Eagles produced a solid first-half effort, extending the lead to 32 points halfway through the third term. Then, like the demolition of a house, West Coast stood still and North Melbourne swung the wrecking ball.

For Eagles supporters, it was a disappointing result to give up a late lead for a thirteen-point loss. For Mick, it was unforgivable. He was furious.

At home, from where we watched, we were just as angry. It can be so difficult to comprehend a loss in which the players seemingly give up. That isn't the case, of course; no player ever throws his hands up in resignation mid-match. But from the comfort of our lounge room, when it appeared that Dad's men had stopped playing with the same fierce intent and physical exertion they'd shown in the first half of football, we couldn't help but feel irritation for the players and frustration for Dad. And regret for the loss.

It had been a difficult year at home. Mum had been called back to Melbourne halfway through the year to say goodbye to her gravely ill mother. Nana had contracted septicemia and, with her health in decline as a result of Alzheimer's, doctors advised the family to gather and say their farewells, fearing the worst. Mum rushed to her side. She was one brave and tough woman, though, my nana, and she recovered from the life-threatening infection, enabling Mum to return home with some good news.

We flew to Melbourne every year for Christmas and Mum travelled for some of the Eagles' Victorian clashes each season, but the time between each visit made the deterioration of Nana's memory all the more obvious when we did see her. So when Mum came back to Perth this time, she did so with a heavy heart: her much adored mother no longer recognised her. Not for the first time since we'd moved to WA, Mum began thinking about moving home.

Dad wasn't opposed to the idea. His father had been diagnosed with an enlarged aorta during the year and had undergone triple-bypass heart surgery. Dad also feared for the ongoing welfare of his elderly parents, who still lived in Ballarat.

As well as winning two premierships, the Eagles had been in the finals every year since Dad had taken the reins, so the hoped-for success had been achieved. But the lingering thought that the club could win another grand final kept raising its hand and demanding attention. So, with the emotional strings that still bound us to Melbourne stretched to breaking point, a move home was put on the backburner.

Dad was awarded life membership at the West Coast Eagles in October 1997 for his outstanding service to the club. It seemed like a sign that staying was a good idea.

8 MILES FROM HOME

THE FREMANTLE DOCTOR IS an afternoon sea breeze from the southwest that sweeps across Perth like a broom cleaning the kitchen floor. It carries away the dust that has settled during the day and makes the smothering heat more bearable. It is a relief to say 'Here's the Doctor' after a morning spent melting in rising temperatures.

After eight years of finals, West Coast Eagles supporters had come to expect a winning season just as locals wait for the Doctor to blow in every day. But they didn't know how exceptional their good fortune was.

Finals football is for the top eight sides of the competition only. That's just half of the teams competing each season. A look at the AFL records reveals that a regular appearance in September is a rarity. The system has been structured deliberately to make it difficult for any club to maintain dominance; the draft and the salary cap are the tools used to level the playing field. Hence the common cycle of a club's rise and fall, up and down the ladder.

The fact that West Coast had been in the finals for eight straight years wasn't celebrated as an accomplishment in Perth, but rather viewed as proof that a premiership was achievable every year. It was a heavy burden for Mick to bear. He never mentioned the supporters' lofty ambitions as being over the top or naive—in fact, it was that passion that inspired him each season—it was more that the Eagles' board and the West Australian media placed so much emphasis on a grand final finish every season. It's not realistic for any AFL team.

A two-point loss to North Melbourne in the opening round of the 1998 season signified the uphill climb ahead. After 22 rounds, the Eagles had won twelve games and lost ten, to finish seventh on the ladder. It was the lowest the club had finished since Mick had lifted them from eleventh in 1989.

The team of 1998 was a very different team to the ones that triumphed in 1992 and 1994. For a start, Peter Sumich, Tony Evans, Karl Langdon and Michael Brennan were among the recently retired. John Worsfold, Chris Mainwaring, Brett Heady and Mitchell White all missed several games of the season with injury, and Ben Cousins, Michael Braun and Chad Morrison were young and still finding their way at the top level. This is called rebuilding, and it happens at every club when senior players make way for rookies.

In August, I began my new job as a sports reporter in Channel Ten's Perth newsroom. My first day was Monday the 17th, Dad's birthday. I did my first ever live cross, from Subiaco Oval, on the Thursday. I was to talk about team selection. It was nerve-racking.

Thursday is the day that AFL teams are named. The cut-off time is six o'clock, though some clubs release their team changes slightly earlier. On this occasion, I called Dad in the early afternoon for West Coast's ins and outs and he gave them to me. He must have already had the opposition's line-up or he wouldn't have been so obliging—even for his daughter!

I remember that Glen Jakovich was in some doubt with an injury; I spent a lot of time declaring him a certainty to play in the Round 21 match against St Kilda that coming Saturday. Captain John Worsfold would miss the match with knee soreness. At the end of the cross I rolled my eyes with relief that it was over and I'd made it through without a stumble.

My phone rang almost immediately; it was Dad calling to congratulate me.

'Very good, darling. I saw you roll your eyes, though.' He laughed. 'No-one else would have noticed, but I was watching closely.'

'Was all the information correct, though?' I quickly asked, concerned.

'Yes. Well done, Lois!'

So now I was a fully fledged journalist working in a two-team town, where my dad was coach of one those clubs. I would have to regularly attend his press conferences, and the Eagles' training. And what a time to begin doing that—when the shit was about to hit the fan.

Leading up to West Coast's first final against the Western Bulldogs at the MCG on 9 September 1998, Mick made a decision not to include John Worsfold in the team. The Eagles' skipper had been struggling with knee problems that extended from his prior reconstruction, for most of the year. 'Woosha was a player who needed to play with grunt,' Mick explains. He'd lost mobility and his pace had become restricted. Without grunt, too, he would be beaten.

John Worsfold had so often been labelled 'Perth's favourite son' in the media that a visitor to the state couldn't be blamed for wondering if 'Perth' was the name of his father. As a brave, tireless and intelligent captain of the club, everyone loved Woosha.

Mick had been in regular discussion with the club medical staff for weeks regarding John's knee—or knees, as it turned out, because they were both playing up. The doctors were far from convinced that he could still play at full capacity. On the Monday after the Eagles' Round 22 loss to Adelaide, the coach spoke to his skipper about the medicos' assessment, telling him then that he wasn't prepared to take a player into the finals who wasn't fully fit. John disagreed and put his hand up to play anyway.

At home, Mick was preoccupied. He couldn't finish a conversation, he couldn't sit still, and he would snap at anyone over the slightest transgression. For three nights, his mind was only on John Worsfold and whether he could risk playing him in the qualifying final.

Mick didn't doubt his courage, a quality he'd always admired in Woosha. Called 'Superman' by his teammates, John would play with pain for four quarters if he had to. But pain wasn't the issue; the loss of agility and speed and the consequential drop-off in form was.

The coach in Mick knew the opposition would 'expose' John with an opponent who would greatly test his pace and movement. However, the footballer in him knew that his captain led by example and his teammates followed; if he didn't play they would be disappointed. The Eagles coach pitted his skipper against teammate Andy Lovell in a mini practice session at Subiaco Oval. John struggled and was beaten, easily. At the match committee meeting on Tuesday night, Mick and his team selectors talked through their options.

On Thursday, when the team was announced, John Worsfold's name was on the list, but only as a deception for the opposition. The Eagles' captain wouldn't be playing and he was told so. The coach waited for his skipper to accept and acknowledge that his knees were letting him down. He needed John to get to grips with his injury omission before his teammates were told.

On the morning of the game, Mick went for a walk around Albert Park Lake with his chairman of selectors, Ian Miller.

Ian said: 'He still wants to play.'

'I know,' Mick responded regretfully. 'But he can't. He's not right. I can't do it.'

John Worsfold sat in the corner of the changerooms as his teammates warmed up for the clash. He didn't say a word but his face revealed his disappointment. He still thought he could play.

On the boundary, Channel Seven commentator and former Eagle Adrian Barich broke the news of John Worsfold's 'late withdrawal'. And that's what began a media witch-hunt in Perth for the 'truth' of the situation. All networks ran stories in their news bulletins following the game that John Worsfold had been 'dropped at the last minute' and was seething about it. It was a very one-sided approach and excluded the fact that John had known for days that he wouldn't be playing.

Mick had known the decision would make him unpopular, and he was okay with that. He had made the call for the 'greater good of the team', not to win a popularity contest. He had lost sleep over it, and it would dent some relationships. But he had to take 22 fit players into the game or he would compromise the whole team. This was always his policy.

West Coast scored just one goal to the Bulldog's five in the first quarter of that semi-final at the MCG. Chris Waterman— in what would be his last game—and Ben Cousins did their best to counter the influence of Jose Romero, Scott West and Nathan Brown, but the Bulldogs midfield was determined and damaging. The nine goals kicked by Chris Grant and Simon

Minton-Connell was more than the Eagles' total score. It was a 70-point disaster.

In his press conference after the game, Mick was asked about the captain's absence. Even on two strong legs, John Worsfold wouldn't have been able to stop the Bulldogs that day. The coach was sure of it.

A medical report on his chronic knee problems led John Worsfold to retire after the season. As the current coach of the Eagles, he has encountered similar situations himself. Perhaps because of this, his initial disagreement with Mick didn't last long, and they remain friends today. Every coach, at some point—probably on multiple occasions—will make an out-of-favour selection decision due to injury or team balance. It's part of the job to make the tough calls.

Something about 1999 felt different. There was lingering resentment in a few circles that John Worsfold's career had ended without a final hurrah. And there was something else, too. Like the stench of sweaty sneakers that remains on your feet even after the footwear is removed, there was a foul smell wafting towards us.

It was Dad's tenth season at the Eagles. He was contracted to remain at the club for an eleventh year in 2000. Across town, Gerard Neesham had been sacked as coach of Fremantle and replaced by Damien Drum, which seemed to pose a series of questions: How do AFL clubs define success? How much time should a coach be allowed to achieve that success? Does the responsibility of that destiny ultimately reside with just one person—the coach?

Mick thought AFL clubs were quick to point to losses and slow to acknowledge wins. They focused on the negative rather than the positive. He agreed and accepted that the buck stopped with the coach, but more often than not the coach was made the scapegoat in a fraudulent 'resolution'.

Four seasons had been played since West Coast had won its second premiership. The Eagles had contested the finals in each of those seasons, reaching the semi-finals in three of the four years before bowing out. They had won more games throughout the 1990s than any other team and Mick's win/loss percentage was 65 per cent. They were all very good numbers, but for some people the only number that counted was number one—the premiership number.

As the season began with a close win over Fremantle in the Derby—making it nine wins from nine Derbies—a former Eagle, Karl Langdon, and a former Bulldog, Brad Hardie—both working on Perth radio—began insinuating that Mick's time at the Eagles was up. Karl Langdon asserted that the coach had 'lost' his player group, that his men were no longer responding to him. Brad Hardie suggested that four years was too long between drinks and that, with the team he possessed, Mick should have won a third or fourth grand final. Other media joined in.

Mick met with his players to ask if they were all on board with him. They were. The Eagles addressed the issue of performance. They understood the volatile world of football and were happy with their coach. These two responses flew in the face of the negative campaign that had been launched against the West Coast coach. It worked to unite the squad.

Playing like a team on a mission, the Eagles won their first six matches, including eleven-goal victories over Essendon and the Western Bulldogs. By Round 16, they had amassed eleven wins. Nothing unites a team more than the feeling of being ambushed—if players can block out the white noise and convert the negative sentiment to motivate them, they can get results, as the boys did that season.

The feeling of satisfaction that usually came with a win was replaced by pure relief for Mick that winter. A positive result eased the external pressure. A loss increased it. It was as tense as it gets.

The brain is a wonderful organ, but when it fails you, it completely deserts you. Nana's health had taken a turn for the worse. Her mind was in a state of constant confusion as she relived a life long gone, and she had to be moved to a palliative care residence for the 24-hour care she now needed. When Nana had first been diagnosed with Alzheimer's, Dad used her memory loss to make us laugh and momentarily forget the awfulness that we were witnessing.

But as the disease further took over her once sharp mind, he stopped joking about it. There wasn't anything funny about her condition any more. She had forgotten how to hold a cup of tea, how to read a book, and that she had grandchildren who loved her.

Mum could no longer live so far from her own mother, and she said so to Dad. He worried that another year in Perth would result in Cain and Troy becoming lifelong 'sand-gropers': they had already lived over half of their lives in WA. Cain was in Year 10 and would be starting the important final years of high school in 2000. My parents had always thought the boys' schooling would be completed in Melbourne, which meant that they had a decision to make.

The Western Derby is a big deal on the Perth football calendar, and this one wasn't any less exciting, particularly for West Coast fans. Chris Mainwaring had pleaded with his coach to help him reach 200 games, despite his chronic knee problems. He'd managed three matches in the season so far, taking his tally to 199, and had performed solidly enough to be selected for the Derby. Mick wouldn't have played Mainy had it been finals, but in the home-and-away season, when he was still a handy inclusion, he was pleased to help his star wingman achieve the important milestone. He realised the significance of the accomplishment when he later heard Chris describe the moment as one of his proudest days.

So the team was set for an almighty showdown, but this time the Dockers gained early control. There seemed to be no match for the former Crow Tony Modra, at full-forward, as he kicked six goals for the game. The 23-point margin didn't alter in a goal-for-goal second term.

A ferocious Fremantle crowd cheered every Docker goal in the second half. I was watching the game for Channel Ten and I could feel myself sinking into my seat with every goal that increased the Dockers' lead. It was a foregone conclusion at the final change, as the 'new boys' sniffed victory and the 'old boys' sensed a changing of the guard. As the Eagles supporters left the ground early, they did so to a chorus of nasty chanting from Fremantle fans. The 'purple army' was elated at the final siren and on the ground the Dockers players celebrated like they'd won the grand final.

I knew my family would face a barrage of abuse when they walked to the car after Mick's press conference, but it couldn't be worse than what I was about to experience.

The Dockers faithful were already gathering at Fremantle Oval when I arrived there with my camera crew to film the celebrations for our news bulletin. I may as well have had a neon sign above my head for the attention I immediately received. I don't think a single person missed reminding me of the result while detailing their loathing of the Eagles and my father. They launched into ecstatic applause when their coach took to the stage in the social club to talk about the defeat. I stood quietly in the back corner. When his speech was over, I had to interview coach Damian Drum.

'They're pretty excited, it was a good win,' he said, referring to the crowd. 'It's hard for you, though—how are you doing, are you okay?' I was taken aback by his mindfulness, although this softly spoken coach had always displayed a kind and polite manner in my presence. 'I don't know how your father has done it for so long. I really don't.' He said this more to himself than to me. This was Drum's first senior coaching job after assisting Ron Barassi at the Sydney Swans for five years.

It was close to this time that gossip of Mick making a house purchase in the outer-Melbourne suburb of Eltham sparked another media hunt for the truth. A real-estate agent was spruiking that he had sold the house to one Mr Malthouse, and before long word had spread to WA. It must have been a Michael Malthouse lookalike, because it certainly wasn't my dad. He and Mum were still deciding if 1999 would be their last year in Perth. They hadn't even discussed their thoughts with us, let alone started looking for a home in Melbourne. But the coincidental timing of the declaration sent the rumour mill into overdrive.

The *Footy Show* personality and former Geelong great Sam Newman saw an opportunity to turn what had become an interrogation of sorts into a joke when he learnt that the host of the show and new Collingwood president, Eddie McGuire, was meeting with Dad in Perth. The 'meeting' was actually a casual catch-up over coffee between the two men and their wives. I attended the morning-tea break also, seeking career advice from a man well experienced in the television industry. In a Subiaco café, just a few blocks from Subiaco Oval, a Channel Nine cameraman caught the get-together on tape as Sam Newman burst into the coffee shop, demanding an explanation from Dad and Eddie as to their secret conduct. The Eagles coach and the Pies boss played up to the surprise intrusion, and then laughed it off.

When the camera and Sam had gone, Eddie turned to Dad with a grin on his face and asked: 'So how can I get you to come to Collingwood?'

Dad laughed. 'You can't.'

'One day I will,' Eddie declared, and that was that. We resumed talking about Carla McGuire's recent work trip overseas. People have always assumed that encounter had more business to it than it did. There was no offer and no acceptance of any coaching position. I even asked Dad in the car on the way home afterwards, 'Do you think Eddie would really offer you the Collingwood coaching job if he thought you'd take it?'

'I don't know,' he replied.

Following the Eagles' loss to Fremantle, a demoralising 100-point defeat to Brisbane at the Gabba increased the urgency Mick felt to make a decision on his future. He had been alerted to some disturbing news, which he shared with his family. A member of the West Coast football department had been in Melbourne recently, sounding out the interest of Hawthorn's Perth-born coach, Ken Judge, in returning home to take over at the Eagles. The visit was also linked to the rumour of the 'Malthouse Melbourne house hunt', as if to undermine Mick's integrity and loyalty to the club.

It was all that we needed to agree with our parents that ten years was long enough to stay in Perth; it was time for them to go home. Danielle and I would stay in WA for work commitments, and while the boys were reluctant to relocate again, they would finish off the school year before departing.

In early August Mick told the club chairman, Michael Smith, and its new chief executive, Trevor Nisbett, that he wanted to return home to Melbourne and outlined the reasons why. He said he wouldn't coach at another club, if that was what it would take to be cleared from his contractual obligations. They were surprised by his announcement and agreed they would impose a sanction on him coaching elsewhere. A week later they lifted the sanction after reconsidering the situation. They wouldn't tell the players or the press yet.

West Coast finished the season with four more straight losses and it became clear that the constant speculation about their leader was affecting the players. Mick went back to his chairman and CEO and asked to be allowed to tell his players of his decision to leave before the start of finals, as the club had finished fifth on the ladder.

In a small meeting room at Subiaco Oval, Mick delivered the news that his players had already guessed. Shortly, he would be saying goodbye. They reacted with gratitude. Guy McKenna and Glen Jakovich produced a short video to Andrea Bocelli's 'Time To Say Goodbye', with farewell messages from a host of players, including Chris Mainwaring.

It was time to alert the public, so a media conference was held on Tuesday, 31 August. Mick signed his letter of resignation, with a brief hesitation, and then walked from his office, with Nanette by his side, to the media room. It was packed. Cameras on tripods stood in a line from one side of the room to the other. Reporters, players and staff members squeezed into the small room, standing, sitting and kneeling on the floor to fit. I was there to work, though I stood to the side with my mum, where we had a clear view of Dad.

He had left all emotion at home, wringing himself dry of the deep sorrow he felt, in order to appear strong and professional in his decision. He stated that there were 'personal reasons' for his departure and was questioned repeatedly about his next move. The answer was simple: he didn't know what he was going to do next. It sounded like a cliché, but all that he was thinking about on that last day of August was the upcoming finals and giving his total dedication to the Eagles' September endeavours. Mum cried when Dad spoke about the friendships he would miss. I fought back tears when he spoke about his highlights from a decade in the west. There were red eyes among his players and the Eagles staff members when he remembered his team favourites.

It was the biggest news story in Perth that week and it was big news in Melbourne, too. Mick's manager, Peter Sidwell, started taking calls of interest from several clubs, though Mick declined to hear any of it until after the Eagles' finals campaign.

✱

For the tenth straight year, the Eagles flew to Melbourne for a qualifying final. For a team so rehearsed in finals, this one at the MCG seemed to have more at stake. It was the end of an era, literally, and they wanted to celebrate that. The Eagles were outsiders to win a game that was tailor-made for the Dogs, with a bitter cold wind and heavy rain.

Trailing by two points at quarter time, West Coast signalled its intention to fight for victory with a five-goal second term, led by Scott Cummings and Glen Jakovich. Always a tough opponent, the Bulldogs made every possession a difficult one and kept the Eagles to one goal for the third quarter. Just twelve points up, a Bulldogs goal early in the final term closed the gap and put everyone watching from Perth into a state of panic.

It's hard to watch the close games. The knot in your stomach tightens like a snake around its prey. It takes a big physical effort to breathe with lungs that feel like wet sand. You get angry at every umpire's decision and every stray kick, until you find yourself clenching your hands with an urgent will to stop proceedings and sound the final siren. PLEASE, END, NOW!

What made it worse was seeing Dad in the coach's box with seconds to go, ripping of his headphones, slamming his hands on the desk and shoving his chair aside as he stood up to storm through the door. At the siren he fell against the wall with his head in his hands.

The Eagles were still up by five points. They'd won. Mick had another game as coach. That coach's box highlight has been replayed regularly over the years and still makes me hold my breath.

Once again, it was a huge week. Media and supporters crowded the Eagles' training sessions. People were talking about where Mick would coach next, even though he himself had no idea and was still refusing to even think about it. The Bulldogs game had left the team sapped of energy and mentally worn out.

West Coast faced Carlton at the MCG, once again travelling when they should have been hosting the final. Mick made his disapproval of the rules known to the AFL's chairman, Ron Evans, who visited the Eagles' rooms before the match. 'This is a disgrace and the sooner it changes the better,' Mick announced, even though he would no longer have to worry about it after the season. Mick had discussed the issue of emotional exhaustion during the week and now he told his players to forget the hype that surrounded them and focus only on winning.

It wasn't a close contest, not from the start. The Blues kicked away to a 30-point lead and held it until three-quarter time. Mick strode onto the ground, aware of the significance of the next five minutes. He didn't say too much. They all knew it would take a miracle to win now. Mick gave a few pointers about the opposition and how to counter their attack in the final term, and then he turned to walk back to the coach's box. As he did so, Glen Jakovich grabbed his shoulder. Mick saw that his defender had tears in his eyes and was struggling to keep his emotions in check. Close by, Michael Braun lingered, also trying not to cry.

Still the coach, the mentor, the leader, Mick put his arm around Glen's shoulders in a gesture of acknowledgement and strength. It was a brief offering in an important moment. Glen pulled away, almost embarrassed by his tearful display, and took his place in the backline. Mick sat down to coach the last quarter, thankful for the distraction from the feeling of loss that was pressing against the centre of his chest like two large hands.

The Eagles lost by 54 points. It had been ten years, and it was over in an instant.

9 A BLACK-AND-WHITE MACHINE

D O YOU KNOW THERE IS a website dedicated solely to the Magpie Army? I was surprised to find that the expression isn't included in any Aussie slang dictionary, and yet astounded that there are millions of results in a Google search of the term.

The Magpie Army is a way of describing the loyal, passionate and one-eyed supporters of the Collingwood Football Club. Their website catchphrase is 'It's Nice to be Hated', and it pretty much sums up their attitude. These football fans know they belong to a club that other people love to hate, and they pride themselves on it. It is why they are so united, and inspiring. They are a true force to be reckoned with.

Growing up, Mick belonged to this group of die-hard followers. His local football club wore the same colours as Collingwood and thus began his black-and-white love affair.

By the time he was old enough to be picked up by a VFL club, he had to put those loyalties aside—he wasn't in Collingwood's zone. But in October 1999, with his manager fielding coaching offers from four different AFL clubs, he thought it was a gratifying irony that one of them was Collingwood.

True to his word, Eddie McGuire had been persistent in his efforts to lure Mick to the Magpies. He'd upped the ante once word got out that the talented coach was available and returning to Melbourne, and he was in almost daily contact with Mick's manager, Peter Sidwell, trying to outbid his competition. Eddie had three teams to beat: Richmond, Adelaide and Hawthorn.

For Mick, it was really only the Tigers and the Magpies in contention. He never discussed the financial component of any offers with Peter, choosing to make his decision based purely on the club—the conduct and vision of the people who represented it, and of course the team list it owned. Mick had been a strong advocate for the Adelaide Crows over the years, particularly admiring the way the club was run in the upper ranks. But while he was impressed with the manner and direction of the Adelaide Football Club, the family needed to get back to Melbourne, not South Australia.

When Ken Judge departed the Hawks for the West Coast Eagles, as Mick's replacement, Hawthorn sought out Mick. But the challenge there failed to grab his imagination.

Richmond's attraction was that it was his former club, where he had won a premiership as a player. Returning had a romantic ring to it, but football and romance rarely go hand in hand without ending in a bitter divorce. At the time, Mick felt the Tigers lacked professionalism, and he was stuck on that point and couldn't get past it.

So he picked Collingwood. Eddie McGuire had big plans for the Magpies and Mick found it hard not to be inspired by the president's enthusiasm about the club's future move to the Melbourne Olympic Park stadium, and his passion for restoring its pride. Mick had complete faith in McGuire's vision.

Collingwood had finished the 1999 season sixteenth on the ladder—rock bottom. The club had gone a record number of years without contesting the finals at all, and it was grossly in debt. This once grand club appeared to have lost its soul and it had become confused about how big it was and how big it wanted to be. Mick was inspired by the massive challenge: how could he lift Collingwood from the bottom rung and return it to its rightful place in the Australian sporting scene as a legitimate powerhouse that was both admired and loathed for its success?

By the end of October 1999, Mick was the new coach of the Collingwood Football Club.

It was an announcement of Hollywood proportions. Mick was introduced on stage to the Melbourne media sitting in the front seat of a Volvo beside his new captain, Nathan Buckley. Lights flashed, music blared and a smoke machine blew a dense fog that dissipated with the arrival of the pair, dapper and dolled up in black Versace suits. Like a peacock proudly displaying its fanned tail of iridescent colour, Eddie McGuire heralded a new era of accomplishment for the Magpies and boasted that his new coach and captain were the best the league had to offer.

Mick looked about as comfortable as a child with nits trying to sit still in church. Given the choice, he picks sneakers over dress shoes and well-worn shorts over a suit every time. Mick is a man who owns a TAG Heuer but prefers to wear a plastic digital Gatorade watch. He took a packed lunch to work most days and rides his bike on the footpath, wearing old bike shorts. No one could ever describe him as flashy. So to see Mick dolled up beside Eddie McGuire and Nathan Buckley was the personification of an oxymoron. For his family, it was highly humorous. For the new Pies coach, it was uncomfortable and disconcerting.

All the kids—including me—actually struggled with the idea of Dad coaching Collingwood. It felt like he was joining the enemy. Perhaps because we were all older and able to form our own opinions, we were totally opposed to the thought of barracking for a team we had despised for so long. The boys swore they would still support the Eagles from Melbourne, and Danielle and I stated that our loyalty would lie only with Dad, not necessarily the club. Our attitude may seem a little petulant, but we had just spent ten years growing up within the realm of another football club. It was tough to switch immediately from one to another.

Even Mick found it difficult.

As his first day on the job approached, he began to feel nervous. By the time he pulled up alongside the rust-coloured train tracks opposite Collingwood's headquarters, Victoria Park, it was as though he had opened the door of an aviary inside his chest. His heart grew wings and fluttered hard against his ribcage, trying to escape. But his mind called the shots and told his heart to settle.

Yet still Mick sat in his car, paralysed with dread. His family was still in Western Australia, his wife and sons packing up to leave the state and his daughters moving into homes of their own. He was alone and felt the reality of the situation like a hammer through his car windscreen. He'd left behind friends, a team with a winning culture, and countless young men he'd tutored in football and life. He felt like he'd deserted them all, and at the same time he felt he still needed them. Mick hadn't yet cut ties with his former club and it haunted him now.

He knew he would have to move soon, to hop out of the car and close the door behind him and walk through the small side entrance of the football club. He reminded himself that he had another class of young footballers to teach, that he had games to win and history to make, that he would meet new friends—not to replace the old but to join them—and that he had family in Melbourne who needed him here.

The sound of the office door slamming shut behind him snapped him back into the present. He was the new Collingwood coach and he would put his heart and soul into this club, no matter what it took.

The rest of Mick's day was no better than that first hour. As he toured the Victoria Park facilities with the club's newly appointed CEO, Greg Swann, he became more depressed with each step through the rabbit warren shambles. He almost fell through the floorboards as he entered the medical room, and he wondered about the mould that occupied the ceiling throughout the changeroom area. The office lacked a kitchen but a fridge sat in the corner of a boardroom—full of beer. The gym was sparse and in need of an urgent upgrade. And he was appalled at the state of the ground, walking through ankle-deep mud along the player's race to the field, after recent rain had left the area flooded. A gusty wind dangerously shook the advertising boards that lined the fence of the arena and threatened to send them flying across the boggy, patchy ground.

He knew it would be bad. Eddie had warned him, reminding him also that a deal for new facilities at Olympic Park was currently being negotiated. It's not like he hadn't been in this situation before—the Western Oval had hardly been in any better shape and Subiaco Oval had just begun a full renovation at his departure. But the stench of decay, the crumbling foundations, the heavy ground, the out-of-date gymnasium—it was all a bit much to take in.

Humans by nature don't like change, so it's not surprising that the initial day of anything—a new job, a new school, moving into a new home—will have your muscle fibres tingling, your raw nerves screaming and your brainwaves buzzing. It's no coincidence either that by the end of the first week in your new surroundings, you'll feel more at ease and comfortable in your skin again.

That's how Mick felt at Collingwood. By the Friday he had formed a close bond with Greg Swann and had been reacquainted with a former Tiger teammate, the Magpies' football operations manager, Neil Balme. He'd also met and clicked with player welfare and team manager Mark Kleiman and had managed to surround himself with loyal, committed and determined assistants: Dean Laidley, Brad Gotch and Michael Broadbridge. It may have taken him longer than in previous football moves but he would feel at home at Victoria Park soon enough. He swore to make the place better, more efficient and more professional.

We kids still had our doubts, but as it happens, when you meet people face to face, your opinion of them can change—for the better or the worse. In this case it was for the better.

I travelled to Melbourne late in the year for a work assignment and met Dad at his new office fresh off my flight. He gave me a quick tour, suggesting I keep the palm of my hand over my coffee to avoid pieces of mould from the ceiling landing in my cup, and introduced me to his new workmates. Everyone was lovely and I could see that Dad would be happy working with them.

Later that day he drove me past the house that he, Mum and the boys would be moving in to. They had just taken ownership of it without Mum even seeing it. It was in the bayside suburb she had grown up in, close to her eldest sister, and close to the palliative care home Nana was residing in.

Cain and Troy would attend the Catholic college nearby for their final years of school.

Mum and the boys met the Collingwood staff next, and hosted the Magpie players for dinner. By the beginning of 2000, a year that to many was the symbol of a fresh start and an exciting new age, four members of my family were settled back in Melbourne, and they were Collingwood through and through.

Over the summer the Collingwood list underwent a big change. Several players had retired—and more would do so the following year—and others had been moved on. It was a young team now, ripe for rebuilding. Mick also had spoken to the fitness staff about a worrying trend he had noticed, mainly that they attended only to the players who were willing to put in the effort, while leaving the other squad members to fend for themselves. He needed every player to participate in weight training and fitness testing.

Then he addressed the elephant in the room.

The club, as he saw it, was loading too much pressure on its captain to win a Brownlow Medal. Many people at the top level seemed be transferring their desire for a premiership win onto Nathan Buckley's shoulders as the one player who could achieve Collingwood success, albeit individually.

In media circles, the Magpie skipper had earned an unkind nickname that suggested he thought he was better than everyone else, and gossip had also circulated that his teammates despised his preaching manner. It was Mick's job to sort the facts from the fiction, and to make things right at the club. The ability of the side to operate as a team had been compromised by the hierarchy within the player group and the club lacked respect in the football world because of its image as the 'Eddie McGuire and Nathan Buckley show'. Neither factor, whether real or imagined, was conducive to September success.

Mick wanted people believing that the Magpies could win a premiership *and* produce a Brownlow medallist—it didn't have to be one or the other. But first he needed a captain who could lead a team and at the same time be part of a team. He got it, eventually, in Nathan Buckley.

The 2000 season started with a bang when Collingwood defeated Hawthorn by 54 points. Then they beat Adelaide by eleven points, then the team's nemesis, Carlton, by a whopping 73 points. Mick thought what a luxury it was to play three straight games at the MCG after years of playing very few games there during the regular season. He also thought it odd that a win over the Blues could create so much excitement at the club. To him, a win was a win, no matter which team it came against, but this hatred for Carlton was a small part of the Magpie culture he was still getting used to.

Two more close victories, over Sydney at the Sydney Cricket Ground, and over the Western Bulldogs at Docklands, had the Pies placed second on the ladder on percentage, behind Essendon, at Round 6. We were all surprised by this excellent start.

The Magpies' new structure was built around a solid defence that included Simon Prestigiacomo, Tarkyn Lockyer and Glenn Freeborn, and a forward line that could kick goals and also limit the run of the opposition backline. It was here that a tough decision had to be made. For the forward line to work successfully, Mick doubted that the two Rocca brothers, Saverio and Anthony, could continue to play there together. Sav was cut from the list at season's end, but Mick was pleased that he quickly found another home at the Kangaroos. In the centre, Nathan Buckley, Paul Licuria and Shane O'Bree were beginning to work together to good effect.

Collingwood's first loss came against the Kangaroos and from there the year got nasty. Nine rounds later Collingwood had slipped to thirteenth without adding another win to its tally of five.

I could only watch the horror from Perth, always waiting until the day after the game to call home, when the disappointment, like dust after a windstorm, had settled slightly. I felt very distant from the scene, not just in kilometres but emotionally. I started having a recurring dream that my two brothers were babies again and I needed to protect them from harm. I didn't need a psychologist to tell me I was feeling protective of my loved ones.

In the middle of May, I became the centre of a football storm and was left feeling very alone in Western Australia.

As part of my job in the Channel Ten newsroom, I watched the West Coast Eagles train, paying close attention for any sign of something newsworthy—an injury, a missing player, an unhappy player—as I had been doing for over a year at both the Eagles' and the Dockers' training sessions. I followed my camera crew into the Subiaco Oval media room and stood alongside journalists from other television networks, various radio stations and Perth's two newspapers. West Coast's new coach, Ken Judge, wandered off the track slowly and took a seat at a table at the front of the room, facing us all. He was asked about his team, who would play and who wouldn't, and he gave vague answers. He was asked about the form of the side, having just come off a 30-point win against his former club, Hawthorn. The Eagles had won half of their games by Round 11.

Then someone asked Judge about Mick and how he might be feeling coming up against his old club. There was an obvious shift in the tone of his answers after that, as more questions followed about the former West Coast coach and his new team.

Then Judge noticed me. I think I asked him a question and he responded by saying, 'Do you want to know for you or for your dad?'

I do not remember his exact words but I do recall the utter horror and humiliation I felt at being accused of being a spy. It was said in jest, of course—he probably even laughed after he said it—but I, like everyone else in the room, heard loud and clear the underlying insinuation that I was doing my dad's dirty work.

Every AFL club has a spy, or two, that the coach can regularly call on to watch opposition training sessions for him. The correct title of an AFL spy is 'forward scout' and he will assess the availability of certain opposition players and look for game structures that may be practised at training or player positions that might vary from the previous encounter. Every coach has pushed to the limit of the unwritten laws of access his spy has to the opposition. Then again, many coaches have also barred from their training sessions someone they have recognised as a spy. It's a sort of game within the game of football, really. However, on this occasion it became a lot more than that.

Word got to Dad in Melbourne that his daughter had basically been called a spy in front of an entire media contingent and he was mad about it. He retaliated with a quip against Ken Judge in his own press conference that afternoon. I know he was trying to defend me, but it didn't help.

The next morning, I was woken early by a phone call from a local radio host, who asked me to respond to the back-page story of *The West Australian*. I declined to comment. I bought a newspaper and read the article. It was a retelling of the previous day's events and essentially pitted Dad and me against Ken Judge.

I called Mum and Dad in tears. They didn't know what to say to me, but Eddie McGuire would, so they asked him to call me. His advice was to dress in my best suit, to do my hair and make-up with extra care, and to walk into work with my head held high and display a bright smile. It was excellent advice and I followed it to a tee—though my smile was more on the dull side.

A journalist from my own sports department did his take on the story for our news bulletin, and his first line stated: 'Usually she writes the news, today she is the news . . .'

I had to sit at my desk, tapping away at my keyboard while a cameraman filmed me for the report. I wasn't smiling any more. I don't think I was sent out on any assignments that day; my producers probably felt the need to protect me a little. At 23, I felt like I was fourteen again. I wanted the day to end immediately and to go home and never go back to work again. And I wanted my parents, but they were on the other side of the country.

I did go to work the next day. We all moved on to another story. Sometimes one day is a long time in football.

The remainder of Collingwood's season was patchy. Like a child learning to walk, Mick felt, the team would take two steps forward and then one step back. But it was to be expected, really, for a young team with a new coach. The Magpies finished fifteenth on the ladder, one spot ahead of the previous year and with three more wins. They'd also done it with a younger, less-experienced squad, which meant the lessons learnt in the season would benefit the club for a long time to come.

For a high achiever like Mick, finishing one position from the bottom hurt, but it was good to have the first season completed. He'd seen some positives that could be built on, and he had a further opportunity now to reassess the make-up of the squad. More players were traded and others retired. When Gavin Brown announced his retirement, Mick asked him to stay at the club in another capacity. He needed good team men like 'Rowdy' around, sharing their knowledge and expertise with the rookies and helping to keep morale up within the group.

Mick also needed a new strength and fitness regime for the squad, as he was dissatisfied with the current condition of his players. He interviewed several candidates for the position of sports science director and immediately gelled with one applicant: David Buttifant, who was fresh from working with the Australian Olympic team. He was appointed to the role and immediately set about changing the way the club trained.

Mick is a fitness fanatic. He had never needed to be motivated to put in the extra gym and track work as a player, and he had pushed himself to stay fit when his playing days ended. Even now, at almost 60 years of age, he cycles or walks every day, throwing in 100 sit-ups and 100 push-ups for good measure. So he was all for David's scientific approach to fitness and his extreme methods of testing and training.

It was a gruelling pre-season, but by March 2001 the player group was fitter and stronger than it had ever been. Mentally, many players were still learning, but their youthful enthusiasm narrowed the gap between a negative mindset and a positive one.

*

I moved home to Melbourne for the beginning of the 2001 season. I'd never felt completely at home in Perth, despite having many friends and having begun a career there. So when I was offered a transfer to Victoria by Channel Ten, I jumped at the chance. My move coincided with Ten's announcement of its acquisition of the joint AFL broadcast rights with Channel Nine and Foxtel for the following season, and I was to play a part. It was exciting.

As I was getting ready to attend my first Collingwood match with my family, my sister—who had also returned to Melbourne after travelling overseas—said to me: 'Get used to losing.'

What she meant was that it happened more regularly here than we were used to from watching West Coast play in Perth. In Dad's ten years there, the Eagles lost very few games at home, whereas the Magpies, in that first season at least, lost many games in Melbourne. Unfortunately, I experienced the sensation that very day, as Collingwood was overrun by the Hawks in a close Round 1 contest at the MCG.

Then the season picked up. It was still a roller-coaster—two wins then two losses, a win, a loss, three wins then three losses—but the numbers were stacking up, and by the end of the season the Pies had won half their games and just missed out on the finals.

James Clement and Shane Wakelin had joined the team for 2001 and instantly boosted the backline. Jarrod Molloy had been another new inclusion and a handy contributor up forward, where Chris Tarrant had also had moments of brilliance throughout the season. Mick saw the year as one of growth. When he'd arrived at Victoria Park, Collingwood sat at the bottom of the ladder because it was 'a poor football side'. Now the players were young, keen to learn and determined to win, and earning credibility within the league. Ninth wasn't such a bad finish.

By the time 2002 rolled around, Mick was confident that his squad was progressing well in all areas. He was eager for the season to start, perhaps more so this year than most.

It hadn't taken long for the family to feel like we had never left Melbourne. Cain had completed school and was undertaking an AFL traineeship before starting a university degree. Troy was beginning Year 12. Danielle was working with a printing company and living with a friend. And I was about to add 'AFL boundary rider' to my résumé. It would be the first time a woman was part of the free-to-air weekly AFL television broadcast. I had moved into my own apartment and, like every young person purchasing their first home, I felt proud and broke!

Mum was pleased to be back in familiar surroundings. She was most pleased, though, to have her mother just a five-minute drive away. She visited her regularly—we all tried to—and even though her presence elicited little response from Nana, it was enough for Mum to know that she was there in person.

At the end of February the call came. I was at work, preparing for a live cross from the Allan Border Medal presentation at Crown Casino.

'You need to come and say goodbye to Nana,' Mum said quickly. 'It might be days yet, but you need to come.'

Mum and her sisters and some of my older cousins were sitting in shifts beside Nana's bed, for comfort and to keep us all updated. That night, dressed in an evening gown and full make-up, I took over from my Aunty Leslee and held my nana's hand until the morning.

Her breath had slowed but she was still fighting, so I went home and got dressed for work. A few hours later I was called back.

We all stood together then—her family, surrounding her bed and whispering for her to go find her Jim, her beloved husband who had passed away so many years before. She took her last breaths and we said goodbye.

Mum's grief was raw and deep and it remained that way for a long time. But she was far from alone. Nana had always been so proud of Nanette's Michael, how handsome he looked on television coaching in those tough football games. She had loved his sense of humour and his appetite for her baking. And she was so pleased that he was a good husband and father. All the jokes about the 'difficult mother-in-law' were never told by my dad; he loved Pat as much as her children and her grandchildren did.

Football always had a way of overshadowing events in our lives, but on this occasion it was welcomed. When the season started, the family was able to refocus its energy on something positive.

Three games in, the Pies were one and two, the second loss coming against Carlton by 20 points. As Mick sat in his office preparing for the club's clash with Hawthorn that coming weekend, Greg Swann walked in.

'They want to sack you,' he said. 'I'm flabbergasted.'

Collingwood's CEO had just been in a board meeting where several members had expressed concern that Mick 'wasn't delivering'. The defeat by the Blues had been the catalyst for the impromptu meeting and was reason enough, it seemed, to dismiss the coach. Losing to the enemy was unforgivable after two seasons of failing to reach the finals.

Mick had always said that he was a servant of the game. He lived with the knowledge that the board could sack him at any time, that they had a right to sack him if his record wasn't good enough. But the family took issue at home, especially because we'd witnessed first-hand the positive results he'd achieved. Already, Collingwood had climbed the ladder and was playing in closer contests. There was a clear improvement in the team's performance. To rebuild a football team can't happen overnight—it takes time.

Those few Collingwood board members—it hadn't been a unanimous decision—were acting from a position too removed from the battlefield. Their knowledge of the game seemed to be limited and they were now letting pride and ego override their logic. Greg Swann had fought for Mick in that board meeting and as a result he was given more time to justify his position.

The Magpies won their next five games. The run included a 41-point win over Hawthorn and an 83-point win over St Kilda. They lost one then, to Port Adelaide, but that five-point defeat was just a pothole on the dramatic new path the team had taken.

By Round 11, they were in the top four and facing Melbourne in the Queen's Birthday clash. In the corresponding encounter in 2001, the Pies had humiliated the Demons with a 77-point thrashing. Melbourne was faring better this season, currently sitting sixth. For Mick, this game would be a good test of how the Pies were improving.

If the 23-point quarter-time lead was anything to go by, they'd come a long way in the last two and a half years. The Pies had more than doubled that margin by the end of the game, claiming a 51-point win.

By that evening, Mick's belief in his troops was at an all-time high. The older, more experienced players were taking responsibility for the game plan, both for their individual roles within the structure and for the tasks assigned to their teammates, particularly the youngsters. Mick could see they had faith in each other now. They could start thinking about finals. But first Round 18 loomed as a big weekend in Mick's mind. It was time to play Carlton again.

As though sensing their coach's extra urgency, the players lifted their game to near perfect. Carlton was held to one goal for the first half and the Pies found multiple goal-scorers. By the final siren, Josh Fraser and Chris Tarrant had amassed eight goals between them. The Blues had kicked four. It was a 108-point message to the Collingwood board: don't write Mick off too soon. The final margin still stands as the Magpies' biggest ever win over the Blues.

That night Mick shared a lesson with the family: 'Be cautious when you win, be highly cautious when you lose, and don't ever treat one as more important than the other.'

The Magpies finished fourth, with thirteen wins, and were headed to Adelaide for a qualifying final. Nathan Buckley was out of the side, injured, and Collingwood was the underdog against the top-placed Port Adelaide.

Football Park is a hostile environment. Supporters there have loyalties to Port Adelaide stretching back to the origins of the SANFL. They particularly despise Collingwood for its use of the name 'Magpies' and its black and white colours, elements held in common with the original Port Adelaide Football Club. Mum and Danielle were in the stands, sitting beside Greg and Leonie Swann and Eddie and Carla McGuire. It wasn't a pretty sight, as Port supporters did their best to have an influence on the game from their seats with a typically passionate display of home-team devotion and opposition contempt.

It was always going to be tight, but Collingwood's nine-point lead at half time signified that it was ready for a fight. Each team scored 4.3 in the third term, setting up a thrilling contest for the final quarter.

The team was led by Paul Licuria, who picked up 40 touches. Shane O'Bree and Scott Burns shared the load in the middle, while James Clement stood solid in the backline and Leon Davis provided the magic up forward. The Pies outscored their opponents to seal a magnificent thirteen-point win. It was one of the greatest victories of Mick's career, he said, for the inner resolve the team showed in the face of adversity.

As Mum and Danielle waited at the top of a steep set of concrete stairs to follow the heavily pregnant Carla McGuire down (she was being shielded by her husband and Greg Swann), Mum was pushed from behind. She stumbled forward, losing her balance on the narrow step, and fell into my sister. Witnesses rushed to their aid as a very drunk and outspoken Port supporter threatened to push them again. Security arrived immediately and escorted him from the scene, as Mum and Danielle ran down the steps to the safety of the Collingwood changerooms. The thought of what could have resulted from such a frightening altercation triggered a panic attack in Mum and she required medical assistance to regain her composure.

Collingwood was inexperienced in finals, which can be a disadvantage when the game begins and the lift in intensity and crowd noise takes the young players by surprise. Then again, 'ignorance is bliss', as they say, and not knowing what's in store can also benefit a team by limiting the tension created during the build-up.

Hundreds of fans lined the fence at Victoria Park for the Magpies' final training session of the week. I was there too, with a camera crew filming it all for the news. I stayed to do a live cross, and between the end of the track run and my cross to the news desk, I was swamped by people wanting to pass on their best wishes to my father. 'We love him,' they all said.

I was on the boundary line for the game, too. It didn't help my nerves that I had to interview Dad before the match and try not to barrack too loudly for his team during the broadcast. I had interviewed him several times already during the season, each time just a short, one-minute chat before he made his way up to the coach's box.

Before the season had started, I had discussed with the gameday producer how I should refer to my father during these interviews. Calling him Mick or Michael seemed lame when everyone knew he was my dad, so that's what I stuck with: Dad. It was certainly a first in AFL broadcasting, but people seemed to love that father–daughter moment when, after the interview was completed, I would switch from reporter mode to offspring and say, 'Thanks, Dad, good luck,' and he would reply, 'Thanks, darling,' and we would hug briefly before he bolted up the stairs.

In those few seconds after he arrived by my side and the producer began his countdown in my earpiece, I could always tell how Dad was feeling about the game. If he walked with his arms loosely by his side and his shoulders slightly rounded, and with the hint of a smile at the corners of his mouth, then I knew he was confident, that perhaps the players had responded well to his pre-game speech and warmed up with drive and vivacity. If he had one arm across his chest, the other raised to his face, his index and middle fingers resting on his cheek, then he was deep in thought, already coaching the game in his head. If he marched towards me, rubbing his hands together in front of his jutting chest, his cheeks red and his gaze penetrating, I knew that he was feeling jittery because of a lack of focus among the team, or—worse—that he felt underprepared because of an unavoidable occurrence, like a late player withdrawal due to injury or illness. Dad always claimed that he slept well before a game when he knew he had prepared as much as he possibly could for the match, but was restless when he felt he hadn't. He is a firm believer in the idea that 'To be prepared is half the victory'.

On this Saturday, I had stomach cramps as I waited for him to emerge from the race. Then he joined me on the boundary with a smile and a wink—he was looking forward to this clash!

It was a close opening quarter, and Collingwood's inaccuracy gave them just a four-point lead. The Crows had finished third on the ladder for a reason, and they reminded the Pies of it with a four-goal second quarter and a six-point half-time lead. Nathan Bassett was damaging up forward, as was Scott Welsh, but the Collingwood backs nullified their impact and the centres curbed Mark Ricciuto's dominance to produce a true premiership quarter: six goals to one and a 25-point lead heading into the final quarter. I found it hard to contain my excitement as I gave my three-quarter-time wrap and told Channel Ten's viewers that Collingwood was injury-free and still seemed to have plenty in the tank.

They did. The Crows couldn't get near them in the last term and I had to stop myself from embracing every one of the Collingwood players at the final siren as we all realised what the result meant. The sound of the MCG crowd, made up mostly of Magpie supporters, was as loud as I had ever heard it. Nathan Buckley was virtually inaudible to me as I interviewed him on the ground and he announced, with that trademark grin, how pumped he was to have earned a grand final berth.

The only downer was Jason Cloke's report for striking, but 'it was nothing, he'll be fine', as Dad said.

Jason Cloke was anything but fine. He'd played every game of the season and certified himself as a key member of Collingwood's defence. In the 263 disposals he'd amassed to that point, he'd made 50 tackles, taken 110 marks and had 168 kicks. It all meant nothing, though, if his striking offence was deemed deliberate and he was banned from the grand final.

A week that should have been one of excitement and hope was laced with trepidation. The tribunal case was held late on the Tuesday afternoon. Collingwood's defence was that the contact to Tyson Edwards' head was accidental and incidental in the play, that Jason had eyes only for the ball in the marking contest. They thought the replay vision validated their claim. After a long deliberation, the Magpies defender was found guilty of striking and suspended for two weeks.

It was awful. He was 20 years old, playing in his first year of AFL football, following in the footsteps of his famous father, David, and now it seemed that his dream of contesting a grand final was shattered because a three-member tribunal panel thought his actions were negligent and rough. Football is played to a code of rules and regulations, but in this circumstance the interpretation of those rules made the code questionable. How could someone be rubbed out of a grand final for an offence that clearly lacked intent? On these grounds, Collingwood decided to appeal the decision, which prolonged the agony further.

On the Wednesday, thousands of supporters turned out at Magpies training. Once again, I was almost trampled as eager fans displayed their affection for my father. He had coached their team into a grand final, so in their eyes he was almost a holy figure. As I viewed the scene before me, I was struck by the thought that to be part of the Magpie family is a powerful thing. A black-and-white machine had taken over our lives and their destiny had become ours.

The appeal was heard and rejected on the Thursday and everyone was devastated, no-one more than Jason himself, who was in tears as he left the tribunal room. For Mick, it 'hurt like hell' to lose a player like Jason for the grand final.

As a hard, courageous and attacking member of the backline, he was always going to be difficult to replace.

Mick knew first-hand the agony of missing the one big game all footballers play for. However, having learnt long ago to repress his true feelings for the benefit of the team, the coach put on a brave face when he consoled Jason and told his teammates that the show must go on. Jarrod Molloy was brought in to replace Cloke, for his ability to play at either end of the ground. Molloy also had something to prove against his former Brisbane teammates.

Friday's grand final parade was an hour of near Magpies hysteria. The city streets looked like a black-and-white ant colony. Supporters of the Brisbane Lions, most of them visitors to Melbourne, were lucky not to be carried away like food to the nearest anthill by the massed Collingwood faithful. Mick wore a smile as he sat next to Nathan Buckley in an open-top vehicle, waving to the crowd and answering reporters' questions. But underneath, something was agitating him.

Jason Cloke's forced absence cut Mick deep, but there was more to it than that. Nerves? Perhaps. Pressure? The club's eight grand final losses between 1960 and 1981 gave rise to the term 'Colliwobbles' and was something every Pies coach had to wear since then. Leigh Matthews was the first coach in over 30 years to shrug off the slur and hold the cup aloft in 1990. He also happened to be the man Mick would coach against on this grand final day. But that was an issue for other people to discuss—it was a long way off being a cause of worry to him.

It was the phrase 'nothing to lose' that had Mick riled.

Collingwood was facing reigning premiers, the Brisbane Lions, a team that ran deep with talent and quality, including three Brownlow medallists and numerous All-Australian representatives. This was why the inexperienced Pies were given underdog status. But as it is for a little brother trying to match the achievements of his older sibling, the Magpies were already being told—by the media and the public—that close enough would be good enough, and that infuriated Mick. He had no intention of accepting a grand final berth as ample reward.

For Mick, 'nothing to lose' is an acceptance of mediocrity—a get-out clause, if you like. Collingwood, in this instance, had everything to lose. It had a grand final to lose, so its one and only aim was to win it. There was actually an air of confidence in the Magpie camp that belied the negativity surrounding the club.

In a week that was far from normal, Collingwood had kept it as normal as possible. The players had handled it well. Everything was new to them but they had met it with poise. Finally, game day arrived, and with it came the wind and the rain. Rather than a day of hope with the promise of glory, it felt like a day of reckoning.

A whirlwind had brought the Magpies to this moment. Mick felt as though the team were caught up in an uncontrollable surge forward that had propelled them in a mad rush to September glory, whether they were ready for it or not. Even now, when he recounts the weeks leading up to the grand final, his voice takes on a strangled pitch and his words spill out in such a hurry that he can't finish a sentence. He'd begun the year still in a rebuilding phase and had almost been sacked, and here he was about to coach a grand final. As though it were a movie in fast-forward, he took the remote control and pressed pause . . . then he took a deep breath and drove to the MCG.

*

As I had been involved in Ten's breakfast coverage from the ground, I was already in the Collingwood rooms and waiting when Dad trotted in, flanked by my brothers, who now towered over him. He seemed vulnerable, as I noticed his loose-fitting uniform and puffy eyes, and I wanted to pour all of my love into him as energy. He said hello and I asked how he was, but he didn't linger—his mind was understandably elsewhere. He was exhausted.

Any coach on grand final day, according to Dad, is the most fatigued person at the ground. They've given everything by this point. Every minute of the year is spent thinking about football. Every day at the club is spent instructing and motivating other people. Every ounce of energy is put into preparing for a game, coaching the match and analysing the result, week after week. Dad says that, by the first bounce of a grand final, a coach, in a way, feels helpless. He's directed and pushed the team as much as he can by then and he has nothing left to give. The rest is up to them.

I stood and talked to Cain and Troy for a while—they fidgeted, a sign of their nerves. Players were still arriving, each one alone with his thoughts. The warm-up began and the mood became serious.

My job in that next half an hour was to interview Dad on camera and confirm the final line-up, but I was loath to disturb him. He disappeared behind a door with his players and the changeroom fell silent. Outside, the pre-game entertainment shook the walls and hovered like a forcefield over the 91,817 supporters, who were already thickly charged with adrenaline. When the team re-emerged they appeared focused and fierce and some of them wiped tears from their cheeks. Dad walked out with his head down, trying to hide his own red eyes.

He had spoken about a brotherhood. A connection among teammates that will never be lost if a premiership is won. He told his players they would never regret the sacrifices they had already made, nor the pain they might suffer in the following hours, if it led to a win. They would have to play hard, they would have to play tough and they would have to play smart. Most of all, they would have to perform better than their best and play out of their skins. It would be worth it, he said, to crawl from the ground at the end of the match, even if it meant carrying the cup on their backs. He said that the glamour of a grand final would eventually disappear, but the result would be etched in stone.

Clearly, his speech had been moving. I *really* didn't want to have to interview him now.

But of course I did, the two of us professional and brief. Off-camera, I threw my arms around him and wished him good luck and then made my way to the boundary. I felt genuinely ill, my whole body shaking with nerves as I reported that the weather was yet to reach the predicted high of fourteen degrees and the afternoon forecast was for more showers and more wind.

I looked for my family in the stands and gave them a wave. They looked tense among a sea of delirious Magpies fans. I watched Dad walk the ground, testing the surface with the tip of his shoe. He held his hands behind his back as he strolled the centre square, keeping one eye on his opponents and the other on his own team. He seemed composed.

We all stood for the national anthem, the opposing teams and coaches lined up face to face across the ground, the crowd singing the words. That's when the tingle of anticipation spreads throughout your body. It's exhilarating and sickening all at once. The countdown had begun.

As Dad and his team of assistants hastily made their way to the box, he broke away from the group at the base of the stairs and ran towards me. I met him halfway and we hugged and I said, 'good luck' again—from the whole family. This time I sensed his confidence.

The weather made for a scrappy start, Collingwood taking the early lead with just one goal kicked between the two teams by quarter time. Brisbane was down a man after ruckman Beau McDonald left the field with a dislocated shoulder. All of a sudden, everyone else realised what the Magpies had known all week—it was game *on*.

Scores were level four times during the remaining three terms and the lead changed hands thirteen times. Ten minutes into the final quarter, the Pies led by four points. My desire for the game to end was physical as I clenched my jaw and ground my teeth. The pressure from both teams was extraordinary; neither side was going to give this up without a fight.

Then Anthony Rocca had the ball 45 metres out on a slight angle. He kicked it long and high and it sailed over the top of the goalposts. Collingwood players started celebrating, Brisbane players ran back to the centre square. The Magpie faithful were up and out of their seats: 'YeahWhatNo!'—it came out as one long word shouted in chorus. The goal umpire had called it a point.

'Booooo,' the Pies cheer squad hissed and I wanted to join them. Television replays showed that it was a goal. My God, it would have put us ten points up—the biggest margin of the match. We needed that goal.

Brisbane moved the ball quickly downfield and looked for Alastair Lynch. A pack went up for the mark and the Lions' full-forward was awarded a free kick. It was deemed soft by the angry Collingwood supporters directly behind me, who had no hesitation in alerting the umpire to another error. Lynch kicked the goal and Brisbane hit the front.

From where I was sitting, on the boundary to the left of the players' dugout, perched on the very edge of my seat, I could hear every call from the Collingwood players to 'get back', 'clear out', 'kick long', and I felt every hit they took.

Directly in front of me, Jason Akermanis roved the pack. In an instant he gathered the loose ball and kicked it over his left shoulder. It was a goal. A heart-stopping, punch-in-the-guts goal.

I didn't let myself react—I couldn't, I had to keep the faith. Behind me, two tiers up, I knew Mum would have stopped watching, unable to bear it, and Danielle might have too. Cain and Troy would be swearing and yelling for the team to 'get it back, boys', their faces red from the effort.

Time seemed to speed up at that moment. The crowd was wild with desperation. Brisbane fans cheered one of their favourites while he celebrated with his teammates as if he had just won them the game. Beside me, an insensitive colleague said, 'That's it—it's over.'

'No,' I responded loudly. 'There's still time.' I felt a hand on my back—our boundary-line floor manager, my friend Cathy Fox, was offering her support.

The players' bodies must have screamed with exhaustion but both teams continued to battle. Overhead, a thunderstorm threatened to break, only adding to the drama of the afternoon. Then I heard it: 'thirty-seconds' came the call through my earpiece as the producer gave us our final-siren instructions. Ten . . . nine . . . It can't be the end already! Seven . . . six . . . I felt a quiver in my bottom lip and bit down hard on it to stop the tears. Three . . . two . . .

The siren sounded and, before me, Brisbane players jumped into each other's arms. The contrast between jubilation and devastation on the field was like the aftermath of a blazing fire, when half of the bush is untouched and the other half is ash. Nine bloody points.

The producer began yelling in my ear again to get a Brisbane player on camera *now*. How in the world was I going to do that? I made the mistake of looking towards the Collingwood players, who had gathered in a group, mostly sitting on the grass, lost in their own heartbreak. Then I saw Dad reach out for a visibly distressed Paul Licuria, who seemed to collapse into him. My God—is Dad crying too?

It was the saddest picture I'd ever seen of my dad and I was overcome with grief. Choking back the emotion, I forced myself to concentrate on my task. With Cathy's support and assistance, I somehow managed to interview several players—Michael Voss, Simon Black and Jason Akermanis among them. I put on a brave face—they were celebrating, after all. When the presentations were completed I made my way to the Collingwood rooms. My job wasn't over yet.

I saw my family, clearly upset after sharing Dad's hurt, but I waved them away for fear that they'd set me off. Neil Balme made my final interview easy, speaking softly about the Pies' disappointment as the players were consoled and comforted by their loved ones behind us. One final address to the camera and I was done. I had nothing left anyway.

Out of the corner of my eye I saw Dad approaching and put my hand up to stop him. The camera was still on and I wasn't ready yet to face him. I had to gather myself before I could give him the same support my mum and siblings were already delivering, the support he needed.

But it was too late—he was in front of me. He released a deep sigh as he pulled me into his arms. I lost it then, not just crying but sobbing into his shoulder. He felt heavy and his lack of emotional restraint made me feel a sorrow for him that crushed my chest. Mum embraced us protectively before Danielle and the boys joined us.

We drew closer together; Dad was going to need us.

10 MATTERS OF THE HEART

MICK COACHED A TEAM of dedicated soldiers, and he was getting the best he possibly could out of them. They too brought the best out in him. But he couldn't help feeling that they were playing out of their weight division. Making the grand final hadn't come easily. Getting as close as they did to their formidable opponents had taken enormous effort and still they had fallen short. Mick wondered if it was an opportunity missed, if it was the one and only chance this team would have of playing for a premiership. That thought disturbed him and depressed him.

He kept his worries to himself, though, and implored his players to learn from the loss, to use the heartbreak as motivation, and to reapply their focus to the new season.

They listened and listened well. The experience of the previous season helped to consolidate their belief that discipline and determination can take you a long way, so they played with grit and applied control. Collingwood opened the 2003 season with three wins, over Richmond, Carlton and Geelong, then the team flew to Brisbane for Round 4 and returned with a fourteen-point loss. It took the edge off their confidence and the stairs appeared higher to climb to reach the Lions' stature.

Still, they rode through the rocky patch that followed as a united team, returning more buoyantly to the path after each stumble. As the season progressed, it became a question not of *if* they would make the finals again, but of whether they could possibly finish in the top two.

On Monday, 7 July, Bob Rose passed away. Like every Collingwood supporter, Mick had idolised Bob Rose the player, but he also felt for Bob Rose the coach. Bobby had played in three Magpies grand finals, and was a member of the premiership-winning 1953 team. He'd then coached the Pies to another three grand finals, suffering losses in all of them. The 1970 match was one Mick would never forget, for the look on the face of the Collingwood coach after 'having Carlton on toast' with a 44-point half-time lead, only to lose by ten points. 'His players let him down that day,' Mick says.

After the Magpies' 2002 Grand Final defeat, Elsie Rose put an arm around Nanette and asked, 'How are you, dear?' before whispering, 'I know how it feels to watch your husband hurt like this.'

Bob Rose was as much a part of Collingwood as the magpie emblem.

'We all loved Bobby,' Mick says. 'He was a gentleman and such a humble man.'

That was why his passing created so much emotion for the Magpie Army and the Pies team. Mick felt compelled to speak of Bobby before their clash with Fremantle on the Saturday after the Collingwood legend's death, so he reminded his team to play with the same spirit and courage and passion as the man they would greatly miss. 'Give him something to be proud of,' he urged them.

By the time they ran out onto the field, his players were buzzing with determination, but the pre-game talk had left Mick feeling raw. I noticed the tears in his eyes when he met me on the boundary to be interviewed. He began to answer my question about Bob Rose but then he trailed off and changed the subject, turning away from me as he did. Sensing how close he was to losing his composure, I wound up the interview and threw back to the commentary box. He had said during the interview that he was feeling upset about the loss of a wonderful person he admired and an excellent footballer he had loved to watch play, but until then I didn't realise just how sad it had made him. I swallowed back a lump in my throat and watched the Magpies produce a brilliantly executed 41-point win over the Dockers, each player wearing a black armband.

Collingwood suffered just one loss in its last nine games of the season, to Brisbane in Round 19. It finished second behind Port Adelaide, with the Lions third.

A qualifying final against the reigning back-to-back premiers followed and Mick predicted that it would be a psychological battle for his players more so than a physical one. Pass this test and they would have the assurance to match their commitment.

Have you ever experienced a moment of panic, like when a cat runs in front of your car and you have to swerve to miss it? Well, that feeling of dread that starts in your chest and drops to the pit of your stomach is what our family felt before the approaching final against Brisbane. Twice Collingwood had lost to the Lions during the year and the media's predictions of torture were piling on the pressure. But while misgivings abounded, Mick's conviction remained. The team was playing to the best of its ability and the players had such a desire to topple the giants from the north that their hunger would lessen the disparity in skill and experience—and that was where Mick's belief came from.

It was goal for goal at the MCG, the Lions managing to stay in front for the first three quarters. As the final term began, Collingwood had a three-point deficit to make up, and it was as though the team had a collective light-bulb moment: 'We can win this, we can beat Brisbane.' They outscored their opponents then, 3.4 to four points. It was a fifteen-point win but it may as well have been a 115-point win for the spirit it sparked within the player group.

The Magpies' next challenge was Port Adelaide in a preliminary final. The top-of-the-table team had dominated the season and beaten the Pies in their one and only encounter.

But that was before *the win* over Brisbane. Collingwood now played with a wind behind its back, pushing it further, faster, higher. The Pies outplayed the minor premiers as if their final ladder positions were reversed. A six-goal last term stretched the final margin to 44 points: 44 reasons to get excited.

Within the space of twelve months, Collingwood had secured its second grand final berth. Brisbane's dismantling of Sydney a few hours later set up a rematch of the 2002 Grand Final. A feeling of déjà vu descended immediately on the Collingwood camp.

It was a strange mood in the Magpies' rooms after the win—instead of elation there was subdued contemplation. Anthony Rocca, the biggest man in the room, must have felt like the smallest as he contemplated his chances of playing in the grand final: he had been reported in the first quarter for striking Port Adelaide ruckman Brendon Lade, and faced a tribunal hearing during the week.

In Mick's view, Anthony Rocca was Collingwood's most valuable player in 2003. He'd kicked 45 goals for the season, but it was his sheer strength and size that made his presence in the forward line so important. He took the best defenders and worked hard off the ball to provide goal opportunities for his teammates. He'd kicked only one goal against the Lions a fortnight before, but Mick knew that Rocca worried Brisbane. Should they cover him with more than one man and risk leaving other Collingwood forwards free, or should they match him one on one and struggle to contain him? Mick felt that Rocca held the key to a Pies grand final victory.

As he was flooded with the memory of his own near miss in 1980—when he had been reported by two umpires for striking Sam Newman in Richmond's semi-final win—Mick could only hope that his player would be as lucky as he had been, and walk free. He worried, though, that more recent history was repeating itself.

While Collingwood's advocate, president, CEO, football manager, coach and player worked overtime on the case, grand final week began. Monday night was Brownlow night. An event that honours the best and fairest player of the league, it's also an evening to celebrate the end of a long season with a few invited teammates and, just as importantly, partners.

On this occasion, the Collingwood captain, Nathan Buckley, was one of the favourites to win the award. Two Magpie tables were positioned side by side, and as everyone seated at them finished their meals in time for the live telecast, they tried to focus on the vote count rather than the approaching tribunal hearing. But it was difficult not to dwell on such an important event.

By the time the Round 17 votes had been announced, it was clear that Nathan Buckley had some competition. Sydney's Adam Goodes and West Coast's Ben Cousins shared the lead, with 20 votes each. Mark Ricciuto was second, with nineteen, and Buckley had eighteen.

In Round 19, Buckley scored two votes to draw level with the leaders. There were three rounds left. A hush descended on the room as people quietly calculated the chances of a tie.

Finally, AFL CEO Wayne Jackson moved on to the last round. Collingwood versus Essendon: three votes, Shane Woewodin; two votes, James Hird; one vote—he paused for effect—Nathan Buckley. A cheer went up at the Collingwood tables: Buckley was in the outright lead. Just as the viewers at home were processing the information, Adam Goodes scored another two votes, and Mark Ricciuto another one. It was a three-way tie. Three very deserving Brownlow medallists.

Nathan was elated. Magpie fans were elated. Mick was elated for his skipper, but cautious about how it would affect his week. In this sense, he says, it's a shame the medal count comes in grand final week, when the shine of the award gets dulled by the need to return focus to the game. If anyone could handle the attention that comes with being awarded this highest of football honours and still retain a steely resolve for the upcoming match, however, the coach knew his skipper was that man.

To Mick, Buckley was one of the greatest players he'd ever coached: a determined footballer, highly professional, remarkably disciplined. Throughout his career he went head-to-head with the greats—James Hird, Michael Voss, Mark Ricciuto, Adam Goodes—and held his own. He was tagged in virtually every game and still came out a great player, which is testament to Buckley's concentration and ability to get the best out of himself.

After the high of Brownlow night came the inevitable tremor of tribunal Tuesday. Collingwood was convinced that

Anthony Rocca would get off the charge and gathered in force to support him at the hearing.

The club's defence advocate rolled video footage that showed Rocca's forearm connecting with his opponent's shoulder. The big Magpies forward told the panel that although he was a physical player, he never acted with the intent to hurt a rival. He pleaded to be allowed to play in the grand final. Brendon Lade testified that he felt a strike to his shoulder, not his head, as indicated by the reporting umpire. The whole thing went for two hours.

When chairman Brian Collis, QC, handed down the verdict, Anthony Rocca momentarily closed his eyes. Mick shook his head and heard a ringing in his ears. Guilty. Reckless and unnecessary. Suspended for two weeks.

The Collingwood group piled out of the room dumbfounded and distraught. How could this be happening again? They decided immediately to appeal, but it would mean hovering in limbo a little longer.

Mick's job, besides preparing his team, was to protect it. His players didn't need another drawn-out process complicating the week. He tried to shield them from the press as much as he could and remained upbeat in their presence. Rocca trained with the team and put on a brave face, even while suffering from shock.

The appeal was heard on the Wednesday afternoon and once again Collingwood had put together a good case. Brendon Lade was flown to Melbourne to reveal a large bruise on his shoulder, the area that Rocca insisted had been the point of contact. Hawthorn coach Peter Schwab, and a former Richmond player, Neville Crowe, testified to the everlasting impact it would have on the Magpies player to miss a grand final for such an insignificant misdemeanour. And Rocca himself made an impassioned plea to be allowed to play, saying that the past 24 hours had already been the worst of his life. Mick just hoped that the three-member board would look at the case objectively and not be influenced by the tribunal sanction.

They deliberated in private and made a decision. 'We find no reason to disagree with the findings of the tribunal,' said chairman Peter O'Callaghan. The ban was upheld.

Rocca was too devastated to speak afterwards. Mick was thinking about Mitchell White. In 1994, the West Coast defender had missed out on the Eagles' premiership because he was dropped from the team. He'd missed a lot of football that year due to a nagging groin complaint and with the return of trusty full-back Ashley McIntosh from injury, someone had to be cut from the squad. Mick chose White 'because he was the least done, fitness wise', and he'd regretted it ever since. The option was the right one as West Coast won the title, but the decision to deny his player the chance to contend for a premiership had remained a stone in Mick's shoe. On this day, when Anthony Rocca turned his gaze towards his coach, his face disfigured with sorrow, Mick felt a familiar pang of lament.

Mark Richardson was the obvious option to come back into the side. He was tall, strong, an accurate kick at goal and experienced. His father was a two-time best-and-fairest player for Collingwood who'd never won a premiership, so there was a fairytale element there also. Unfortunately, a spell was cast on Richardson before he could become Collingwood's knight in shining armour and he broke down at training with a thigh strain. Mick couldn't believe it.

So Tristen Walker, an eighteen-year-old rookie of nine games, came in to fill the void instead. Rocca was a giant of a man and a giant of a character, at the peak of his form, so replacing him was impossible; 'Tex' Walker would have to bring his own game to the MCG. After another grand final parade in which the city of Melbourne was painted black and white with thousands of Magpies fans, and one final training session cheered on by those same hysterical supporters, Mick felt as though he had been riding the ocean waves on a lifebuoy for a week.

We always gave Dad a good-luck card at the beginning of the season and another one at the start of the finals. He kept every one of them, which means his sock drawer resembles a Hallmark stand.

Usually we kept it simple, something like, 'Best wishes, Dad, we're right behind you,' but that September we added another line: 'You deserve it.' For all the effort, all the hard work, all the headaches and chest pains, the broken sleep, the public enquiries and the eternal faith, you deserve to be rewarded with a premiership. We wanted him to win it so much that it was our only thought for a week. A collective consciousness willing the team to victory.

And then it was the morning of the game. Grand final day. Say it aloud and it sends tingles to your toes. The wind whispers messages of hope. The earth surrounding the MCG trembles from the energy of almost one hundred thousand wishes being carried into the stadium by supporters. No matter how many times you've been there, the thrill of the occasion always takes your breath away. It was a magnificent morning.

Just like the previous year, I was at the ground early for Channel Ten's grand final coverage. I waited outside the rooms to meet Dad as he arrived. He'd told our family the night before that many people at the club were feeling drained after a week that started with celebration and turned into frustration. It had been seven days of extreme emotion. But now, three hours before game time, Dad was wearing a cloak of confidence.

There had been a lot of talk during the week about Brisbane's injuries. We had covered it all in our newsroom. The Lions had gone to the extraordinary length of chartering a plane to fly at a lower altitude to that of a domestic flight, so as not to hamper the recovery efforts of several players. One of them was Nigel Lappin, who had a broken rib; he had declared he would play regardless of the injury.

There was widespread talk that Brisbane was overusing painkilling injections to aid its injured players. At his final chat to the media for the week, Leigh Matthews had appeared bemused by the suggestion that the Lions' injury treatments were bordering on illegal. He wasn't a man worried about the ramifications of going to extreme lengths to get his best players on the field. I thought the Brisbane coach had a swagger about him, a sense of immortality. It made my longing for Dad's team to beat his even stronger.

Mick had ignored all of the grand final preamble to prepare to face a full-strength Lions team, whether that was the side that ran out onto the park or not. It was a case of over-preparing rather than under-preparing and being caught out.

His concern, hidden by an armour of optimism, wasn't about the opposition but about his own line-up. They were severely weakened by the loss of Rocca—no-one could deny that—but the Magpies also lacked depth. Below the first tier of skilful talent, Mick felt vulnerable to the idiosyncrasies of the less gifted and less experienced players. He hoped that the men who had performed poorly in 2002 would redeem themselves in this grand final, and he implored them to think of their teammates and the group effort it would require to bring down the reigning champions. He appealed to their egos: play like heroes and you will be heroes; don't lairise—a show-off never wins. And he reinforced it all with a positive message: we have beaten them once, we can win again. We will win.

'Let's go, boys.'

The national anthem filled the air above the MCG and I prayed for a Collingwood win. My family took their seats among the partners and parents of the players for the grand final hurricane. It was a ride they were now familiar with. They hoped for a better ending than the last time.

The Brisbane team lined up as named, with Nigel Lappin present. It wasn't a surprise.

'Go Collingwood,' I called out from the boundary, but it was drowned out by the thunder that erupted with the first bounce.

The opening quarter was tight, the Lions edging out to a two-goal lead. A manageable deficit, I thought, this is okay. In the Pies' huddle, Mick repeated his pre-game words: 'Lift, boys, give it everything—there is no tomorrow.'

The next thirty minutes were almost impossible to watch. Simon Black had the ball often. Jason Akermanis and Alastair Lynch finished off his hard work. And Collingwood fell apart, one mistake at a time. It was torment to witness. My mum, I knew, would be grinding her teeth in desperation, and my siblings would be tearing their hair out.

Dad was in a rage at half time. The door of the Magpies' changerooms barely contained the anger inside. I stood near it, glaring at anyone who looked my way, wishing to be upstairs with my family instead of hovering in the foyer with a camera crew. Collingwood was down by 42 points. The coach challenged his players' commitment, the one thing he hadn't had to question before now.

We kept out of the way as the team emerged from its dressing-down, and as much as I wanted to give my dad a reassuring pat on the back, I stayed out of sight. Better to keep his mind on the game.

Collingwood responded with a two-goal opening burst to the second half. The margin was back to 28 points. The Magpies cheer squad came back to life and the heartfelt noise was invigorating.

Then it all went pear-shaped again. Unable to maintain their intensity, the Magpies hesitated and Brisbane pounced. The all-conquering Lions took a 39-point lead into the final term and ran with it, piling on six further goals. I could only cringe, and I wasn't the only one.

Three late goals saved the final margin from being utterly humiliating, but 50 points was bad. *Really* bad. The Lions had just won their third successive premiership but they celebrated as though it were their first. Collingwood had suffered its second straight grand final defeat, and felt the deflation like death.

As I interviewed jubilant Brisbane players on ground, odious in my thoughts but respectful in my manner, I didn't have to look at Dad to feel the fury radiating from him across the field. He stood next to his players but couldn't look at them—not that any of them could meet his eyes. They watched Brisbane receive the cup and hold it up to their supporters, again. Then the Magpies trudged off the ground to the comforting arms of their families.

Dad's mood didn't change even after seeing his wife and children. He was livid about this loss. It would torture him for a long time, and that in turn would torture us.

*

The second grand final loss was a catalyst for Mick to shake things up at the club. He made an important decision and, with the backing of the board, acted on it. He chose to start again. Hanging on to what you have is easy, but for success to happen in football, change is necessary.

Making the assumption that Collingwood wasn't going to win a premiership with its current group of players, Mick decided to refresh the list. Players were moved on and more rookies brought in. Mick warned the club and the supporters that it would take time to regenerate the team, but it would be worth it. They should brace themselves for the inevitable crash that comes with upheaval, he cautioned, but never lose sight of the big picture.

We knew the drill and we knew the reasons, but it didn't make it any easier to deal with the consequences. Losing is never fun. When it happens regularly, it erodes your spirit and denies you any relief.

Halfway through 2004, Eddie McGuire's promise to give Collingwood the best facilities from which to prepare for a premiership assault came good. The club moved its headquarters and football department into the fully renovated Olympic Park, complete with a state-of-the-art gymnasium, ice baths, an altitude room, a players' lounge and fully equipped kitchen and, most importantly, a training ground with a pristine surface.

It was here that Mick would now be able to nurture and advance the talented youth that came under his care. He was rapt with his new surroundings after so many years of dealing with substandard facilities at each club he coached; it was a wonderful reward to go to work in a modern and high-tech setting that was the perfect environment for creating success. After three years of turbulence, in a strange way it felt like things were finally falling into place.

But Collingwood lost fourteen games in 2004 and finished thirteenth. Nathan Buckley's hamstring problems began during the season and kept him out of seven games. The Collingwood coach faced a backlash from unhappy supporters, and heavy criticism from the media. He also had to ward off a fidgety Magpies board.

Things got worse in 2005. Anthony Rocca snapped his Achilles tendon in a Round 4 clash with the Kangaroos, ending his season immediately. Mick had often referred to the Pies' big man as the barometer of the side: 'If he played well, the team played well.' His unavailability would hurt, as would the omission of Buckley for half the season after hamstring surgery.

Midway through the season, when the team had suffered its eighth loss, Collingwood announced that there would be 'a thorough review of the football operations' at the end of the season.

In Round 16, the Pies faced Essendon, after a 78-point defeat at the hands of Brisbane a week earlier. By three-quarter time the Bombers' lead was 56 points. Some gutsy football helped the Magpies pull it back in the last term, but there wasn't enough time to erase the damage and Essendon won by four goals. Afterwards, the Collingwood football department was put on notice by a ropable club president.

✳

We gathered for a family meal over the weekend, needing to schedule appointments to see each other due to the rapid pace of our lives. Dad told us about Eddie's outburst, which had stemmed from the complaints of the restless Magpies board.

'So I'm going to resign,' he announced.

We didn't believe him. He was always miserable when losses mounted up and the media repeatedly pointed the finger at him, often saying, 'I'm sick of it, I've had enough.' Then he would get a win and the press would turn on another coach and his spirits would be revived.

This time, though, he was serious.

'They're not happy, they're impatient, so I'm going to give them what they want,' he said.

We implored him to think on it for longer but he was pretty adamant that the club would be better off without him. He was going to quit the next day.

The following morning he walked into Greg Swann's office and offered his resignation. Just like that.

Greg looked at him from behind his desk and shook his head. 'No, I won't let you,' he said. 'I don't accept it.'

The two men sat and talked. Mick said he was putting the club first. The team had been without two of its best players for most of the year; there were seven players in the top 22 with less than 25 games' experience and several other players close to retirement. The Collingwood coach was doing his best and he had warned everyone that rebuilding would take time. 'But if they can't wait and they're that unhappy, I'll go,' he told the CEO.

Greg responded: 'I'm talking you out of this. I'm not even going to take it to the board. This club needs you.' And that was that.

In an industry where there is little positive feedback for a coach, it can be easy to believe the negative talk and begin to doubt your own abilities. So often Dad had said to us, 'When we win, it's the players that did it, when we lose, it's my fault.' And he didn't mind this take on things, always maintaining that 'the buck stops with coach', but sometimes it was nice for him to hear that he was doing a good job. On this occasion, it made all the difference.

Two weeks later, I was asked by a Channel Ten colleague if my dad had recently offered to stand down. I was used to living in two worlds, where any private information I had remained secret, so without hesitation I denied it. Still, he ran with the story, stating that he had received information from a reliable source. That evening Collingwood, including

Mick, categorically refuted the claims and nothing was ever said about it again.

The Magpies didn't win another game for the season, slumping to fifteenth after seventeen losses. We all thought it couldn't get much worse than this. The only way was up.

By the end of 2005, David Buttifant had convinced the Magpies board that altitude training overseas would benefit the team enormously, so in November they headed off.

Nanette was worried for her husband. Never being a man to back down, always wanting to lead and win, and too casually shrugging off his age as an excuse to slow down, Mick, at 52, would be at the front of the pack for every challenge the team undertook in Flagstaff, Arizona.

'Be careful,' she insisted before he left. 'Remember, you're not as young as your players.'

He scoffed at her remark and replied, 'But I'm just as fit as them.'

Every time he phoned home to recount another completed challenge—such as climbing up Mount Humphreys to its peak, 4000 metres above sea level, at minus 35 degrees in howling 120-kilometre winds, before descending to the base, all in one day—Nanette breathed a sigh of relief and slept a little easier. Until she remembered that next they were going to hike down the Grand Canyon.

When he returned from the 'incredible experience', exhausted and sore, having lost weight and had his back freeze up on the flight home, Mick boasted that he had led his players for each treacherous hike and was never once overtaken. He said it with pride but his family thought he was stupid. Everyone agreed the trip would profit the team not just in fitness, but also psychologically for the adversity they had encountered and overcome together. It was totally and utterly Mick's cup of tea.

Mick began the 2006 season feeling energised and motivated. A familiar excitement was starting to build in him, like pins and needles, spreading from his feet to his face.

Collingwood lost its first match but won its second. There was a story going around at the time that Eddie McGuire had called for Mick's head at half time of the clash with Hawthorn, when the Hawks led by nine points. Anthony Rocca—in his second match back from injury—kicked five of the Magpies' eight goals in the third term and greatly contributed to the eventual 35-point victory. Afterwards the president made no mention of firing his coach. Mick dismissed the tale as nonsense; the game is fickle but surely not that capricious. The post-game media concentrated on Rocca's absolute domination of a young, second-year rookie, Zac Dawson.

After another victory, the Anzac Day match loomed as a big battle. It fell on a Tuesday and, as always, drew a massive crowd. Over 91,000 spectators saw Essendon jump to an early lead and maintain it—just—for a one-goal lead at half time.

I was at work, filming a story at a golf course for a children's football program I hosted for Channel Ten, but I had regular updates from the clubhouse staff. Late in the afternoon, as I was wrapping up an interview, the staff happily told me that Collingwood had kicked nine goals to five in the second half and won the match by seventeen points. Hooray, I thought.

Dean, my boyfriend of six months, picked me up and announced we were going out for dinner, a surprise date he'd organised days earlier. I was excited, until I got a phone call from my sister. She was in tears.

'Dad's had a heart attack. He's been taken to hospital,' she blurted out. The words hit me like a sledgehammer.

I could barely talk. 'What?' I asked, signalling for Dean to pull over.

'I don't know how bad it is—they're doing tests now. Mum will call you.'

We went home and waited. And waited. And waited. I'd tried to call Mum but her phone was off. Our presence at the hospital would tip off the media that something was up, so we'd all been told to stay put.

I thought back to 1994, when the West Coast Eagles' fitness coach, Brian Dawson, had done an experiment on Dad by strapping a heart monitor to his chest for a match. On two occasions his heart rate became elevated to 160 beats per minute—during the pre-match address, and when the Eagles trainer gave away a free kick. The typical resting heart rate of an adult is between 60–80 beats per minute and it wasn't good, he was told, that his heart was put under that kind of strain every week.

Finally, Mum phoned.

'He's okay,' she said before I could ask. She sounded tired but relieved now that the worst had passed. He would have to remain in hospital overnight, with a heart monitor and other medical equipment still attached. It hadn't actually been a heart attack—it was arrhythmia.

Dad had had chest pains throughout the match and tightening across his heart. By the last term, he'd felt nauseous and lightheaded, his heart literally skipping a beat before he momentarily blacked out.

On his release from hospital, he was put on medication, but he had an adverse reaction to it, so eventually he had to learn how to live with the condition. He has had arrhythmia episodes since but he also knows not to panic. It is something he will live with for the rest of his life.

The remarkable thing about the entire incident was that the media was none the wiser. Mum and Dad had been rushed in to Royal Melbourne Hospital by a side entrance, and once admitted, the staff had politely remained quiet about his visit. There was a rumour—he had skipped his post-match press conference, which had raised some suspicion—but the club had shrugged it off as a stomach upset so it was left alone, for the time being. Dad was thankful for this; he didn't need his health questioned as well as his ability to coach.

Collingwood's season improved. With the addition of Dale Thomas and Scott Pendlebury, the team had a good, albeit young, look about it, and it was getting results.

They defeated Carlton by 72 points in Round 6 and in Round 8 they landed a knockout blow on Geelong, kicking six straight in the first quarter to trap the Cats against the ropes, only easing up in the final term when they were sure their opponent was down for the count. The Pies won by 102 points: 22.14 (146) to 6.8 (44).

The Pies' biggest loss that season occurred against St Kilda, when Brendon Goddard and Luke Ball couldn't be contained and helped the Saints to a 59-point win. Collingwood rounded out the season with an eleven-goal victory over the Kangaroos to seal fifth spot on the ladder, behind four non-Victorian teams: West Coast, Adelaide, Fremantle and Sydney.

Mick felt that finishing fifth was a great effort for an emerging side and a promising sign for the future, but he was in two minds about the elimination final. Collingwood had defeated the Western Bulldogs in their one clash during the season, but this was the team's first final since the 2003 Grand Final loss and he wondered how his players would handle it.

The eighth-placed Dogs were a good team and perhaps should have finished higher. Their pace troubled the Pies and matching up on them was difficult because of the unorthodox way they lined up, with medium men playing tall. The Bulldogs always performed well against Collingwood.

Theory translated to practice and it was a dogfight in the opening term. In the first minute, Brodie Holland ran through the centre square and straight through Brett Montgomery—he served a six-week suspension for the hit—setting up a physical encounter. Only ten points separated the teams at the first change, with the Pies leading.

As fast as you can say 'supercalifragilisticexpialidocious', the Bulldogs executed a 20-point turnaround to take the lead into the half-time break. Montgomery made a remarkable recovery and kicked four goals for the game to help the Dogs increase their lead further in the second half. Matthew Robbins and the young Adam Cooney backed him up.

Dale Thomas, returning from a collarbone injury, took a specky over Rohan Smith in the final term—his trademark leap just one of the talents that had already earned him cult status at the Pies—but it was Collingwood's only highlight late in the match, resulting in a disappointing 41-point loss.

The pressure was on immediately after the game.

It had been a rough year. There had been off-field incidents involving high-profile Magpies players. There had been persistent rumours that Mick was suffering from ill health, possibly even cancer, because he had lost weight due to a winter cough. Reports had been denied that Port Adelaide coach and former Collingwood player Mark Williams would replace Mick for 2007 because his health was a grave concern. And the Magpies had just surrendered an early lead for a miserable end to their season.

By the start of the working week internet chatrooms were abuzz with talk that the Collingwood coach was about to resign or be sacked. Neither happened. On Friday, 15 September, Collingwood issued a statement:

The Collingwood Football Club emphatically denies reports that coach Mick Malthouse has resigned from the club. The reports are nothing more than malicious gossip. Malthouse is contracted until the end of next year and is eagerly planning Collingwood's assault on the 2007 season.

Collingwood's bosses brought in an outside company to conduct another internal review of the club's football department and in October Neil Balme was replaced as chief of football by North Melbourne CEO Geoff Walsh. Football operations manager Mark Kleiman was also moved on, as was army officer Reg Crawford—ironically, the man they had brought in a year earlier to analyse the running of the department. Balme declined the offer of a different role at the club and took on the job as general manager of football at Geelong. It was a big restructure, but one the Magpies board felt was necessary.

It was so much to deal with that we were all glad the season was over; we had felt trapped and slightly claustrophobic. When the media finally left Mum and Dad's doorstep and the second week of finals began—without Collingwood—we emerged into the daylight.

Mick's only solace was the thought that he was building an outstanding team capable of anything, one block at a time.

Travis Cloke, Cameron Wood, Harry O'Brien and Heath Shaw all debuted in 2005. When Mum and Dad hosted a young group of players at our family beach house on Victoria's west coast at the end of that year, it included Scott Pendlebury, Dale Thomas, Harry O'Brien, Jack Anthony and Alan Toovey. They presented Mum with a thankyou gift 'for all of her delicious cooking'. Mick looked at the names signed on the attached card and said, 'This is the nucleus of a premiership team.'

Mick was very excited about those young players and several more who joined the club the next year: Ben Reid, Chris Dawes, Nathan Brown, Sharrod Wellingham, Brent Macaffer and Tyson Goldsack; and talked about them all the time, for he was never just a footy coach. He took on the role of mentor, teacher and father-figure to so many of his players because he genuinely cared for their welfare. Sure, most of that applies to helping them fulfil their ambition to become elite footballers. But to develop into well-rounded human beings, many of those young men needed further support and education in other areas of their lives, and Mick was more than happy to provide it. His greatest joy as a coach was to see his players grow into upstanding, well-balanced men, as well as successful footballers. He did this by listening, advising and caring.

In March every year the AFL holds a swanky cocktail party to launch the new season. In 2007, Nanette and Mick spent most of the evening talking to close friends Greg and Leonie Swann. Neither couple stayed late, eager to enjoy a long weekend before the beginning of the season.

The following day, as they drove to their beach house, Mick received a phone call from his president. He almost drove off the road upon hearing what Eddie had to say: Greg Swann was leaving to go to Carlton. To say Mick and Nanette were shocked is an understatement—they simply couldn't believe the news. They understood why it had been kept from them— football secrets don't often remain secret if they are whispered to too many people—but Carlton? The Blues had taken the wooden spoon for the last two years. New president Richard Pratt must have played hardball to get a man of Greg's ilk on board. Mick knew why Eddie was so upset about it: he despised Carlton and losing his CEO to them was like a stinging slap in the face.

Mick felt like he was losing a mate. He and Greg had shared a close bond from the beginning, each using the other as a sounding board, and they worked well together, which was important for the efficiency of the football department. Mick admired Greg for his professionalism and integrity and it would be difficult to maintain a tight relationship with both men working at different clubs. He would miss Greg greatly.

It took Collingwood six weeks to find a replacement and it came in the shape of former Magpie—and Eddie's Channel Nine colleague—Gary Pert.

In 2007, at the start of a cold winter, when Collingwood was gaining momentum but still missing something, Mick was struck by inspiration.

Together with David Buttifant and Guy McKenna, who had joined the club as an assistant coach, he devised a plan to maximise the energy expenditure of the Collingwood players and in turn nullify the opposition's playmakers. The Pies needed to be different, to work to the strengths of their team and try something that no other team was doing. They decided to significantly increase rotations off the bench during a game.

The Magpies had a host of players who were slowing down, tiring after years of football; many of them would retire within two years. The second-tier group was young and inexperienced, but full of potential. To make the most of every player's output, the coaching staff had to work the bench effectively to rest players enough for them to compete at a higher workrate. It was simple: if the Pies were fresher than their tiring opposition, they would have more chance of beating them. In this way, they could turn a mediocre side into a good team.

By the end of the season, Mick had doubled the average number of rotations made in a game to 88. Collingwood won six of its remaining games and finished sixth on the ladder.

There are defining moments in everyone's life, sometimes several—events or people or sudden flashes of thought that pick you up, shake you by the shoulders and turn you around to push you in another direction.

Grandpa had been battling ill health for years, but more recently he'd been getting worse and had become weak. In the days leading up to the Magpies' Round 18 clash with Carlton, he had fallen in the bathroom and couldn't get up. Dad rushed to Ballarat when he learnt of the fall and of Grandpa's admission to hospital.

On the Saturday after Grandpa's return home, Dean and I kept my grandparents company in their small lounge room. We rearranged the house to make it safer and more comfortable for Grandpa and when we left he laughed at my bossy orders for him to keep using his newly hired walking frame.

It was unexpected, then, when he collapsed a second time, before Collingwood's next match, and went downhill fast. We were told he had a cancer that had previously gone undetected. He was put on morphine to ease his pain as the doctors revealed that he didn't have long to live.

We witnessed grief overwhelming Dad, numbing him and hijacking his mind. He drove back and forth between home and Ballarat each day that week, sometimes with Mum, other times alone. The Pies lost to Richmond by 20 points, and early the next morning Dad and Mum travelled back to the hospital, where they sat all day beside Grandpa and Grandma.

On the Monday morning, they asked us all to go to Ballarat. By the time we arrived at the hospice, Dad's grief had broken open and spilt from him like lava. Every time Grandpa groaned Dad leant down to ask him if he was in pain, if he needed more morphine, and every time he did, his heart seemed to break again, releasing a fresh set of tears. I don't think any of us had ever seen Dad look so vulnerable, his sorrow weighing heavily on us and blending with our own grief.

Grandpa passed away holding the hands of his son and his wife of 55 years.

Dad's misery was so palpable that he was offered the option of not coaching the Pies in their Friday-night clash with Melbourne. He would wait until the day to decide, he said. He was well supported at the funeral by many Collingwood people—the president, the CEO, the football manager and several players. When Grandpa's coffin was lowered into the ground, beneath rain clouds and with a chill wind blowing, Eddie McGuire began a chorus of 'Good Old Collingwood Forever', and everyone who loved Ray joined in. It was a surreal but moving moment.

The next day, Dad did coach. He was drained and sad but he wanted to do his father proud. He said he would draw from Grandpa's courage, and he did, instructing and guiding his team to a big half-time lead and through a late Demons fightback to an eleven-point win.

He says now it was one of the toughest nights of his career, but it was worth it to honour his father.

In the 2007 finals, Collingwood met Sydney at the MCG. The Pies needed to win to keep their season alive and were well ahead at quarter time by 31 points. The Swans had played off in the last two grand finals, winning one of them, and they were intent on making another one. Off Michael O'Loughlin's boot they had reduced the margin by 21 at half time.

Collingwood's new rotation policy was telling in the second half as it pulled away again. With energy in reserve, the team further increased its lead in the last quarter. The 38-point win was the club's first finals victory in four seasons.

They flew to Perth with boosted confidence to tackle the reigning premiers, West Coast. In a first term in which defence dominated, the score mirrored the effort of both teams: 1.5 (11) to 0.4 (4) in the Magpies' favour. Dean Cox had too much muscle for Guy Richards, and Matt Priddis was in destructive form, giving the home side enough of an edge to hold a narrow lead at the next two breaks.

The match remained low-scoring, with both sides struggling to penetrate solid walls of defence. Paul Medhurst was magic, first pouncing on a loose ball and kicking a goal from outside 50 before setting up Dale Thomas for another major to put the Pies in front with minutes remaining.

In Mum and Dad's Hampton home, where we had gathered to watch the match, there wasn't a cool head in the room. We breathed with relief when the Eagles' Darren Glass missed a set shot from a contentious free kick against Anthony Rocca for a high tackle. And in unison we screamed out 'dive' as though Shane O'Bree and Shane Wakelin could actually hear us as they chased Andrew Embley, who ran into an open goal and missed to the right.

The camera concentrated on Dad in the coach's box, yelling instructions into his headset as the ball was held up at the top of the Pies goalsquare. Time ticked down. The next shot showed him throwing off his glasses as he bolted from the box to the ground. The siren had gone with the score at 72 points apiece. An extra quarter of time-on was announced.

Mick could sense that his team still had energy as he approached the huddle. They were determined and confident, but better than that, they had the fuel to play another 20 minutes of finals football. He knew then that this was proof that the increased rotations had benefitted the squad.

Collingwood's onballers, now resting for two minutes, three times a quarter, were brilliant. The forwards, who came off once or twice a term, were accurate. And the backs stayed strong and were supported well by the midfield. They trounced a weary Eagles team, 3.3 to 0.2, and progressed to a preliminary final against Geelong.

On the night before the match, Mick received a phone call from Josh Fraser, who was pulling out of the team with a sore back. Mick threw down the phone in annoyance. He needed his number-one ruckman in the side against the talented Cats duo of Brad Ottens and Mark Blake, and he felt let down. Chris Bryan would come back into the team but Mick would need to use several options in the centre.

Geelong had finished on top of the ladder with a team in blistering form. Rain and a slippery surface would keep the game tight and interesting. After Scott Burns' opening goal from a boundary throw-in, Matthew Stokes replied immediately and, four minutes later Brad Ottens converted a set shot from 45 metres out. Struggling against his speedy opponent, Tyson Goldsack was left behind as Stokes drilled his third for the quarter to give the Cats a handy eleven-point first-quarter lead.

Two early goals in the second quarter handed the lead back to the Pies before Geelong skipped away again. The pace was furious and the ball hard to control. Alan Didak used his soccer skills to produce a goal, leaping over Corey Enright for a midair kick over his head. Another goal to Sean Rusling and the deficit was back to a straight kick at half time.

The Cats failed to convert early in the third term and a Cameron Ling fumble allowed Leon Davis to put the Pies within two points. It was gritty and desperate football as the lead bounced from team to team, with never more than eight points separating them.

It all came down to the final term and when Travis Cloke put the Pies in front, an almighty cheer went up as the biggest MCG crowd in ten years—98,002—sensed an upset. By now, we couldn't—or wouldn't—breathe, holding the air in our lungs between each goal as we followed the play with our eyes and contorted our bodies in our seats, contesting the ball through will alone, finally gasping for breath when it sailed through the goalposts and the players ran back to the centre square to do it all over again.

Each time the Cats gained momentum, the Magpies would wrestle it back, doing it now without their skipper. Nathan Buckley had re-injured his hamstring and was resigned to the bench. Not a single person at the game could lounge in their seat, instead edging forward to get a better view of an unbelievable contest that had just been made closer by goals to Travis Cloke and Alan Didak. Five points.

Gary Ablett junior kicked a goal sideways off his right foot. Eleven points.

Paul Medhurst took a kick for Anthony Rocca as he limped off with a broken ankle; he put it through the middle. Five points.

A minute left.

We couldn't move. We couldn't speak. We couldn't breathe. We could only hope like hell for a win.

We watched as the Pies got the centre clearance and Geelong ambushed the midfield to hold it up. Back and forth, back and forth, the ball moved barely two metres at a time as players tackled, dived and fought for it.

Finally, a clean disposal came as Didak picked up the ball on the wing and kicked it long into Collingwood's attacking zone. Jimmy Bartel grabbed it first but Cloke swung him to the ground. Ball-up inside the 50. With seconds remaining— we weren't sure how many—all we could yell was: 'Kick it!'

As the umpire threw the ball in the air, the siren blared. Game over. Five points.

We slumped, defeated, in our seats: upset, angry, disappointed, sad and unbelieving, all at once. The Cats were in the grand final. We weren't.

Mick still bristles at the memory of that loss. In many ways it was the grand final, as the Cats went on to humiliate Port Adelaide the following week to win the premiership. We watched the game together at the beach house. Dad spent the two hours of the game outside gardening, unable to bear the contest and the result. If disappointment can be summed up in a single match, that preliminary final is the game.

Nathan Buckley, James Clement and Paul Licuria all retired after the season. Clement's decision was based a need to return home to Perth, while Buckley and Licuria reluctantly succumbed to their tired and sore bodies. Each player would be immensely missed by the club and by their coach. More change was on the horizon.

Dean and I got married in November 2007. We had two weekends to choose from on which we could hold the ceremony, between training camps, trade week, the draft and the pre-season beginning. Not long after we met, Dean knew he was entering a life consumed by football. He had barracked for St Kilda until then, but after watching a single game with us he switched immediately to Collingwood. He couldn't bear to see the effect a loss had on the family, so each week he barracked for a win.

I have a photo that was taken just before I walked down the aisle. My arm is linked with Dad's and I am looking across at him, my eyes wide with wedding-day anticipation.

'Are you nervous?' he had just asked me.

'Yes.' I answered, my throat dry.

'Don't be. You look beautiful. I'm happy for you, darling. Just as long as he makes you happy, that's all we care about.'

Then he laughed as I blew out a deep breath through my tight lips.

It was one rare moment in my life when there were no thoughts or talk of football and everyone present could see Dad as his children saw him: as a loving father.

11 DEALING IN NUMBERS

COLLINGWOOD HAD APPOINTED Scott Burns as captain for the 2008 season. Mick saw him as steely, reliable and very team-oriented. Diligent and unflappable defender Simon Prestigiacomo was sidelined with a nasty and nagging foot injury that had required surgery. Nathan Brown and Sharrod Wellingham both debuted in the early games, joining a long list of young men who were replacing the retirees and rebuilding the club.

The team changed shape with each new addition. The dynamics shifted and the batteries got recharged. The side had more speed now, with Dane Swan and Dale Thomas setting the pace. They had a powerful marking forward in Travis Cloke, who had the potential to be a Coleman medallist. Nathan Brown, Ben Reid, Nick Maxwell, Heath Shaw and Harry O'Brien formed the basis of a tough and hard-running backline. And Scott Pendlebury, Sharrod Wellingham and Ben Johnson were working as tirelessly in the centre as Nathan Buckley and Paul Licuria had before them.

By Round 8, Collingwood had won just three games. Then a nine-point victory over St Kilda started a four-game winning run.

In Round 9 the Pies faced the reigning premiers, Geelong. They weren't going to take them on at their own game, which consisted of high-possession football and a highly corridor-conscious structure. Mick had already tried that and it hadn't worked with his squad, which lacked the ball carriers to possess the footy in high numbers. His new structure, working to the strengths of the Collingwood team, was based around steady frontal pressure, like an army advancing on its enemy, forcing opposition turnovers and errors. In attack, they would spread to the widest part of the field and move the ball along the boundary in a plan aimed at protecting the ball and the scoreline.

The players had redemption on their minds as they entered this match against the team that had sent them packing from the 2007 finals series, and that was exactly what they achieved.

After Leon Davis opened the Magpies' account at the six-minute mark, they scored three goals before the Cats had kicked one. Holding a commanding 26-point lead at the first break, Travis Cloke kicked his third goal halfway through the second term and a win was almost a given. The Cats began the second half with three quick goals before Alan Didak answered and Cloke booted his fourth—the Pies were away again. By the end, the margin was a huge 86 points—the result was confirmation that the planets were aligning for Collingwood and its coach. It would take some tweaking and refining over time, but the plan was in place. Mick believed, 'You can't replace champions but you can give anyone a chance to become one.' So in 2008, he fed his future football stars a game plan to mature their strengths.

The following weekend they faced West Coast at the MCG; kicking 27.11 to 10.13, the Pies annihilated their opposition by 100 points. On the Queen's Birthday Monday, the Magpies defeated Melbourne by 21 points.

Still it was difficult to get hold of that elusive thing called momentum. The following week the young Pies were given a lesson in playing four quarters of football. Level at three-quarter time with Carlton, after wasting a half-time lead, Collingwood lost concentration. Three unanswered goals within six minutes gave Carlton the ascendancy and they went with it, Brendon Fevola kicking four for the quarter—eight for the match—and turning what was a tight contest into a blowout. The Blues won by 30 points.

This is the big issue with an inexperienced team: youthful enthusiasm is wonderful when it lasts, but more commonly, it's the young mind that becomes restless, the young body that gets sore, and the energy of the young person that fades as quickly as it was switched on.

'So how much longer will it be now?' We were sitting in a café discussing the construction of my parents' new home, an apartment in a beautiful old building near the city.

'Well, they're saying another six months, at least,' Dad muttered, clearly annoyed.

'And you'll have a spare bedroom that can fit a cot?' I asked, trying to be casual.

Mum screamed and Dad blushed an excited pink and grinned.

'Are you really pregnant? You'll look funny on the boundary with a baby bump,' Dad laughed, happy.

At my twelve-week pregnancy scan, the radiologist noticed an abnormality in the baby's kidneys.

'We'll need to keep an eye on it,' the obstetrician told us. 'But it could be nothing, so don't worry.'

Of course we worried.

As my stomach grew, it was amusing to hear comments from the crowd as I walked the boundary line pre-game to my position near the player's bench.

'Is it a boy or a girl, Christi?'

'Will it play football?'

'How are you feeling?' Even big burly men with football club tattoos inked around their arms enquired after the wellbeing of 'the bump'. The baby in turn would kick and squirm inside me as the crowd noise grew louder throughout each match I worked, until I was sure it was a boy and he wanted to play football.

My second scan revealed that the kidney problem wasn't 'nothing'. It would require further monitoring before delivery. My pregnancy coincided with Danielle's planning of her 14 December wedding to Simon, which had been booked before she knew I was pregnant. I was due that same day. It was possibly the first time that the events of our own lives occupied more space than football.

Collingwood's 54-point loss to Hawthorn in Round 18 was the club's third defeat in a row and it slipped to eighth on the ladder. So on Monday, 4 August, the last thing the club needed to be announcing was the indefinite suspension of two important players.

Mick was woken by a phone call in the early hours of the morning to be told that 22-year-old Heath Shaw had crashed his car and blown almost three times the legal blood alcohol limit. There was also talk that Alan Didak had been a passenger in the car, though both players initially denied it; they broke down after an intense media witch-hunt and revealed the truth. The boys were suspended for the remaining four games of the season, and the ban would extend to the finals—if the Magpies made it to September.

The decision had been made by the head honchos of the club, Eddie McGuire and Gary Pert, and the football department leaders, Geoff Walsh and Mick. The captain and his deputies also had a say on the incident. But of all of them, it was perhaps the coach who suffered the most from the suspension, trying to fill the gaps left in his team and in his game plan by a brave and strong defender and a quick and skilled goalsneak. The rest of the squad was put on notice and it seemed to spark in them an extra desire to succeed that year.

In three matches the Pies defeated St Kilda at the MCG by fourteen points, Port Adelaide at Football Park by 31 points, and Sydney at the Docklands by 45 points. They were on a roll, until Fremantle hit them hard in the first quarter of their Round 22 clash at Subiaco Oval, kicking five straight goals to Collingwood's 1.4, and going on to win by 24 points.

Collingwood finished eighth and flew to Adelaide to play the Crows in an elimination final. The team was without Sharrod Wellingham, Alan Toovey and skipper Scott Burns, who were all injured. Anthony Rocca had played just eight games of the season due to nagging injuries and was still a way off returning. Simon Prestigiacomo was back, though, after his welcome return to the team against the Dockers, his first match of the year.

I was in Adelaide for Channel Ten. Outside the Collingwood rooms before the game, Scott Burns stopped to ask how my pregnancy was progressing. My swollen stomach was protruding through my winter coat by now. A father of two, he talked about the joys of parenthood. Then we were joined by Paul Licuria, who had remained at the club after his retirement in a mentoring role and as team manager of the Pies' VFL side. Married earlier in the year, he revealed how clucky he was. Then Anthony Rocca, who was injured but had travelled, joined in. And Travis Cloke, whom I have known since he was a baby, came over to say congratulations. I remember thinking to myself at the time: 'This is bizarre! Here I am standing in a cold, concrete tunnel underneath the grandstand at Football Park talking to a group of AFL footballers before a final, about—of all things—pregnancy and babies!'

The game began and minds refocused. The Pies had eleven players aged 21 or younger; eight of them had played fewer than five games. Another five team members hadn't yet played a full season of senior football. Needless to say, they all were about to experience a bumpy finals ride.

The Magpies took the early lead through Shannon Cox and Chris Dawes, though a seven-goal second quarter swung the match back in the Crows' favour and they led by twelve at half time.

Again I waited in the dark and narrow corridor outside the Collingwood rooms. Simon Prestigiacomo had been injured and I asked how bad his shoulder was. 'We're not sure, too soon to tell, but he probably won't come back on,' said a club physio. Damn it, I thought. I could hear things getting louder inside.

Mick had told his team to think about how much they had achieved that year. He told them to draw on the energy reserves he knew they possessed from their annual altitude training camps. And he told them to get back to the game plan—to be relentless in their endeavour, in their pursuit of the football, and in the pressure they applied to their opponents.

Collingwood kicked the next seven goals, with just two Adelaide majors in between. Up by 20 points in the last term, the Pies forwards chased hard to keep the ball in their forward zone. The midfielders tackled fiercely and pounced on the lose ball and the defenders played high to support their teammates, who dropped back to fill the gaps. They were relentless, just as their coach had asked, and they achieved a 31-point win.

At the airport that evening a group of Collingwood supporters stopped Dad to say congratulations on the win. When they looked at me they added, 'You wouldn't want to go into labour on grand final day.'

'Let's hope not,' I said.

'We have to make it first,' said Dad, always the diplomat.

Simon Prestigiacomo succumbed to his shoulder injury and was replaced by Shane Wakelin. Scott Burns remained sidelined. Playing at the MCG, Collingwood faced St Kilda, one of two clubs it had beaten twice during the season. If the Saints lost, it would be Robert Harvey's last game. Mick knew from experience that this would provide a lift for the St Kilda team, who would be playing to ward off the inevitable for their club champion. Mick warned his team to get on top at the opening bounce or risk the Saints gaining a momentum they could ride for the match.

It was tight in the opening term, and the Saints led by three points at quarter time. Tyson Goldsack kicked the first goal of the second quarter but his teammates failed to capitalise on some golden opportunities as the Saints kicked four straight.

As St Kilda's lead increased in the third term, keeping the Magpies to a single Travis Cloke goal, it became obvious which team was more desperate for a win. The Saints out-kicked and out-marked their young opponents, but what angered Mick more than anything else was that his team was also out-tackled. St Kilda won by 34 points in the end, although they had six fewer scoring shots.

Mick could only use the loss as a lesson to his team. Finals football cannot be taught; it's an experience that has to be lived, and not every player—no matter how highly skilled—will pass the pressure test. For this, then, the coach was pleased with the overall season, pointing out that with so much experience lost through retirements, the young squad could have struggled to adapt, but instead they had learnt from it. A winning culture had been retained at the club, and built on. They hadn't bounced outside the eight. They hadn't taken any shortcuts. And, importantly, they had won a final, and lost one. Scott Burns, Shane Wakelin and Brodie Holland all retired in September, but even with extra holes to fill, it had been a season that showed Mick his team was ready to advance, no matter how great the challenge.

In the final weeks of my pregnancy, we found out the baby would need to undergo several medical tests after it was born, for a condition called kidney reflux. We also found out it was stuck in the breech position, head up and feet down, so I was scheduled for a caesarean section on 4 December.

It is a surreal experience to be wheeled into a sterile operating theatre knowing that your baby will be delivered in a few minutes. As the nurses gave Dean his instructions for the procedure—basically, to sit still—and I was numbed from the chest down, I was introduced to the pediatrician who would care for our baby. I was also told that he was a Cats supporter. Geelong had lost the grand final to Hawthorn and he asked what I thought about the game. I couldn't believe it—even as my first child was being brought into the world, football was present.

Zachary Dean was born a minute later, pink and screaming, and the first man to hold him was saying loudly that he had a strong pair of legs that would aid him well as a future 'Geelong' footballer. When Zac was placed in my arms, I felt an intense love flood through me and instantly I wanted to protect him from the world.

'Don't worry, little man, football won't rule your destiny,' I whispered, though I wondered if it already was.

Collingwood sent him a club membership that very day and his arrival even made the newspaper, complete with a peaceful photo.

Zac was the star attraction at his auntie's wedding ten days later. Dad walked Danielle down the aisle of a picturesque garden setting, proud, emotional and wearing a grin that could only be matched by the greatest of football triumphs.

*

For the superstitious who look for 'signs' in every action of the universe, the events at the start of 2009 didn't bode well for a rosy year ahead.

On 7 February, fires roared through 450,000 hectares of Victoria's bushland, killing 173 people and destroying over 2000 homes. It became known as Black Saturday and struck every Victorian, and most other Australians. There was an outpouring of communal grief and help, as people witnessed the fire's rampage on their television screens and set about assisting the victims and their families in any small way they could. The AFL moved a scheduled NAB Cup pre-season clash from Darwin to Melbourne as a special bushfire appeal match, and Collingwood raised its own funds to help the casualties, as well as one of their own, Anne Martin, whose house had been ruined.

One morning later that month, Mick received a shocking phone call from David Buttifant. His eldest son, Nick, had taken his own life. Mick rushed to the Buttifants' home, not yet knowing what to say to David and Maria, but knowing that being there was more important than anything else. Nick's death touched everyone who'd known him as a bright young man from a loving family. His parents and siblings were devastated. Mick and Nanette joined a large group of people from the club in offering as much support as they possibly could to the grieving family. At a time when words meant nothing and actions were everything, the Buttifants had many people to lean on. This is when family becomes bigger than football, and a football club becomes like family.

Less than a fortnight later, Harry O'Brien grieved the loss of his father in similar circumstances. He took extended leave from Collingwood and stayed in Perth with his family as they took time to recover from the shock. When he flew back to Melbourne for the start of the season, he was still distraught with grief and spoke to his coach about his ongoing anguish. Mick said, 'Your father took his own life, Harry, don't let him take yours, too.' The advice was solace for the defender and gave him permission to get on with living, which for him meant, among other things, playing football.

A dark start to the year had rendered the Pies emotional and drained. When they met Adelaide in Round 1, the players appeared to merely go through their paces, playing without passion or commitment. At the long break Mick blasted them. It was time to dig deep and show respect for two important members of the club who were dealing with loss in a brave and admirable fashion. The team fought to level the scores at the last change but fell short by four points. At least they had given it a crack.

Collingwood's early results reflected the team's combined state of mind. By Anzac Day they'd won two and lost two. Mum invited the Collingwood wives and girlfriends for lunch before the match, sensing a need to bring them together after a difficult couple of months. As they chatted, they seemed to relax into each other's company and, Mum hoped, they felt more supported. It's always easier in tough times if everyone is working together.

Collingwood jumped to an early lead in a battle that the whole team looked forward to every year. But as Patrick Ryder's influence in the centre began to reflect the Anzac spirit, Essendon rebounded and scores were level at half time. The Bombers extended their lead to nine points at the last break and set up a thrilling contest in the last.

Two goals in six minutes put the Pies back in front by three points. Then Essendon returned the favour. Two more to Collingwood. Two more to the Bombers. A rushed behind at the 29-minute mark made it a one-point game. With less than a minute remaining, Patrick Ryder got his hand to a wayward Magpies pass and the Bombers swooped on the ball, delivering it straight to David Zaharakis just inside 50, who turned and kicked on the run. It was a goal. Moments later the siren went. Essendon had won by five points.

Mick was angry. Surrendering a lead, particularly on a day that commemorates the Aussie fighting spirit, was disappointing to him, to say the least. But he forgot his irritation with the events of the match when he learnt that his grandson had been taken to hospital before the game. Zac's kidney condition had led to an infection and he had become very unwell very quickly. Months of prior testing had revealed that he would need surgery to 'rewire' his kidneys and bladder and now it was imperative that it happen soon. He was booked in for surgery in June.

In May, Collingwood won three more games and were on the end of two big losses, to St Kilda and Carlton. Dad's manager, Peter Sidwell, and Eddie McGuire began contract negotiations.

On the day of Zac's surgery, Richmond confirmed that its coach, Terry Wallace, was stepping down.

In the children's centre of the hospital, my six-month-old baby was prepped for surgery. I cried as I kissed him and left him in the hands of the surgeon; the fear in his eyes was like a knife through my heart.

Three hours later, the doctor walked through the double doors of the waiting room to tell us that the operation was over and we could see our baby. Zac looked tiny and vulnerable in recovery, attached to machines with tubes and wires, and I was almost too scared to touch him.

Proving the true resilience of children, however, two weeks later he flew with us to Sydney for his pa's 600th VFL/AFL match. Dad carried Zac onto the ground before the match as photographers scrambled to get a shot of the two of them together, looking intently ahead, courage and determination etched in their stares. Collingwood won by 23 points. A photo taken on that day hangs on Zac's bedroom wall, a reminder to me every time I see it of how brave they both are.

Dad's tenure at Collingwood was suddenly thrust into the spotlight: a powerful beam hovering over his football future until the glare became too much to see straight without shielding his eyes. Dean Laidley had become the second coach in a month to walk away from his club, and with his departure began the speculation of who would take over at North Melbourne. Nathan Buckley's name was mentioned. He was in his second year of a commentary role with Channel Seven, but the moment he raised his hand and expressed an interest in coaching his media career was all but over. One minute the former Collingwood captain was being touted as a good choice for North or Richmond and the next the papers were pitting him against his past Collingwood coach and asking readers to vote on who should coach the club in 2010.

We wondered why Mick was being dragged into it and the answer came when Eddie McGuire and the Collingwood board made the suggestion of a succession plan.

Mick was astounded when his manager put forward the proposal the Magpies' president had delivered. He'd been hoping for and expecting an extension to his contract, which was coming to an end that year. Instead, he was being offered five more years at Collingwood, on the proviso that he handed over the senior coaching reins to his newly appointed and untried assistant coach, Nathan Buckley, at the end of 2011.

Mick felt that he was on the verge of something special at Collingwood, and he wasn't the only one. In a recent meeting between Eddie McGuire and Geoff Walsh, the Pies' football manager hadn't minced his words when he declared, 'We're not far off a premiership,' and listed the reasons why: a talented and determined group of footballers; a structure to maximise their individual and combined strengths; and an experienced coach with the knowhow to get the best out of his team.

With that meeting on his mind, Mick told his manager: 'I need to think about it.'

Mick didn't know if he would be ready to stop coaching in two years, and that was the sticking point, because by committing to this deal he would effectively be agreeing to give up the one thing he loved almost as much as he loved his family. He still prized the contest. He still treasured 'his boys' and the challenge of developing them as elite footballers and good men. He still cherished being the coach, the man who led and motivated the team and made the final decisions and called the shots on gameday.

He felt like he was coaching well, almost at his best, if he was being honest with himself. His team played for him, enjoyed playing for him, and deep in his heart he knew that together they had every chance of winning a premiership in the next couple of years. Would that change the equation? No, because a deal is a deal.

Mick still loved being part of the Collingwood Football Club. If he signed this contract, he wouldn't be able to coach anywhere else when he stopped coaching the Magpies, but he doubted he would want to anyway. He was realistic. He knew that an extra two years on top of the decade he had already coached at the club was excellent, really, but while he was being truthful with himself, he thought that he deserved an extension.

Didn't he?

The team, and the club with it, was on the way up. As he searched further inside himself, Mick realised he was hurting. Actually, it hurt like hell that his own people were more than predicting his demise—they were making it happen. He wondered if the contract was more about keeping Nathan Buckley than keeping him. He didn't dislike Nathan—in fact, they had formed quite a tight bond in the eight years that they were coach and captain at Collingwood, and Mick enjoyed the evenings when he and Nanette dined with the Buckleys and the McGuires. Nathan had a dry sense of humour that had made his coach laugh. If the Collingwood favourite son hadn't entered the media game, Mick probably would have sought him as an assistant coach, on his own terms and when the time was right. There was something about this timing and this deal that felt manipulated and awkward.

As for Mick's family, we were aghast at the notion. We thought it strange and disrespectful to suggest that Nathan Buckley could come in without any prior coaching experience and take over the senior position in just two years, regardless of how well Collingwood fared in that time under its current coach, our dad.

'Don't sign it,' we told him.

*

The Magpies were travelling well. They hadn't lost a match since Round 8. Round 15 was coming up and they were to face the Western Bulldogs.

The Bulldogs caused a scare for Collingwood when they narrowed a 34-point gap to one point with just over a minute remaining in the Friday night game. The Pies held out and crawled over the line victorious.

That week, Mick met with Nathan Buckley and Eddie McGuire to discuss the only option that had been left on the table. It was a done deal, Mick realised as he entered the room—they were just waiting on his signature. He sought further clarification of the two roles: Buckley as assistant in 2010–11, and Mick as director of coaching from 2012 on. Usually the coach picks the team that will surround him in the box; this time, though, Mick was being told who to use.

'Who will Nathan replace?' he asked, feeling protective of the men who had put their hearts and souls into their coaching roles for a long time. It was still to be decided, he was told, although Brad Scott's appointment at the Kangaroos just weeks later left a gap on the panel.

Further discussion about Mick's future duties revealed that the new job would be 'all-encompassing': Mick would oversee the coaching department as mentor and advisor, he would play a large role in recruitment and he'd be part of match-day preparation.

Mick posed a question directly to Buckley: 'When you are coach, will you want me in the box with you?' The answer was no, and the silence that followed seemed to say much about the proposed roles that had yet to be revealed.

The next Saturday, Collingwood let a narrow half-time lead slip to Hawthorn and a very determined Luke Hodge and a very accurate Lance Franklin. A 45-point loss was the result.

The pressure intensified. In the press, the Magpies' game plan was criticised for being too defensive and not attacking enough through the corridor. Only St Kilda matched their percentage of boundary-line play, and they sat on top of the ladder. Mick said: 'Let them criticise. It doesn't work for everyone but it works for this team.' The Kangaroos were pushing hard for Buckley, naming him as their number-one candidate in their search for a new coach.

On Friday night the Pies stunned Carlton into submission and won the Round 17 match by 54 points. They now sat fourth on the ladder.

Mick's mum, Marie, had been diagnosed with cancer and she had no will left to beat it. Refusing to leave her comfortable Ballarat home, her son had made arrangements for a daily nurse's visit and for her meals to be delivered.

Mick regularly made the hour-and-a-half drive to see his mother, and he used the time to think about his future. His family was feeling the strain of the drawn-out contract nego-tiations. His wife and children were sick of reading articles that bagged him. They were upset with the club and angry at the media. They'd been through a lot in his years of football, but this time he could see the damage it was doing to them.

Recently he'd been made to appreciate life more. His father's death had shaken him but also taught him to deal with what you're dealt. Marie was showing signs that her time was nearing, but instead of fearing it, she seemed in harmony with her eventful life. Mick's grandson had shown him the vulnerability of life and the pleasure of living. It would be years before Zac would be given the all-clear but he had come through his surgery well. Danielle's recently announced pregnancy was a reward for her determination to keep trying to conceive after two miscarriages, and it reminded him that hope and fight can mean the same thing.

On Sunday, 26 July, Mick told his family: 'Anything can happen in two years. I'm not going to fight against this any more, and I don't want to keep dragging you through it. I'm going to sign the bloody contract.'

The following day, Nathan Buckley alerted North Melbourne that he wasn't interested in coaching there. Collingwood quickly convened a board meeting. At eleven am on Tuesday, 28 July, a rapt Eddie McGuire, a grinning Nathan Buckley and a reserved Mick Malthouse announced to a packed press conference that the Collingwood board had unanimously voted to retain its coach for a further five years, two as senior coach before he would pass the baton to his new assistant, Nathan Buckley, at the end of 2011, then becoming the Pies' director of coaching for another three years.

'The two years we were able to get is an outstanding outcome for the Malthouses,' Mick announced.

'I've got a lot to learn as coach,' said Nathan.

The Herald Sun summed up the succession plan as a 'transition of power'. They reported that it came after months of planning, manoeuvring and engineering by Eddie McGuire's administration, that the president had been 'obsessive about his preferred plan . . . stoutly resisting pressure to reappoint Mick Malthouse before securing Nathan Buckley'.

Other football journalists wondered how it would all play out. We wondered that ourselves.

Collingwood won three more games, including a 93-point drubbing of Richmond. Then, on Tuesday, 18 August, Grandma died, almost two years to the day after her husband's passing.

We had all gathered at the hospice the previous day, Dad's birthday. She had been weak but alert and she knew we were there to say farewell. She said goodbye to us too and told us how much she loved us. It made it harder to leave, so we waited until she was asleep before we drove home to Melbourne with sorrowful hearts.

During the night, when Dad sat alone with her, she said she worried for him. She had seen how the recent weeks had taken the colour from his eyes and she was concerned by the pressure—greater than she had ever witnessed before—that had been placed on his shoulders. Her last piece of motherly advice was for her son to take care of himself and to look after his family.

Her sentiment hovered in his mind as he coached the Magpies to a 41-point win over Sydney that weekend.

Collingwood finished the season with a loss but it had already secured fourth spot on the ladder. The most dominant team of the season was to be its opponent in the qualifying final: St Kilda had won 20 games to finish top, two more than Geelong in second.

Mick was looking forward to this finals campaign. There were three first-year rookies in the team, but the rest had tasted finals by now. In the fifteen games they'd won that year, his players had shown maturity and a clearer comprehension of the structure and how he wanted them to play.

Collingwood began the final well. The eight-point quarter-time lead was handy. It lasted until Nick Riewoldt kicked his second goal in a row at the midpoint of the second term. From there, no matter how much they wrestled and fought and tried, they couldn't outmuscle the Saints' big guns. Scott Pendlebury had come off with a cracked fibula and the Pies midfield missed him as Nick Dal Santo, Lenny Hayes and Leigh Montagna ran riot. Riewoldt's fifth goal sealed the 28-point win for St Kilda and the Magpies were left to pick up the pieces of a disappointing loss.

Still, Mick had faith that his young team could rebound, although Pendlebury's absence unnerved him: he was a match-winner and his poise and precision were rare qualities in a footballer.

Adelaide came at Collingwood with venom in the semi-final. By quarter time the game was in danger of becoming a one-sided farce. First-year captain Nick Maxwell helped to steady his teammates and the pace eased up. The gap had been marginally reduced by half time, but the Pies still had 26 points to make up. It took them seventeen minutes to dismantle the Crows' lead, and in the final term the coach saw the true potential of his team. Like lightning in a storm, Adelaide's hits kept coming but the Pies continued to fend them off. A Crows goal at the 27-minute mark put them in front by a point.

'Get back, set it up,' Mick yelled into his headset.

As precisely as it was practised at training, Collingwood got the centre clearance and moved the ball quickly into its forward half. Jack Anthony launched himself at a high ball and was awarded a free kick for his efforts. He took his time setting himself up, then took even longer to run in and boot it, but he kicked straight and the Pies were back in front. It was the last score of the game. The Magpies were home by five points.

Mick was as pleased with this win as with any in his time at Collingwood. He praised his team for their effort in withstanding Adelaide's ongoing attack and for sticking to their own game in the process. It was a win to encourage them all.

It was a highly talented and experienced Geelong outfit that Collingwood faced next.

Mick looked at his team on paper. No Scott Pendlebury. Dane Swan had a sore hip—not bad enough to miss the game but he would feel it. It wasn't ideal, but he would have to cover Paul Chapman and Gary Ablett junior with Dayne Beams and Steele Sidebottom, his two youngest players.

Ben Johnson kicked the opening goal from the first passage of play and it set a force into motion. Collingwood pushed forward another three times, peppering the goals before Harry O'Brien claimed one and put them two goals up. Then, like a car changing gears, Geelong took over the momentum. With the margin ten points in the Cats' favour at quarter time, Geelong increased its lead by just a point after a second-term arm wrestle. Mick could see the fatigue in his players at half time, and he worried that they were already conceding the battle. It had been a long year, an emotionally draining year at that, and he couldn't help but feel that it had finally caught up with them. He hoped he was wrong.

A single Magpie goal in the final minute of the third quarter gave him his answer. Mick didn't give up—he never gives up—but it was clear that his team was shot. Geelong finished the game with a flurry of goals, while Collingwood kicked a solitary behind. They lost by 73 points. Game over. Season complete. Year done.

To look back at that year is to feel regret at what took place. Mick felt like he was bombarded and trapped in a corner with only one way out. In a year that held so many on-field highs for the club, he faced a lot of lows off it. He is a private person who doesn't dwell in his own misery, so his personal business stayed at home. But in a year when it was more important than ever for the club to pull together, it became divided. Instead of feeling supported in his own time of grief, Mick felt compromised, and hung out alone to fend for himself.

*

Dad was in Mount Gambier when Danielle went into labour. Collingwood had just beaten Port Adelaide in a NAB Challenge match and now he was hoping for a quick flight home. He made it to the hospital with an hour to spare and his second grandchild, Holly Grace, was born. We all concluded that her entry into the world, before Round 1, was a good omen for the year.

Two games and two wins into the season, Mick was happy with his team's form. In Round 2, the Pies were slow to take off against Melbourne but quickly made up ground in the second term, holding off a gutsy and persistent Demons outfit to win by a point. The fact that Mick's boys didn't give up was pleasing.

The following Friday night, Collingwood played St Kilda. There was already tension between the clubs after Luke Ball, unhappy at Moorabbin, had defected to the Magpies after the 2009 season. The Saints led by four as the two coaches made their way onto the ground at quarter time. Alan Toovey was unwittingly drawn into a scuffle with two St Kilda players and several of his Magpies teammates jumped to his defence. There was a heated exchange between the two factions as they divided and walked towards their respective huddles. As they did so, Steven Baker and Stephen Milne continued to fire derogatory shots at Travis Cloke and Mick told them get over it and move on. Milne spat a crude insult at Mick.

Within earshot, Paul Licuria immediately jumped in. 'Show some respect,' he told Milne, who abused him in return.

Angry, fired up and without thinking, Mick had a go back at Milne. He knew instantly that he had overstepped the mark, but what could he do? He'd seen and heard worse before on field and always the game went on. Collingwood lost by 28 points.

When the quarter-time clash was labelled a 'tirade' by the media and Mick was asked about it in his post-game press conference, he responded by denying it. Why make it worse by repeating it? It happened on-field, in the heat of the moment, and it should be left there. He was sure Stephen Milne wouldn't want to repeat his part in the exchange either.

But later that evening, Mick was advised by Collingwood CEO Gary Pert to apologise to Milne via a memo to be sent to St Kilda officials. I'll admit that, as a former member of the football media, I told Dad it would be a mistake to do it, that it felt like the club was distancing itself from him.

But Mick said sorry because he was sorry, and it blew up in his face. He was deemed a liar as well as a name-caller by the media. His outburst was taken out of context and blown out of proportion in subsequent media reports in which the coach was labelled the instigator and the player as the victim. Mick admits it was his mistake to enter a slanging match between players, but as Leigh Matthews said from the commentary box after witnessing the incident, 'It shows the emotion that's out there tonight.'

Football is an emotional game and no-one is immune to being swept up in a moment of undiluted fervour. It will forever remain a moment of regret for Mick, an out-of-character eruption that went against his philosophy of leading by example. But it's not something he dwelt on, or gave further thought to, because you can't change the past.

Everyone moved on, eventually, and the Pies won five in a row before meeting Geelong in Round 9. Collingwood was playing good football. The interchange rotations had reached an all-time high, 130 per match on average. It kept the players fresh, allowing them to apply constant and intense tackling pressure on their opposition from front to back. They were wearing rival teams down and attacking when they were vulnerable. It was working well.

Then the Cats turned the tables on Collingwood. There was a point the difference at the first break, before Geelong pulled away. Each time the Pies got back into contention, the Cats wore them down again. Gradually, the gap widened until a goalless final quarter left the Magpies lifeless. It was an inexplicable 36-point loss, an aberration on a good start to the season.

But a second loss a week later to Brisbane had Mick concerned. A lucky escape against the Western Bulldogs and then a draw with Melbourne had him very worried. So he meditated.

David Buttifant had implemented the practice of meditation at the club in 2009. Mick had joined the original classes, though it wasn't until his youngest son, Troy, was struck down with chronic fatigue syndrome and sought alternative therapies to recover from the debilitating illness that Mick took the process to heart. He'd had trouble stilling his mind initially and struggled with the concept of 'enlightenment', but as Troy began to feel the healing effects, Mick, too, realised the positive benefits of meditation. He began to take a quiet moment to himself before each game, appreciating the clarity it gave him. When he closed his eyes this time, the answer that came to him was to stick to his guns. With great belief in the structure, he told his players to stay focused and to play to their roles.

For the next eight weeks Collingwood dominated, including a 22-point win over Geelong at the MCG, in which a six-goals-to-three second half overcame a half-time one-point deficit and a hungry opponent.

In a low-scoring match against Adelaide in Round 21, the Pies struggled to maintain their intensity against a team that fumbled and erred and dragged down the level of the contest. It was a difficult match to watch, but in a final quarter in which Collingwood missed several 'sitters' the coach remained encouraged by his team's will to win. They did so, by three points.

On top of the ladder and clear by a game and a half, the Pies' final-quarter meltdown against Hawthorn in Round 22 didn't alter the team's course, but it did put an element of doubt into the minds of the supporters and gave the media something to criticise. Mick worried that his team was fatigued. His structure called for an enormous effort each week by his players to maintain the pressure required for the team to perform at its peak.

It was time for some light relief. The entire club gathered at the palatial home of board member Alex Waislitz for a Monday evening of frivolity and fun. Everyone relaxed. Like a detox diet, it worked to erase any lingering doubt and negativity, and let them start the finals fresh and re-energised.

Before the qualifying final against the Western Bulldogs, Mick was nervous, really nervous, as nervous as he had ever been before a game. He tried to join in a conversation with his family, as they gathered in the kitchen of the inner-city apartment, but he was too tense to laugh at the jokes and too focused to give in to his grandchildren's pleas to play. He left for the ground early to a chorus of 'good luck'. He met Ben Johnson in the rooms as he arrived.

'Are you toey, Mick?' asked Ben.

'I am, I'm really nervous, Benny.'

'We'll thump them, don't worry.'

And with that confident statement from a key player, Mick calmed down and prepared for the match. Perhaps his team was more ready for the challenge than he'd given them credit for.

They were. Collingwood stormed to the lead with a ferocious first term, adding to the advantage at every change. There were contributors from all over the field as ten players shared in the goal-scoring—Dane Swan and Steele Sidebottom pinched three each—and the Bulldogs forwards were kept quiet. In a complete performance, the Pies won by

62 points, and with a week off to recover, they were named as the premiership favourite.

Mick was cautious. His team was determined; they were hungry and committed. And they were confident. It all tallied to being a good thing, but they had a long way to go to prove that they were the best.

Mick and David Buttifant agreed they should take it lightly on the training track during the fortnight before the preliminary final—there was no need to flog the team now. The players were fit and healthy, so why risk injury and exhaustion?

The Magpie Army was warming up too, enjoying the tag of favouritism. Supporters came from everywhere and clambered to get a good view of training, hailing their heroes and wishing them well against the Cats. They barked at the suggestion that Geelong would again prove to be Collingwood's stumbling block.

On the morning of the preliminary final, Mick woke with a start. He'd struggled to fall asleep when he'd gone to bed and remained restless through the night, tossing and turning until the early hours of the morning, when a calm finally swathed him. He didn't dream. Now, with a pounding heart, he wondered if he'd overslept.

'It's seven o'clock,' Nanette told him, knowing his question before he asked it.

His stomach churned and his head ached. He escaped to his den to meditate when his family arrived. He didn't feel like talking or thinking. Why was he so nervous again?

Because he didn't have forever. The time was right to strike with this team.

He looked for Ben Johnson in the rooms. 'I'm nervous, Benny.'

'They're just in our way,' Johnson said, unaffected by the apprehension his coach was feeling.

Geelong wasn't in the way for long. The Magpies played with passion and determination and raw desire in the first term. Kicking seven goals to one, they claimed a 37-point lead, and then continued to be brilliant, running down the Cats' midfield, burying their forwards and humiliating their backs. The lead got out to 66 points before Collingwood decelerated, keeping some energy in reserve for the following week. The 41-point win earned the club a berth in the 2010 Grand Final.

So it was here again—grand final week.

Mick had been voted the AFL Coaches' Association Senior Coach of the Year, so the family arrived at the Tuesday night dinner to surprise him. He was chuffed to receive the award— it was clear in the way his cheeks turned pink and his eyes danced as he walked to the stage, trying to hide a wide grin behind a cough. He was embarrassed to accept the accolade in front of the men he coached against every week. But this award was voted on by his peers, so it was special.

I was fifteen weeks pregnant, so I told myself the butterflies in my stomach were related to the baby growing inside me, not the approaching game, because I only wanted to project positive vibes for this grand final. But as Mick talked in front of a captivated crowd about the sixth grand final he would coach in, I started to feel a little sick about it.

I took Zac to Collingwood's main training session on the Wednesday morning. We walked past thousands of Magpies supporters decked out in full black and white, crammed against the wire fence, hoping to get close enough to reach out and touch their idols. When Zac saw his pa he made a dash for him across the ground and ran straight through a set drill. Dad swept his grandson up into his arms, gave him a hug and a lolly, and returned him to the sidelines until training was over. Ten minutes later, when the session was finished, he took Zac back out onto the field to wave to the fans. Wearing a Collingwood jumper with 'Coach' printed on the back, Zac cuddled into his pa, suddenly shy and overwhelmed by the noise and attention. It was a lot to take in for a little boy. It was a lot to take in for his grandfather.

On Friday, the grand final parade was a chaotic clutter of black, white and red, as the colours of Collingwood and St Kilda were mixed and meshed in a tangle of football frenzy. We tried seating Zac and Holly in the car with Dad as it slowly lapped the city streets, but they were too frightened by the shouts and cheers of almost 100,000 excited people. Dad's sister, Gerardine, and brother-in-law, Bill, had flown from their home in Brisbane for the big game and they stared wide-eyed at the crowd before them, mesmerised by the frantic activity.

Mick had been told earlier that Simon Prestigiacomo was pulling out of the team. He felt like crying for his defender. Presti had strained a groin muscle at training during the week but kept it quiet, hoping it would come good. It didn't, which left him with only one choice. He couldn't risk letting his teammates down in perhaps the biggest game of their careers so, selflessly and nobly, he withdrew his name from the team list. Mick consoled his player and took on his sorrow, ready to use it to spur on the men whom Presti had put before himself.

The nerves had gone, almost, replaced by composed assurance. Mick had been waiting for this day for a long time and now that it was here, he was ready for it. His team was ready for it.

They were all at their best—right now. His players knew the game plan like a mother knows her child. It worked to their strengths, so they felt strong playing it. They were no longer parts of a puzzle—they were a team playing as a whole, with trust and acceptance. It was very effective and it gave Mick a thrill to think how far they'd come.

He addressed them: 'Give it everything you have and then look at your teammates, and find more to give. Leave nothing out there. Not a "Wish I had've . . ." Not a "Why didn't I?" There is no tomorrow, there is only now.'

The opening play was perfect. Straight out of the centre, deep into the forward line and on to a running Darren Jolly, who kicked straight and true. Collingwood goal—24 seconds gone.

It was a game of defence as the ball ricocheted from backline to backline. Collingwood held sway by a goal as Mick entered the quarter-time huddle. His A-listers were down; already he knew he would have to pump them up. Scott Pendlebury had been sick for days and lost five kilograms of weight; he was weak and tired now. Dane Swan was being tagged, which was not unusual, but unusually he was fading beneath it. Find more to give, he told them, and stick to the game plan. They lifted on the back of three goals. Collingwood was up by 24 now; it could have been more but for the misses. The pressure was heavy.

St Kilda returned from the half-time break angry and proud. Brendon Goddard and Lenny Hayes led the storm, raging around and through and between their opponents, who went goalless for the quarter.

Eight points up at the final change, it took another eight minutes for Collingwood to kick a goal. Like boxers at the end of a ten-round bout, every player ached, leaning into each other for support, to stay on their feet. The Saints chipped away at the Magpies' lead until a high ball was sent forward into their attacking zone. Goddard climbed an imaginary ladder, launching himself above the pack to take the type of mark that kids replicate in the playground. He kicked a goal and St Kilda hit the front. It was nineteen minutes into the last term.

Two minutes later, Travis Cloke missed an attempt from outside the 50 and players scrambled for a kick in the Pies' goalsquare. Bodies piled up in an attempt to get a possession. To stop a possession. The ball was rushed through for a point.

The game was so evenly matched that it seemed like the teams had blended. It was a battle of wills now, of character and resolve. Leigh Brown took a mark on the outer wing and was crunched for his efforts, sent off with the blood rule. Harry O'Brien took the kick and bombed it long but it bounced off a wall of men too exhausted to take it cleanly.

Momentum sprang between the two back halves as the ball became like gold. Sam Fisher booted it forward and Nick Maxwell leapt, grabbing it overhead and sending it back all in one motion. The Pies worked it forward. It slipped through Heath Shaw's hands to Chris Dawes on the ground. He handpassed to Travis Cloke, who ran into an open goal and kicked it. They were back in front by a point.

As Nick Riewoldt took a mark on the MCG wing, Mick yelled for his defenders to get back: 'Plug the hole!' One kick was all they'd need to get a score, he knew, and he willed his team to shut it down. The kick was long and the ball bounced forward, Hayes ran on to it, kicking it over Stephen Milne's head as the Saints forward gave chase. But he was beaten by the bounce of the ball as it richocheted to the right and went through for a point. Scores were level. One minute remained.

I worried for my unborn baby as I held my breath until my heart felt like it would explode from my chest. Danielle left her seat and didn't return. Cain, the worrier, and Troy, the deep thinker, alternated between shouting encouragement at the team and hanging their heads in their hands. We thought of Mum sitting next to Jayne Walsh on the opposite side of the ground to us: would she still be watching? Vision of Dad flashed up on the big screen, frantic and desperate. I looked again at my brothers, who had bloodshot eyes and skin as grey as ash and knew the relief they felt that it wasn't a goal, but we were equally shattered that St Kilda had scored at all.

Someone shouted that ten seconds remained.

'Shit, it's going to be a draw,' I couldn't help but say it aloud.

There was a boundary throw-in near the top of St Kilda's 50-metre arc. There was time enough for them to score with one long kick—Collingwood had to close it down or they would lose. Mick shouted, 'Cover his left shoulder,' but instinctively Scott Pendlebury moved to sit between the ruck contest and St Kilda's goals. Goddard got the tap but Pendlebury got the ball, pulling it in and killing the play. It lay beneath a pack of depleted players when the siren finally sounded.

The grand final had just ended in a draw.

12 THANKS, BUT NO THANKS

MICK WAS NUMB. HIS thoughts had scattered like a group of naughty children at the final siren, so he sat in the box for several minutes trying to pull them together. It's like winning the lotto after losing the ticket, or buying your dream home a day before it burns down. A hurricane had raged around him and then stopped and an eerie silence ensued.

As if the two teams of the 2010 Grand Final didn't have enough to deal with, a sewerage problem had left the changerooms flooded so both Collingwood and St Kilda were directed to the opposite side of the ground. Mick knew then that he had to take control. Without a clear result, his players were distressed and emotionally and physically wrecked. They'd been left stunned.

Mick made the decision for the team to attend the planned post-game dinner, with partners and families, and once there he told everyone to put the game to rest. 'It's done, it's happened, now we get a second chance. This is half time.'

Mick was grateful for a week without grand final fanfare— no Brownlow Medal, no parades, no distractions. Geoff Walsh handled the logistics of a further week of football, David Buttifant led the team recovery, and Mick planned for another assault. During Sunday-morning recovery he heard his players laughing at a Dale Thomas antic and knew they were back on track. He had told them before the game that there was no tomorrow, and he'd been wrong. They had been given the gift of a second chance and this time he was convinced they would graciously accept it.

As the week progressed, Collingwood's confidence increased. Club staff had been directed to stay positive and upbeat around the player group, and they did. The players had been told to call the time before the rematch 'half time' in any media reports, as if the pause button had been pressed and they were ready to pounce when it was released. They put a positive spin on every interview, talking up how the team was feeling. When they heard St Kilda speak of fatigue and a lingering disbelief of the drawn result, they were validated: there was a psychological gap between the two teams now and the Magpies had the edge.

By the morning of the grand final replay, Mick was eager for the game to start. The buoyant mood in the Collingwood rooms contrasted greatly with the feeling of apprehension that had been evident a week earlier. The draw had given his players a chance to rid themselves of any grand final demons and nerves; today they were all switched on, healthy, fit and resolute.

There had been one change made to the team: Leon Davis was out and Tyson Goldsack was in. Mick and the Pies' selectors had agonised over the decision right through the week—and the coach would forever feel for the player who missed out—but it was made on the basis that Goldsack gave the team more options.

In a small room, Mick made his pre-game speech: 'They are tired, they are sore, they are wondering if they can get through another four quarters. *We know we can.* There will be no easing up. There will be no taking your foot off the accelerator—keep it hard to the floor and maintain the pressure. Let's go.'

Around the ground, the vibe was upbeat as Lionel Richie performed his past hits and sent waves of electricity through the crowd. People danced in their seats and joined in the lyrics and everywhere supporters smiled. Within a week we had all shed our anxiety and taken on a sense of calm. It felt like it was going to be a good day.

We watched Dad run off the ground after the national anthem and then turned our attention to the centre of the field. We were surrounded by Collingwood family and friends. Within minutes of the first bounce, Tyson Goldsack's mum jumped out of her seat with her hands in the air. Her son had just taken a mark in front of goal. He kicked it and the Pies were away. Wendy Goldsack squealed with delight and pride.

Collingwood looked like a different team as it controlled the play and left St Kilda lagging behind. Ben Johnson kicked the second goal and the Magpie Army got louder.

With six minutes left in the first quarter, the Saints were yet to score. They worked it forward. Leigh Montagna got a handpass to Adam Schneider, who kicked to Nick Riewoldt on the run. He was in the clear, in an open goalsquare. As he dropped the ball to his boot, Heath Shaw sprinted from the half-back flank and lunged at the kick. Somehow he got his hands to it in time. *Smother!* The kick was rushed through for a point. Magpie supporters went wild. It was a stunning act, an unbelievable highlight, and it sent shivers through us. The St Kilda captain could only shake his head. Within a minute, the Pies responded with a straightforward goal to round out the term with an eighteen-point lead.

Under heavy pressure and close contact, the Saints missed early chances; when Brendon Goddard scored a goal halfway through the term, it was their first of the game. So Collingwood lifted again, and answered it, twice, and by the half-time break their lead was 27 points.

In the stands everyone was talking about 'that smother', suggesting that the Pies were looking as good as at any stage during the season. It was exciting to see the team in front and playing great football. There was a scent of victory in the air and we all inhaled it, hoping and praying that it would last another two quarters.

As the Magpies were about to run back onto the field for the third term, Mick had the sudden inspiration to alter a key match-up. It was at this stage the previous week that Brendon Goddard and Lenny Hayes had stepped up and brought their team back into the contest. The Collingwood coach certainly didn't want a repeat performance and he was concerned that Goddard was once again looking dangerous. So he moved one of his own premier ball-getters, Dane Swan, onto the Saints' midfielder. There was great risk in throwing Swan into a tagging role—mainly that it could affect his own ability to gather effective disposals—but Mick had faith that he could defend and attack in equal measure, so he made the move.

When Swanny crumbed off a pack and slotted through a goal nine minutes later, the coach knew it had worked. Goddard's impact had already been reduced and the goal would give Swan an extra boost.

Justin Koschitzke got one back for St Kilda, but when Alan Didak smothered a pass midair and hooked the ball across his body for a spectacular goal, his teammates surrounded him, applauding his brilliance. Their bliss was infectious and I finally dared to look at the scoreboard—it was 67–21 nearing the end of the third quarter. What a wonderful sight!

A goal for each team maintained the gap and when Mick walked onto the field to address his players at the last change, he was cheered by a fired-up and passionate Collingwood crowd.

The decider came early when Chris Dawes scored from a tight angle in the opening minutes of the final quarter, putting the Pies eight goals clear of their rivals. Moments later, some Dale Thomas determination in the Collingwood goalsquare sealed the win. Six more goals were scored between the two teams as time ran out, but Magpie supporters were already celebrating a premiership.

When the siren sounded and Alan Didak held the ball in the air, it was made official. The 56-point victory was the club's greatest ever winning margin in a grand final.

There are hardly words to describe the ecstasy and jubilation that formed into one gigantic happy thought: we are the champions!

As we embraced each other and let warm tears spill down our cheeks, we watched Dad rejoicing—first with David Buttifant and then with his players, before Mum found him on the field and they stood tightly together, stealing a private and emotional moment of celebration. He emanated relief, seeming barely able to carry his own body, but as rapture engulfed those around him, joy crept into his smile and was reflected through his eyes.

Standing on the podium, ready to receive the cup, he finally gave his emotion permission to spill free: 'They are my boys and I love them dearly, they have been outstanding.' The team responded with shouts of satisfaction.

Mick will admit he cherishes all four of his premierships at Richmond, West Coast and Collingwood, but the ecstasy he felt as a player is entirely different to the pure relief he experienced as a coach. As a player, the joy is shared among teammates, each knowing they have played their part in the victory. As a coach, he put his entire being into winning each grand final, feeling responsible for the failure or success of a season. At the final siren, he was left with nothing but the energy to exhale a breath of thanks to the universe.

Collingwood won the premiership in the year Mick was born, and as he held up the cup with his captain in 2010, it felt like his life had in some way come full circle. It was a moment of raw delight that is rare in football.

Mick coached the Australian International Rules team to a series win over the Irish in Ireland in October 2010. Then Collingwood claimed its second title in five months when it won the NAB Cup in March 2011. Chris Tarrant had returned to the club after five years at the Fremantle Dockers and was desperate for another premiership tilt. Nathan Brown, the player who kept St Kilda captain Nick Riewoldt goalless in the grand final replay, was a big loss, sidelined for the season with a torn ACL. After winning every pre-season game convincingly, the Magpies beat Essendon by 22 points in the Saturday-night final. The win came after a summer of respite.

Collingwood's first premiership in 20 years opened the floodgates for an outpouring of gratitude. If Mick took a simple stroll through the Fitzroy Gardens, it became an opportunity for supporters to show their appreciation to the man they hailed as the 'Bringer of Good Fortune' like the

Indian god Ganesh. In any situation—a trip to the shops, a coffee in a local café, leisurely days spent on Victoria's west coast—people everywhere were in a hurry to shake Mick's hand and say, 'Thanks for the premiership—it brought so much joy to my life.' He felt lighter in that time than he had felt for many, many years. Less weighed down by expectation and near misses and judgement. His prime emotion was still relief, but reliving Collingwood's day of triumph gave him an added sense of pride.

As the AFL prepared for the arrival of its seventeenth team, the Gold Coast Suns, I was eagerly anticipating the birth of my second child. Dad was interstate for football duties when I was induced a week before the start of football season. Twelve hours later I was wheeled into an operating theatre for another caesarean section, while Mum raced to the airport to collect Dad. As the anaesthetist—a Russian woman with a thick accent—inserted a large needle into my spine, she said; 'The nurses tell me that your father is Mick Malthouse. How exciting! Will this baby play football?'

When Lillia Mae was delivered a few minutes later, I thought, She can do whatever she wants to do with her life.

Two weeks later she was being passed around in the Collingwood rooms after their second big win from as many games. She wore black and white, and her older brother and cousin ran amok in the changerooms, just as their mums had done three decades earlier.

*

Already the speculation had started. As soon as Mick's final season at the helm of the Magpies began, the press clambered for news of how the transition from coach to coaching director would take place. If they didn't have news, they speculated. What they didn't know then was that only one thing was certain: Nathan Buckley would be senior coach at season's end. The rest of the 'succession plan' remained up in the air, as a detailed job description for Mick's new role had yet to be drawn up. He waited, along with everyone else, to see what would be offered.

In the meantime, he didn't think about the end. He couldn't. If his mind even deviated slightly close to the destination he had avoided since midway through 2009, he grew sombre and reflective. And he couldn't afford to be sombre and reflective, not while he was giving every inch of his fortitude to the team he coached.

Collingwood kept winning, easily accounting for Richmond in Round 4. Then it beat Essendon by 30 points in a determined and spirited performance. It was after this match that Mick realised he wouldn't get to coach another Collingwood–Essendon Anzac Day blockbuster. It was the one game of the home-and-away season that, to a man so intrigued by war, represented the ultimate battle of courage and respect. He felt honoured and grateful to have had the chance to take part in so many of these contests, but he also knew now that he would miss it.

A win and a bye followed. Missing several players through injury, including Darren Jolly and Nick Maxwell, the Pies then took on the Cats. Geelong dominated possession in the opening quarter but failed to convert it on the scoreboard and Collingwood took advantage, turning a fourteen-point deficit into an eleven-point half-time lead. With the teams evenly matched in the third, it made for a gripping final term. The Cats' wayward kicking got accurate, and when Jimmy Bartel scored a goal from a set shot, they hit the front. It was a two-point game when Cameron Wood was hammered in a ruck contest and Scott Pendlebury ran on to the lose ball and drilled a goal. The advantage was disallowed and the Pies' ruckman was given the free kick. It fell short and the Cats turned it around in an instant, a goalsquare tussle in their forward 50 resulting in a rushed behind. Moments later, the siren went—Geelong had won by three points.

Andrew Krakouer made his mark at his new home in the next game against Adelaide and no one was more pleased than Mick. The former Tiger and reformed prison inmate kicked three inspirational goals for the match; his first, late in the third term, triggered the Pies' scoring spree. After trailing for three quarters, Collingwood kicked eleven goals in the last term to run over the top of the Crows for a 43-point win. To Mick, Andrew Krakouer's story is proof that everyone deserves a second chance if they are willing to take responsibility for their mistakes and put in the effort to turn their lives around.

There had been discussions by now, verbal proposals but nothing concrete, about how Mick's new role as director of coaching would look. International travel was an option, to scout the resources and tactics of sporting giants from around the world. Recruiting was mentioned. On match days, Collingwood's various coterie groups needed a guest speaker . . . So far the job description showed little resemblance to the role Mick had signed on for.

The Magpies' game continued to improve. The team as a whole was playing confident football, each player at ease with his role in the structure. The AFL had responded to the escalating numbers of rotations per game, led by Collingwood, by introducing a 'substitute player' for the new year, effectively reducing the number of men available on the bench to three. The Pies answered this by increasing their bench moves even further, though it still meant players would spend more time on the field. By Round 16, the Magpies were second on the ladder, with twelve wins, one loss and two byes.

By now it was early July and speculation about the future of the Collingwood coach had reached boiling point. Rumours abounded that Mick might not stay at Collingwood, that he might possibly coach elsewhere in 2012. Mick was in his office when a player tapped on the door.

The young man in front of him looked nervous. 'Can I talk to you?'

As the coach listened, his player revealed to him that several senior players wanted to sign a petition to have him reinstated as senior coach for the following year. It was nothing against the 'coach in waiting', he insisted, but the boys were concerned. They loved Mick, they needed Mick, and they weren't prepared to stand back and do nothing as he was replaced. Especially after winning a premiership.

'I would like to take it to management and the board,' said the player.

Mick's heart thumped inside his chest and echoed in his mind. What an amazing gesture, he thought, but what a disaster it would be.

'No. Put those ideas away. I appreciate it, I really do, but it will only do more damage than good.' He was firm. 'It's not going to change anything. Nathan will be your coach next year—you have to get used to that. The only thing that can derail our season this year is if our focus is taken off winning.' Mick was desperate not to let that happen.

They talked some more, and in the end it was agreed that everyone was better off concentrating solely on playing good football. They could worry about next year later.

That Sunday, the Magpie boys showed just how focused they were, demolishing North Melbourne by 117 points. They moved into top spot on the ladder.

In the early hours of Wednesday, 13 July, Mick's first VFL coach, Allan Jeans, passed away after a long battle with illness. The former pupil and teacher had spoken just the previous evening when Mick made one of his occasional phone calls to Jeans. The Hawthorn and St Kilda coaching great congratulated Mick on his recent efforts in the box and after a short conversation about football and life, the call ended.

Mick had been left feeling that his mentor didn't have much time left. He was glad that he'd had a chance to say goodbye.

Dad called me the morning the death was reported in the media. Together we wrote a tribute to the Aussie Rules legend for Dad's weekly newspaper column and revealed how pivotal and inspirational he had been to a country boy with grit and ambition.

Later that day he was asked to appear on Channel Nine's *The Footy Show* the next evening.

'You know what they want to talk to you about, don't you?' I asked Dad.

'Yes. But I can handle it.'

He didn't really like doing live media interviews. As a naturally shy person, he was nervous of the spotlight. It was part of the job, though, and over the years he had become more comfortable with answering questions in a concise and professional manner.

He would be going out on a limb to talk about himself in this interview. It was something that he normally avoided, preaching team over the individual whenever he could, but the constant speculation about his future and the 'succession plan' was harming his team by distracting its focus—not to mention the stress it was causing his family. He wanted to put an end to it, to tell the football world that nothing had changed—Nathan Buckley would coach the team next year, Mick wouldn't be coaching anywhere, and the details of the new role were still being finalised. End of story. What he really wanted was for the media to leave him and his boys alone to play football and, he hoped, finals football.

Sam Newman posed two questions to kickstart the interview. 'Could we definitely say that you will be at Collingwood next year, and it's only a matter of you dotting the i's and crossing the t's about your role?' and 'Could you say unequivocally . . . that you don't want to coach after this year again, ever?'

Mick didn't have simple answers to those questions, but he spoke honestly and poignantly. He told them: 'I cannot turn the passion off like a tap. It will always be there.' He meant it.

The fallout from that interview was horrendous, both from the media and from within Collingwood ranks. Mick was accused of being selfish, of putting himself ahead of the club, of disrespecting the decision-makers, everything that he'd so desperately tried to avoid by agreeing to the interview in the first place. Some reporters questioned his integrity and loyalty and commitment—the three qualities that, in truth, could best be used to describe Mick's personality. For a week it was relentless and the negative publicity and intense scrutiny threatened to destabilise his team and the season they were all working so hard on, so Mick made an important decision.

As a family, we were distraught. And fuming, and upset, and we had finally had enough. Mum always said it was like water off a duck's back, the way Dad shrugged off any criticism he received in the press. But we couldn't do that. We felt defensive and angry and tearful, and we struggled to cope with the ongoing pressure and the stinging attacks.

Adding to our distress was Dad's submission. At work, he watched as the CEO and the coach-in-waiting had regular meetings behind closed doors. He saw new office furniture being delivered to all the rooms but his. New computers for everyone, but not him. He heard decisions being made about the next year without his consultation. Did being the director of coaching not warrant a say in the drafting of new players, or the appointment of an assistant coach and new coaching structures?

Dad seemed to be sinking into a hole that had been shovelled for him. If it wasn't for his boys, who trained like mad and played like Trojans, he might have lost his spark entirely. But that competitive light that twinkled inside him and burned brightly during a game was still there, and he continued to shine it on his team and cast a shadow over everything else. And we supported him.

On 20 July, Mum and Dad attended a funeral service for Allan Jeans held at the MCG. It was an emotional congregation that shed a collective tear for a much loved and respected man of football.

One of Allan's four children, Liz, read aloud a raw and honest letter she'd written as a twelve-year-old. It mentioned how sad she was every time her father's Hawthorn team lost a match. She would cry following the defeat, not for the team but for her Dad, whose footsteps up the hall 'became slower and heavier'.

'When the footy season is around I don't see very much of you . . . I can feel your strain and pressure in my heart. Please take this season easy. It hurts me to see you age ten years in a few months.'

My mum cried harder and my dad shifted uncomfortably in his seat, flinching at the words. For him, it was a pivotal moment, as he realised any one of his children could have written the same words at any time throughout his career.

Then grown men wept as they spoke of their cherished former mentor as a father-figure. 'Yabbie' was an eternal coach, they said, his passion to lead and compete never left his soul. Dad could relate to this.

It was an outpouring of love for a father devoted to football and adored by his children.

Later that night, as Mum and Dad reminisced about their own time in football and the effect such a life had had on their family, Dad decided to retire.

*

Collingwood was still on top and still winning. They beat Essendon by 74 points at the MCG. Danielle whispered a thankyou to the player who had proposed the significant gesture for her father weeks earlier.

'Our family really appreciates it,' she told him. He hugged her in return.

When they defeated Port Adelaide at Football Park a week later, by a record 138 points, the players embraced each other. Their intentions for the season were loud and clear.

St Kilda loomed large in Round 21. The club was making a comeback in the second half of the season and posed a threat to all teams. Nick Riewoldt kicked the opening goal as if to prove that point. But by the first break, Leon Davis had kicked two and the Pies led by nineteen points.

Intent on causing an upset, the Saints began the second term with a three-goal rush and when Adam Schneider sealed the fourth, the gap was a single point. With a new confidence and ability to wave off opposing danger and lift in response, the Magpies piled on five unanswered goals. With little obstruction for the remainder of the match, they won it by nineteen points. It was the club's twelfth straight victory.

It was also time for Mick to tell the president that he would be retiring after the season.

The definition of Mick's new job had become muddied. All along, people had feared that he wouldn't be able to release the reins. While it hurt him to think of handing over his team, he had accepted it long ago, as soon as the ink was dry on the contract. But he did want to retain an element of supporting the coaching group, in a teaching and mentoring capacity. He didn't need to be involved in team selection and game structure—that is the job of the senior coach—but he did want to assist in the development of the coaches and the team as a whole. And to do this, watching the form of the assistant coaches on match day was vital. Otherwise, what use was it for him, with 28 years' coaching experience, to be paid well to stay on doing not very much? The decision on that wasn't his to make, though.

At the last club presentation Mick was offered a job that looked more like a glorified promotional role than one that would improve the club and keep him personally motivated. He considered resigning, to get out of his contract and take up one of the coaching offers that had been put to his manager. But his stomach churned at the thought of coaching against the young men with whom he'd built an amazing rapport over twelve years, and he knew that it wasn't an option. This confirmed for him his decision to retire.

Eddie McGuire wouldn't even hear of it, asking Mick to sleep on it for longer. He wouldn't tell anyone in the meantime, Eddie said. Collingwood beat Brisbane at the MCG by eighteen points that weekend.

During the week, Mick called a senior player, whom he admired for his wise and methodical approach to the game, into his office for a chat. He told him he was retiring, but that he worried about the effect it might have on his team if he delivered the news too soon.

'How will they take it, do you think?' Mick asked. 'Should I tell them now or later?'

'It could motivate them more,' mused the player, before going away to think about it.

He returned a day later. 'I think they will get too upset,' he told his coach. 'Tell them after the finals.'

They talked some more and offered each other good luck for the remainder of a very important season. The Magpies travelled to Perth and thumped the Dockers by 80 points.

In the final game of the home-and-away season they faced Geelong. Chris Dawes was back after time off with a broken hand. Nick Maxwell was missing through injury and Dale Thomas was suspended. Heath Shaw was still a week off returning from an AFL ban.

Collingwood got off to a flier—four goals on the trot—before the Cats reined it in, slightly . . . then galloped away with the contest. They were unstoppable, obliterating the Pies' previously impenetrable zone defence. Scoring goal after goal after goal, they pressed forward in high numbers and took chances that paid off. It was a 96-point demolition that gave football commentators licence to attack.

Geelong became the premiership favourite over the ladder-topping Magpies. Collingwood's only two losses for the entire home-and-away season were to the Cats.

We had all come to accept Dad's decision to retire. There was a profound sense of finality among us, and a great sadness that it was coming to an end, and there was also a longing to complete our football life with a premiership.

Time would stand still for us until Dad's season, and football career, ended.

The first challenge was West Coast, one of the big threats of the competition after turning a wooden-spoon season the previous year into a top-four finish. They started solidly and looked dangerous. Sharrod Wellingham's goal before quarter time reduced the margin to eight points.

Again West Coast got the jump in the second term before a familiar fire in the belly roared for Collingwood and the Pies prevailed. Six goals to two in the second term turned the game on its head, and from there the Magpies kept their distance, holding off a dogged Eagles team for a 20-point win.

Mick labelled it a significant victory. His team had played with grit and class to outdo a formidable opponent. They now had two weeks to prepare to face Hawthorn, an equally fearsome task.

One of the Collingwood boys had privately been dealing with personal hardship for many weeks, and in the fortnight before the preliminary final he turned to his teammates and coach for support as the situation became grave. Chris Tarrant's father was battling cancer and his son was heartbroken. He'd returned to the Magpies for the 2011 season with a fierce will to win a premiership, and now he dedicated that mission to his dad. He had everyone's backing. There was even more reason to win now.

Before the preliminary final against Hawthorn, Mick confirmed his decision to retire to the Collingwood president, and it became very real.

It was with overwhelming emotion that the Friday-night final against Hawthorn began. In the rooms pre-game, the Pies' coach calmed his troops down and directed their focus back onto the match: they were going to slowly pull apart the opposition's game structure.

It was obvious from the first quarter that this was going to be an almighty battle. The big guns from both teams stood up as the midfields scuffled for supremacy and the forwards at each end hit and missed in equal measure. Travis Cloke and Chris Dawes had a goal each by half time, while the Hawks' Lance Franklin had two. Hawthorn led by eight points.

Luke Ball, Scott Pendlebury, Dane Swan and Leon Davis went head to head with Jordan Lewis, Sam Mitchell, Brad Sewell and Luke Hodge as war was fought in the centre. Slowly and steadily, Hawthorn increased its lead until we felt sick with concern in our seats as Cyril Rioli snatched another goal and stretched it to eighteen points. Would this be Dad's last game? We fought off the thought as we tried to cheer the Magpies home.

At three-quarter time Mick directed his players to compose themselves: 'We have just gained the initiative. Stay true to the game structure and we will win.'

Within a minute of the opening of the final term, Leigh Brown crunched Jordan Lewis and Collingwood's spark was reignited. As Hawthorn advanced again, Harry O'Brien outmanoeuvred Cyril Rioli in the goalsquare and the Pies' backline worked the ball out of the Hawks' attacking zone and sent it forward. Chris Dawes marked and goaled. The deficit was ten points.

Again Collingwood intercepted Hawthorn's forward push and got rewarded as Leon Davis gathered the loose ball and scored from outside 50. The crowd was in an absolute frenzy as Luke Hodge and Dane Swan each added to the score. Travis Cloke's strong overhead mark and goal put the Magpies back in front and had the supporters in a fist-pumping fit, which soon turned to rage when Lance Franklin slotted one along the ground from an unbelievably tight angle. Chris Tarrant, who had worked tirelessly to nullify his opponent's impact, looked inconsolable. There were three minutes left and Hawthorn led by four points.

But as the pendulum swung again, Luke Ball roamed the back of a ball-up inside Collingwood's 50, a set play that had been rehearsed at training. It landed in his hands and he snapped across his body. Goal! We were launched out of our seats on a rush of adrenaline. With a shake in our hands and quivering lips, we asked God for a favour. We got it when Dale Thomas lunged at Cyril Rioli mid-sprint towards goals, and tackled him to the ground. 'Daisy' got a free kick and Collingwood ran down the clock.

As the three-point result registered, Dad's image flashed up on the big screen. He clapped his hands together above his head and then buried his face in them as he fell back into his seat. Without warning, he was hit with relief and his tears spilt unchecked. He was a picture of torment. We were there to catch him as he entered the changerooms and we all stood as one, emotional wrecks, to say thanks for another week.

It began with the Brownlow Medal presentation. Once again, Collingwood had a medal favourite, but Dane Swan had been outright favourite to the win the year previously and had gone home empty-handed as Chris Judd won the prize.

This time it took until Round 22 for the Magpie midfielder to take the outright lead, with a three-vote game against the Lions. He scored another two in Round 23, against Fremantle, and didn't need any votes in the last round to become the highest-tallying Brownlow medallist in history, with 34 votes.

Dane was a humble recipient and made everyone in the room laugh with his quick wit and dry sense of humour as he thanked his parents and his sister, his teammates and his coach. Mick couldn't have been more proud of him. In Mick's opinion, Swanny got the just rewards for some incredible games played throughout a wonderful and consistent career.

We watched Collingwood train on the Friday morning, along with 10,000 crazy Magpies supporters. It was Dad's last training session. Darren Jolly and Ben Reid had been under an injury cloud during the week, but both trained and declared themselves fit to play. Everywhere we turned, people grappled for our attention, 'We're going to miss Mick,' they said. 'Tell him that we love him.' Little did they know how much that meant to us, and to him.

By the time the city parade began and Zac and Holly climbed on board with their grandfather, the Collingwood coach, the stress and emotional reality of the week was starting to wear on his face. Zac and Holly waved to the crowd and fought among themselves and all the while their pa wore a fixed grin and tried to take it all in. But the noise of over 100,000 excited fans was nothing compared to the notes of the sad song that was playing in his head.

*

Then it was grand final morning. For Mick, it was the *last* grand final morning. He'd slept the sleep of a newborn baby, waking every few hours, disoriented and still tired. But by the morning he had rested enough. He felt good, really good, surprisingly good. He'd tweaked the game plan during the week, adjusting the defensive structure, and his boys were excited to play it. A change was needed after their recent loss to the Cats.

He was in a talkative mood when his children arrived, and he shared a joke with them as he made his pre-game cup of coffee. He had an abundance of support from Nanette's family and Gerry and Bill were once again in town to cheer him on in person. It was time to leave for the ground and everyone wished him luck for the last time.

For a week, for a month, for a whole season, he had tried to deflect the inevitable and shield his players from the ordeal that was his alone. He walked through a curtain of emotion as he entered the rooms and he knew that he could no longer protect them.

He walked around, talking to each player, reminding them of their roles, instructing them again on the moves and match-ups, and enjoying their company. Alex Fasolo was brought in for the injured Dayne Beams. Then the coach called everyone into a small meeting room. This would be his last pre-game address.

'We've gone from being the favourites because they do not trust us. But they do not understand our friendship. They do not understand how much we care for one another. Show them the courage. Show them the mateship. Show them the want. Show them the discipline.'

He spoke from the heart. He had stopped once, briefly, admitting that he was about to get emotional, and he leant against the wall and wiped the tears that were forming, and carried on. His players barely moved, their focus entirely on him.

'This is going to take one of the greatest efforts of all time because they are a good side . . . When the whistle goes you're going to go together. No-one left behind. No-one lagging. Anyone who can't do it, think deep in here what you're doing to your teammates, the people on the ground who are going shoulder to shoulder, down the race and through the banner.'

He was getting louder now, each word more pronounced, his body language more aggressive.

'This is going to be eleven degrees, not minus bloody 40, which we've climbed through. This is going to be ground level, not 4000 metres. There's going to be 25-knot winds, not 150 kilometres an hour. You've been through it, you pushed yourself through it to the other side, but you got each other there. *No-one didn't make it*. Because you had your teammates there.'

With a clap of his hands he wrapped it up: 'All the best, boys.'

The singing of the national anthem had always made the hairs on the back of Mick's neck stand up—this time it gave him goose bumps. As he made his way to the box, he didn't think that this was his last game; he thought, This is the grand final.

The Cats were hungry—it took less than fifteen seconds to prove just how ravenous—kicking the opening goal in an instant. They were two goals up before Collingwood had hit the board. Travis Cloke did that, booting two from outside 50 on his preferred right side. Then Andrew Krakouer snapped one through to put the Pies in the lead. It wasn't long before Steve Johnson replied. Geelong led by one point at the first break. *Oh God!*

But Collingwood had the momentum and ran with it. Three goals and a downed Cat later—James Podsiadly was carried off with a dislocated shoulder after landing awkwardly in a marking contest—and the Pies looked good.

Andrew Krakouer leapt high to out-mark two opponents and a teammate, and extended Collingwood's lead to sixteen points with his goal. *Keep going, boys!*

But two late majors—to Joel Selwood and Jimmy Bartel on a tight angle—brought the Pies' lead back to three. It was as nervous a half-time wait as we'd ever experienced. *Please, let us win!*

The second half began. Three minutes into the third term, Geelong's Tom Hawkins got a toe-poke in the goalsquare and it was all he needed to gain some confidence, his second goal coming a short while later. But it was under duress as the Magpies fought hard to maintain their lead.

The rain clouds that had hovered for most of the game finally burst open and so did Geelong's midfield. The Cats kicked three of the next four goals and held a seven-point lead when Mick walked out to address his team for the final time. As his players stood arm in arm before him, he implored them: 'Give every part of your mind, give every part of your body, for the next thirty minutes. It will leave you with success or regret.'

Still he didn't let himself think of the end; if he was to coach another quarter of football, he couldn't. But it became too much for his team as Geelong muscled its way further in front. The Magpies had three shots at goal and missed all three. Geelong kicked five goals. *No, not this, not like this!*

Danielle began crying before the game had finished. Around us, Collingwood people turned to look and we heard them whisper, 'So sad. Such a disappointing way to finish.'

Geelong had won by 38 points, but in the end all that mattered was that we had lost. Dad didn't get to finish with a win, no matter how hard he tried, despite how hard his boys tried.

Mick made a beeline for his family when saw them in the rooms. They hugged him and their cheeks felt wet against his. He could feel his own anguish building, boiling and bubbling in the depths of his core, but he pushed it back. He had to say goodbye first. He needed to take his one opportunity to speak to the people who mattered most, while they were all together. This could be his only chance to tell them, in private, his secret.

In the same small meeting room in which Mick had given his pre-game speech two hours earlier, the players sat alongside his family. The Collingwood board, staff and volunteers of the club surrounded him.

'You don't plan for these things,' he began. 'I never even remotely thought I'd be up here saying bad luck. Will there be regrets? Of course there will be—only you will know if there's something missing or a shortcut taken. Now those that will go on in life have to learn from this sort of stuff.'

He told his team never to forget that the club had been built on the back of hard work and to continue to be that type of football club going forward.

Then he paused. His family sensed what was coming and braced themselves.

'I just want to say, on behalf of my family, what a great pleasure it has been working here for twelve years. It's just been one of those great times of my life and I'll never forget it . . . I didn't want to make this about me, but I'm not coming back, boys . . .' His words disappeared as he struggled to maintain his composure. His anguish poured out. It was reflected in the faces around him.

Quietly, he continued: 'I'll leave it to some great people in this football club, they'll take you forward.'

People wept openly now—his family, his boys.

'I know deep down we'll be hurting like hell right now and tomorrow morning but, boys, you've made this football club from sixteenth, broke and shithouse, and you've converted it into a powerhouse. Thank you so very much.'

A sound of sorrow filled the room.

Eddie McGuire stepped in. 'All Mick ever wanted to do was look after his boys,' he said, and he thanked him. And then it was over.

Later that evening, at Collingwood's grand final dinner, Mick sat with a glass of wine in his hand. It was only when he began coaching that he learnt to enjoy an occasional red. It worked well to relax him now. From all areas of the large conference room, people descended on his table to congratulate him on a career well done. His childhood hero, Peter McKenna, took a seat beside him and shook his hand and said, 'Well done, Mick,' and the little boy inside him grinned and wriggled with pride.

Mick made his way to the stage and told the audience not to despair at the loss; the team was in good hands going forward. They would have more success in the future. He didn't say it aloud, but privately he thought of the team as a diamond. Once rough and uncut, it had been ground down and chipped away at and polished up, to become a magnificent sparkling jewel. Look after it, he thought, because it will continue to shine. It is one hell of a valuable possession.

Then he sat back down with his family, his greatest supporters. His greatest prize.

The following day he would get to farewell the supporters, the loyal and lively Magpie Army. He had been asked to clean out his office at the same time.

*

Mick was still aching from the loss when he walked with his two sons and brother-in-law to Collingwood's headquarters the next morning, but he knew that this defeat, perhaps more than any in his career, would leave a lingering wound.

He swallowed the lump in his throat and said goodbye to the thousands of adoring fans, standing on stage beside his players, promising everyone there that Collingwood would bounce back.

It was quiet in his office as Cain and Troy handed him two cardboard boxes and they began to pack up 40 years of football experience, and memories, and treasures. The new Collingwood coach stood in the doorway and watched over the room as the Malthouse men packed in a dull silence.

Mick was going to miss the place. The people. His boys. And he was going to miss the game. As they walked away, Mick glanced back, once more, over his shoulder. Then he was done.

EPILOGUE

ON THE EVENING OF Saturday, 7 April 2012, Dad took a journey around the MCG. It was only short, in the back of an open-top car, with his grandchildren beside him, but it lifted him higher than he had been for a very long time.

The score on the board didn't matter at half time of this game, as Collingwood and Richmond fans stood and cheered for him, every person positive and grateful in their applause. Half time ended for Dad then and a new game began.

For the first time in 50 years, Michael Malthouse was no longer part of a football club, after first wearing a team guernsey as an eight-year-old with Wendouree West, and playing against a team from the local orphanage. He was hooked from the start. It broke his heart to give it up.

My siblings and I had no choice but to live a life of football, all born between seasons and between clubs, each one affected in a different way by the pressures and joys of a life lived season to season. Through football's ultimate highs and shocking lows, we've remained tight. In the grief of death, the joy of birth, and the many ups and downs in between, we've formed an unbreakable union.

We have shared our dad with his football teams and the footy-loving public for as long as we can remember. Still, everywhere we go, people whisper: 'Look, it's Mick Malthouse!' He never sought the limelight in becoming an AFL coach, but it found him anyway. Even his grandchildren are used to it now. Every child of a professional coach understands the demands on his time and his attention, and though they may at times resent the fact, for the most part it is with pride that they wave him away before a game and watch him sign an autograph in the playground.

Kevin Sheedy's youngest son, Sam, once said: 'In my eyes, he's a legend at football but he's also a legend of a father, so I don't see him as a superstar or legendary coach, I just see him as a dad.'

When Allan Jeans passed away, his four children grieved the death of a father, not a football coach. Though he was devoted to the game for so many years, they knew they always came first.

I'm sure they all will tell you as I do, that football took their father away on many occasions, but ultimately it brought our family closer together. When the waves are crashing and the boat is rocking, you huddle together for safety and protection. When one of your own is under attack, you fight and defend.

When the game is over and the reward is won, you sit back and smile as one.

In our last year at Footscray, in 1989, my four-year-old brother suffered a near-fatal asthma attack. He had been sick with asthma before, but on this occasion it was touch and go as my parents rushed him to nearby Box Hill Hospital in the middle of the night. Mum and Dad took turns sitting beside Troy as the doctors worked attentively to aid his breathing and open his airways.

The Bulldogs faced Collingwood in a night-series game the following evening. The players gathered at our house, just minutes from the Waverley Park ground, for a team meeting. One look at their leader revealed the strain and distress of his past 24 hours.

The club desperately needed the win for the prize money that was on offer, but at half time Footscray trailed. Its captain, Stephen Wallis, gathered the team together as they made their way out onto the ground, after the coach had delivered his message.

In the second half, the Bulldogs scraped and fought their way back into the game and snatched it by a point. Afterwards, reporters asked the skipper what he had said to the team. The headlines the next day read 'We did it for Troy', and there was a photo of Dad with Troy, who had overcome the worst, on his lap.

When I think of that now, I am reminded that, at every football club we belonged to, our family had a larger family that loved us, cared for us, tangled with us in the backyard, slammed doors in our faces, appreciated us and supported us. We were lucky to grow up with football kin.

It took some adjusting for us all to live without football in our lives. No weekly games to attend, no team to barrack for or worry about. No stress. For Dad, it was about learning to leave the family home of a football club and to be independent and free.

His life in football stopped so suddenly that it felt like losing a limb. He was sad for months, and restless. He missed the routine that had been a part of his life for 40 years. He missed the camaraderie that exists within every football club. He missed the football scene, the mates, the conversations about footy, the constant planning and learning and strategising. Mostly he missed the contest. When the 2012 season began and he was no longer coaching, no longer competing, every weekend, it hurt him—and it hurt us to see him ache.

But with time his spirit was restored. He didn't miss the pressure and the constant scrutiny. He didn't miss waking up in the middle of the night to think about injuries and opponents. He didn't miss being judged and ridiculed for trying his guts out every day.

Growing up, we were the ones who faced the teasing at school. We saw the pained expression on his face and the worry in his eyes. We lived with the strain and tension at home. We were the ones who defended him. We also rejoiced with every win. We experienced some historical moments. We met wonderful people. And we radiated pride and pure delight with each premiership victory.

Supporters with a lifelong loyalty to one club have often asked my siblings and me which team we barrack for: St Kilda, Richmond, Footscray, West Coast or Collingwood? And now, Carlton?

Our answer is always the same: 'We barrack for Dad.' He is our team and we are his.

When his lap of honour around the home of football that April night ended, to the cheer of nearly 60,000 people, Mick walked back to his seat to watch the game as a supporter—for the first time in four decades. His heart was pounding.

He has loved the game as much as anyone, and because love is complicated and profound, no matter where he's watching it from, he will always love it.

'I will be a coach until the day I die.' His journey continues.

It was Sir Edmund Hillary who said, 'It's not the mountain we conquer but ourselves.' Mick Malthouse has accomplished so much in his football career—four premierships, 50 finals games coached, countless players developed into elite footballers and brave young men—but perhaps it is what football has given him that is the most significant part of this story.

It has given him life. A football life.

ACKNOWLEDGEMENTS

THERE ARE SO MANY people I need to thank for making the publication of this book possible.

Of course, I have to start with the obvious—Dad, thank you for letting me chronicle so much of your life. Thank you for being a loving, caring, generous, honest and supportive father and for always moving football to the side when we needed to come first.

Mum, thank you for not only being Dad's memory prompter and pseudo editor of this book, but more importantly for the sacrifices you made to always be there for us as a strong, devoted and amazingly selfless wife and mother and friend.

To my siblings Danielle, Cain and Troy, and their partners and children, what a wonderful life we've led, but boy am I forever grateful that we always had each other to lean on in the not so wonderful times.

To the editing team at Allen and Unwin—particularly Stuart Neal who worked with me from the first typed word until the end, and Foong Ling Kong who came in with a wonderfully fresh perspective. I owe you so much. Your dedication, professionalism and experience created a final manuscript that I at times doubted would be possible, but one I am proud to put my name to.

To my Dad's teammates and players, all of them, from the various clubs he's been involved with in forty years of elite football, thank you for the memories!

To the staff of each football club we have been a part of, again thanks for your support of our Dad and our family.

To the crazy and loyal supporters of the Saints, the Tigers, the Bulldogs, the Eagles and the Pies, please let me tell you how important and cherished your commitment and support has always been to us. When you barracked for our Dad and his teams, you barracked for us too, and for that we will always be thankful.

And last but not least, a big, big thank you to my husband Dean and my beautiful children Zac and Lillia for putting up with my disappearing acts to the library to write, and my moodiness as I tried to meet deadlines. Your love and amazing smiles always inspire me.

INDEX

Loewe, Stuart 95
Lovell, Andy 149
Lynch, Alan 'Dizzy' 23
Lynch, Alastair 193, 209
Lyon, Constable 8

Macaffer, Brent 222
McDonald, Beau 192
McGuinness, Tony 129
McGuire, Carla 157, 182, 183
McGuire, Eddie 61, 156, 157,
    164, 165–6, 174, 182, 211,
    216, 223, 226, 237, 246,
    247, 250, 252–3, 286, 297
McIntosh, Ashley 95, 105, 123,
    205
McKenna, Guy 83, 95, 105,
    117, 130, 133, 136, 158,
    224
McKenna, Peter 4, 7, 297
Madden, Simon 93
Magpie Army 163, 199, 262,
    272, 297
Maher, Robyn 135
Mainwaring, Chris 83, 92, 95,
    104–5, 109, 123, 140, 146,
    154, 158
Malthouse, Cain x, 35, 44, 54,
    65–6, 79, 100, 102, 104,
    111, 124, 135, 138–9, 154,

170, 178, 190, 194, 267,
    298
Malthouse, Christi x–xii, 23,
    25, 27–8, 29, 33, 41–2, 54,
    58, 60, 64, 79–80, 117,
    128–9, 136–7
    journalism 137–8, 147–8,
        173–5, 177, 184, 190,
        195–6, 199, 214–15
    Lillia Mae (daughter) 276
    pregnancy 236–9, 241–2,
        263
    wedding 231
    Zachary Dean (son) 242,
        245–6, 252, 264, 291
Malthouse, Danielle x, xi–xii,
    25, 28, 29, 32, 33, 35, 41–2,
    54, 58, 60, 62–4, 75, 79–80,
    86–7, 100, 102, 104, 110,
    111–12, 117, 129, 135–7,
    138, 177, 178, 182–3, 194,
    217, 267, 295
    basketball injury 135–6
    Holly Grace (daughter) 257,
        264, 291
    wedding 237, 242
Malthouse, Elizabeth (great-
    grandmother) 2
Malthouse, Gerardine (sister)
    2, 5, 6, 18, 264, 292

most valuable player award
24
post-game functions 41–2
Riewoldt, Nick 254, 267, 272,
275, 285
Rioli, Cyril 289, 290
Riverside Inn Richmond 41–2
Roach, Michael 26, 28
Robbin, Matthew 220
Robertson, Graeme 22
Rocca, Anthony 172, 193,
201–2, 204–6, 212, 216,
227, 230, 238
Rocca, Saverio 172
Romero, Jose 150
Rose, Bob 198–9
Rose, Elsie 198
Rowlings, Barry 42
Royal, Brian 50
Royal Melbourne Hospital
217–18
Rusling, Sean 229
Ryder, Patrick 245

St Kilda Football Club 4,
10–11, 43, 94, 124, 127,
147, 181, 231, 234, 238,
240–1, 246, 251, 254,
257–8, 264–74, 280, 285
debut 14
final match 19

recruitment to 11–15, 19
St Patrick's Cathedral 6
Salmon, Paul 131
Sandilands, Laurie 14
Sandringham Men's A Grade
26
Schimmelbusch, Wayne 77
Schneider, Adam 272, 285
Schwab, Alan 77, 88
Schwab, Peter 205
Schwarz, Denny 62
Scott, Brad 250
Scrimshaw, Ian 22
Selwood, Joel 294
Sewell, Brad 289
Shaw, Heath 221, 233, 237,
267, 272, 287
Sheedy, Geraldine 132
Sheedy, Kevin 23, 24, 64,
131–2, 300
Sheedy, Sam 300
Sidebottom, Steel 255, 261
Sidwell, Peter 66, 159, 174, 246
Smith, Michael 158
Smith, Rohan 220
Smith, Ross 13
South Australian Football
League 45, 49
South Melbourne Football
Club 23, 43 *see also* Sydney
Swans

Wood, Cameron 221, 278
World of Sport 61, 62
Worsfold, John 'Woosha' 83,
    95, 105, 110, 122, 126,
    141, 146, 147, 148–51

Young, George 106
Young Talent Time 60
Your Sport 66

Zaharakis, David 245